THE WIZARD'S GUIDE TO PERL AND CGI

Don Gresswe

THE
WEB WIZARD'S
GUIDE TO
PERL AND CGI

DAVID A. LASH

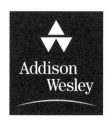

Addison
Wesley

Boston San Francisco New York
London Toronto Sydney Tokyo Singapore Madrid
Mexico City Munich Paris Cape Town Hong Kong Montreal

Executive Editor: *Susan Hartman Sullivan*
Associate Managing Editor: *Pat Mahtani*
Executive Marketing Manager: *Michael Hirsch*
Production Supervision: *Diane Freed*
Cover and Interior Designer: *Leslie Haimes*
Composition: *Gillian Hall, The Aardvark Group*
Copyeditor: *Jill Hobbs*
Proofreader: *Holly McLean-Aldis*
Cover Design: *Gina Hagen Kolenda*
Prepress and Manufacturing: *Caroline Fell*

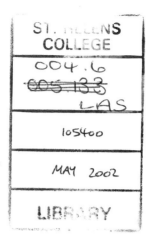

Access the latest information about Addison-Wesley titles from our World Wide Web site: *http://www.aw.com/cs*

Many of the designations used by manufacturers and sellers to distinguish their products are claimed as trademarks. Where those designations appear in this book, and Addison-Wesley was aware of a trademark claim, the designations have been printed in initial caps or all caps.

The programs and applications presented in this book have been included for their instructional value. They have been tested with care, but are not guaranteed for any particular purpose. The publisher does not offer any warranties or representations, not does it accept any liabilities with respect to the programs or applications.

Library of Congress Cataloging-in-Publication Data

Lash, David A.
    The Web Wizard's guide to Perl and CGI / David. A. Lash
       p. cm.
    Includes index.
    ISBN 0-201-76436-9 (pbk.)
    1. Perl (Computer program language) 2. CGI (Computer network protocol)
    I. Title.

    QA76.625 .L37 2002
    005.2'762--dc21
                                           2001045797
                                         CIP

2345678910—QWT—04030201

TABLE OF CONTENTS

PREFACE

About Addison-Wesley's Web Wizard Series

The beauty of the Web is that, with a little effort, anyone can harness its power to create sophisticated Web sites. Addison-Wesley's Web Wizard Series helps students master the Web by presenting a concise introduction to one important Internet topic or technology in each book. The books start from square one and assume no prior experience with the technology being covered. Mastering the Web doesn't come with a wave of a magic wand; but by studying these accessible, highly visual textbooks, readers will be well on their way.

The series is written by instructors who are familiar with the challenges beginners face when learning the material. To this end, the Web Wizard books offer more than a cookbook approach: they emphasize principles and offer clear explanations, giving the reader a strong foundation of knowledge on which to build.

Numerous features highlight important points and aid in learning:

☆ Tips — important points to keep in mind

☆ Shortcuts — timesaving ideas

☆ Warnings — things to watch out for

☆ Do It Yourself — activities to try now

☆ Review questions and hands-on exercises

☆ Online references — Web sites to visit to obtain more information

Supplementary materials for the books, including updates, additional examples, and source code, are available at `http://www.aw.com/webwizard`. Also available for qualified instructors adopting a book from the series are instructor's manuals, sample tests, and solutions. Please contact your Addison-Wesley sales representative for the instructor resources password.

About This Book

This book is designed for people with little or no programming experience who want to use the Perl language to develop Web applications. It describes the relevant Perl language constructs using dozens of diagrams and short incremental examples (about 10 to 20 lines long). The book strives to introduce CGI/Perl and show how it can be used to develop useful Web applications.

The book begins with the basics of the CGI/Perl development process (obtaining Perl, finding an ISP, developing a first program, and so forth) and then describes the details of the Perl language that are useful for Web application programming. These descriptions not only include language basics (such as if statements, looping statements, functions, and so on) but also include Perl features that support Web development (such as generating HTML, receiving arguments from the Web, and setting and reading cookies). The basics of several useful Web applications are used in the examples that include dynamic HTML document generation, guest books, Web Page counters, Web surveys, product order entry, form verification, e-mail notification, and remembering end user preferences between sessions.

I owe thanks to my wife and family. They provided endless support, encouragement, and understanding throughout this project. (Yes, Dad, it's finally done!) Also, the Addison-Wesley staff (Susan Hartman-Sullivan, Elinor Actipis, and Diane Freed) have been terrific to work with. They helped pull this project together and keep it on track. I owe special thanks to Jill Hobbs for her excellent copy editing of this material.

In addition, the book reviewers offered many excellent ideas and changes, all of which truly made this a better book. These reviewers include

Dr. Gerald R. Viers, California Polytechnic Pomona
Malcolm JW Gibson, Devry University – Atlanta
Craig Kapp, The College of New Jersey
Todd A. Gibson, www.augustcouncil.com
John Degallier, Mendocino College
Parag Doshi, Bell Labs, Lucent Technologies
Ray Trygstad, Illinois Institute of Technology
David Raney, Cuyamaca College

Finally, I owe the greatest gratitude to God for giving me the ability and patience to write this book.

David A. Lash
September 2001

CHAPTER ONE

INTRODUCTION

Writing your own computer programs that can dynamically respond to Web forms or generate HTML pages on the fly may sound like rocket science. Writing your own Web programs does not need to be difficult, however. You don't have to spend weeks reading computer manuals or years taking technical courses. In fact, writing such programs can be fun and easy to understand with a little work.

This book shows how Perl and CGI programming can be used to create dynamic Web pages. No previous programming, Perl, or CGI experience is needed. Simple, incremental descriptions and examples cover the CGI/Perl basics. It is not intended to serve as a complete Perl or CGI reference manual, although this book describes the HTML tags needed to work with CGI/Perl, it does not provide details on all features of HTML.

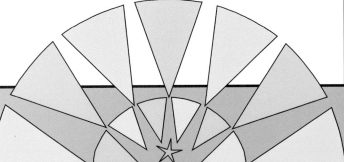

◎◎ Chapter Objectives

☆ Give background information on the World Wide Web, HTML, and Web browsers

☆ Explain what CGI is and how it can be used

☆ Introduce the Perl programming language

☆ Explain how to get started with CGI/Perl programming

◎◎ Some Background Information on the World Wide Web

Before focusing on how Perl and CGI can be used to build Web pages, let's review some basics about Web pages and the World Wide Web. The **World Wide Web (WWW)** is a collection of millions of documents and files that are accessible via the Internet. **Web browsers** (for example, Netscape Navigator and Microsoft Internet Explorer) are special computer programs that know how to retrieve and display files from the World Wide Web. Web browsers can work with files in several different file formats. A **file format** is a way of encoding data for a particular computer application. For example, when a browser accesses a file, the browser might do any of the following:

☆ Play a file in the *wav* format (a sound file)

☆ Interpret and then display a file in a *gif* format (a digital picture file)

☆ Interpret and then display a file in the *HTML* format (a text-based Web page)

◎◎ How a Browser Accesses HTML Files over the Internet

Figure 1.1 shows how Web pages are accessed across the Internet. In the upper-left portion of the figure, a browser requests a Web page from the sample Web address `http://www.myserver.com/funstuff.html`, entered on an Internet-connected PC. The domain name portion of the Web address (that is, `www.myserver.com`) refers to a specific **Web server**. Web servers are computers that store files and make them available over the Internet. The Web server accepts the Web page request, finds the file (`funstuff.html`) on its disk, and then returns the proper page to the Web browser over the Internet (shown on the right). Next, your Web browser looks at the file and decides how to display it on your computer screen (see the lower-left portion of Figure 1.1).

HTML and Web Pages

Ever since the birth of the World Wide Web, Web pages have used the **Hypertext Markup Language (HTML)** to create coded commands called **HTML tags** that provide instructions to Web browsers indicating how to display each page. These standardized HTML tags are used to define links, text size, color, picture placement, tables, forms, and many other aspects of Web pages. For example, if you want to

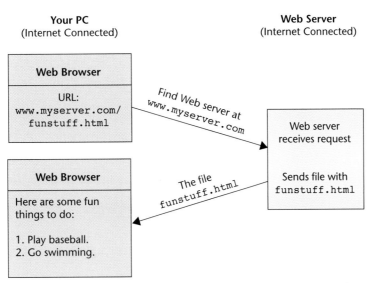

Figure 1.1 A Browser Requesting and Receiving a Web Page across the World Wide Web

insert a new paragraph into a Web page, you would insert a new paragraph instruction (<P>) directly into the text of the HTML document. Web browsers understand such HTML tags and know how to properly display the new paragraph in the Web page.

Figure 1.2 shows an HTML source document and its appearance when displayed in a Web browser.

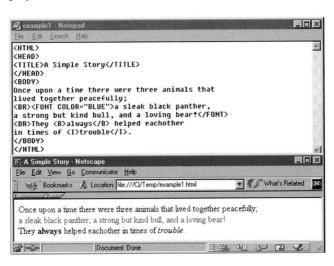

Figure 1.2 HTML Code for a Simple Document Shown in Notepad (top) and the Web Page Displayed in Netscape (bottom).

☆**TIP**   **HTML Generation Programs**

Programs such as Macromedia's Dreamweaver and Microsoft FrontPage are available that generate HTML tags for you. Note, however, that having some knowledge of the basic HTML tags and the way in which they work is very useful when you write your own CGI/Perl programs.

Static versus Dynamic Web Pages

Web pages written in HTML work well for displaying information that does not change much. However, these static HTML pages are not able to interact with the Web browser user. For example, static HTML Web pages cannot search a database and generate reports. HTML Web pages need the help of a **Web application program** to carry out many dynamic tasks, such as the following:

☆ Input a search term from a page, search the WWW for the term, and return the results

☆ Calculate and display the number of times that a page has been viewed

☆ Verify the input fields on a Web form

☆ Save a Web form into a database

☆ Display a special graph or return the results of a calculation based on data input from a form

Web Application Programs

Web application programs are similar to other application programs, such as Microsoft Word, Microsoft Excel, and computer games. Both are types of *computer programs*; except that Web application programs are designed to interact with a Web server. **Computer programs** are files that contain sets of instructions encoded in a specific computer programming language (such as Perl, C, C++, or Java). When a computer executes these instructions, the program may direct the computer to perform many different tasks, such as computing complex mathematical calculations, updating or searching a database, sending data to a network, or updating a computer window.

☆**TIP**   **What Is a Web Server?**

The term *Web server* can refer to both a physical computer and a type of software that runs on it. In the first sense, a Web server is a computer that stores Web files and Web application programs. This computer also runs special Web server software that provides data files, executes application programs, and returns results over the Internet. Some popular Web server software includes Apache for UNIX and Windows systems, Microsoft's Internet Information Server for Windows systems, and StarNine's WebStar for Macintosh systems.

◎◎ The Common Gateway Interface

To work with Web browsers (and become Web application programs), computer programs need a way to work with Web servers. The **Common Gateway Interface (CGI)** is not a programming language, but rather a standard that enables Web browsers to exchange data with computer programs located on a Web server. For example, when a Web form needs to send a name, address, and phone number to a Web application program, using CGI ensures that the Web application program knows in which format to expect the input data.

CGI as a capability first appeared in the **NCSA HTTPD** Web server software built by the National Center for Super-computing Applications (NCSA). The NCSA HTTPD Web server software was one of the first widely used Web servers. Because its CGI implementation was simple and the program source code was made available for free, CGI was widely adopted by most other Web servers since developed. Today CGI remains a popular method for developing Web applications and is available on Web servers built for Windows NT, UNIX, and Macintosh systems.

CGI's main advantages are twofold: It is simple to use and available on a variety of Web servers. Consequently, you can easily create Web applications and move those applications to different Web server platforms (such as UNIX and Windows NT). It's worth noting that several competing technologies for Web application program development have emerged, including PHP (a free language that embeds statements within HTML), Microsoft's Active Server Pages, and Alaire's Cold Fusion.

How Browsers and Web Applications Work with CGI

Although this chapter has described the capabilities of CGI, it hasn't explained how a Web browser, Web server, and Web application work together to use this interface standard. In Figure 1.3, the example illustrates how a Web form and a CGI application program interact. This example accepts a phone number from a Web user, looks up that number in a database, and returns the owner's name for the phone number. This application proceeds through the following steps:

1. The end user enters a number and clicks the Submit button. The form's data are then sent over the Internet to the Web server.

2. The Web server receives the request, executes the correct application program, and forwards the input data to that program.

3. When the Web application program is started, it looks up the phone number in its database and then generates output back to the Web server (in the form of an HTML page) consisting of the user's answer.

4. The Web server receives the output data and forwards it to the Web browser over the Internet.

5. The Web browser receives the new HTML page and displays the results on a browser window.

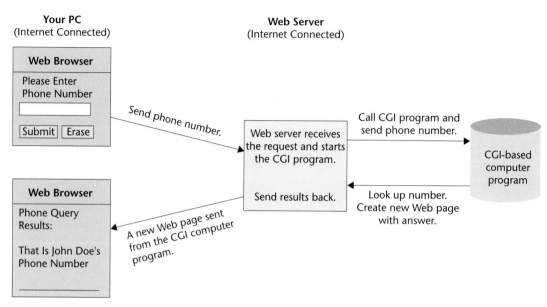

Figure 1.3 The Interaction between a Form on a Web Browser and a Computer Program Using CGI

An Interface with Different Programming Languages

Web application programs that are developed specifically to work with the CGI standard are known as **CGI programs**. Programs written in a variety of general programming languages can be CGI programs. For example, a Web site designer can choose among different languages including Perl, Visual Basic, Java, C, C++, and UNIX shell scripts when creating CGI programs. Any of these languages can be used as a Web or non-Web application programming language.

For a program written in any language to work as a CGI program, it must follow the rules required to work with the CGI standard. Such rules may dictate how the program file is named, where the file is located, or how the program reads its input and outputs its results.

◎◎ The Perl Programming Language

Perl—Practical Extension and Reporting Language—is a programming language that was invented in 1987 by Larry Wall at NASA's Jet Propulsion Laboratory. It was originally developed as a utility programming language for the UNIX operating system and was first used by technical people working with the UNIX operating system. The language gained popularity because of its ease of use, free availability via the Internet, and its powerful combination of features. Over time, it has evolved and added features. Perl is still used extensively by people working with UNIX and by those seeking to develop CGI programs. It is also available for free on many different operating systems, including UNIX, Windows, and Macintosh.

☆ **TIP** **UNIX Influence on Perl**

If you are familiar with UNIX-based tools such as *sed, awk, grep,* and *pipes,* then you will likely recognize the influence that UNIX has had on some of the Perl features described throughout this book. If you are not familiar with these tools, don't worry! Prior knowledge of the UNIX operating system is not required to learn CGI/Perl programming.

Explaining Perl's Popularity for CGI Applications

Perl has at least four features that explain its popularity as a language for developing CGI programs:

☆ *Perl is a free language with lots of free applications.* The Perl language is available for free on the Internet. As a consequence, it is widely available and many developers have written all sorts of interesting stuff with it. Many Web sites offer free CGI/Perl programs available for downloading.

☆ *Perl is easier to work with than many other languages.* Perl has several features that make it easier to use to develop programs than many other programming languages. For example, Perl does not require the inclusion of lengthy headers at the start of the program. Also, no separate compilation process is required to translate Perl language statements into computer machine language. Finally, the language provides several features for working with character strings—for example, features useful for verifying HTML forms, generating reports (and HTML output), and working with input files.

☆ *Perl provides a CGI interface module.* Perl has several special modules for performing a variety of tasks. The popular `CGI.pm` module makes using CGI with Perl a snap. Since the introduction of Perl version 5.004, this module has been part of the standard Perl release.

☆ *Perl applications are portable.* Perl programs can be easily moved between Web servers that run on different systems (such as UNIX and Windows NT). Thus, if you find a Perl program on the Internet that was written for a Windows-based Web server, you should be able to quickly get it to work on your UNIX Web server.

☆ **WARNING** **Using Free CGI/Perl Programs**

Be careful when you download free programs from the Internet. Just because an application is free, it doesn't mean that the program works well, is secure, and is virus-free.

Getting Started

Before you start writing Perl Web application programs, you must make a decision: Will you run your own Web server, or will you work with an Internet service provider (ISP) and use its Web server? Running your own Web server may sound like an expensive and complicated proposition. In reality, Web server software that you can install own your own PC is readily available for free on the Internet. For example, the Apache Web server software is available at `http://www.apache.org`. The Apache Software Foundation provides documentation on how to install and configure its software.

You can also download and install the Perl programming language for free onto your PC (`http://www.perl.com`).

☆**TIP**   **Perl Size and Download Time**

When I downloaded the Perl software onto my PC, the files were about 8MB in size and took about 30 minutes to download using a 56K dial-up modem.

This book will not describe all of the steps needed to install and configure your own Web server software (check the Web server software documentation for that information). Most people will probably use an existing ISP's Web server with CGI and Perl already available. Recognizing this fact, we will concentrate on the use of an existing ISP to host your CGI/Perl programs.

To get going with an ISP you will need two things:

1. A client machine

2. An account with a Web site through an ISP that allows CGI/Perl application development

The Client Machine

Your client machine can be a PC (running Windows or Macintosh) or a UNIX workstation. It needs network or dial-up access to the Internet. You can follow one of two paths: (1) You can develop your programs on your client machine and then copy them to your Web server or (2) you can use Telnet (described later in this chapter) to log directly into your Web server and work there.

The Internet Service Provider

In addition to a client machine, you will need access to the Internet and to a Web server through some ISP. Not just any ISP will do, however. You must know some pretty specific information about the ISP. Oftentimes, you can find this information on the ISP's Web-site; sometimes, however, you might need to e-mail or call the ISP to find out the necessary information. Find out answers to the following questions before you attempt to write CGI/Perl Web applications:

☆ *Does your ISP allow CGI programs to execute on its Web-server?* Many ISPs do not allow subscribers to write their own CGI-based programs, mainly because of security concerns. Because such programs execute on the ISP's Web servers, an intentional or accidental subscriber might create a CGI program that does evil things such as plant a virus or somehow affect the stability of the Web server itself.

☆ *Does your ISP have Perl and, if so, what version?* If your ISP does not have Perl available, you might want to look for a new ISP. You might try suggesting that it get the language via the Internet for free—but don't hold your breath. If it does have Perl available, check which version of the Perl interpreter is provided. This book focuses on Perl version 5.6. If you have an older version of Perl, some of the features described in this book might behave differently or might not work at all.

☆ *What will be my login and initial password on the Web server?* You will need a **user ID** and an initial **password** to connect to the Web server so that you can create programs and copy programs on to the Web server. Once you establish an account with your ISP, it should supply you with these items.

☆ *Where do you put your Perl programs on the ISP's Web server and what are the special permission settings?* Depending on the optional settings of the Web-server software, your ISP may dictate that all of your Perl programs be stored in a special directory on your Web server account. Typically, CGI application programs are stored in the `cgi-bin` directory. Of course, different Web server software installations can have different requirements, so be sure to check it out.

Regardless of where Perl programs are stored, you may need to set special security access permissions for your Perl programs to allow them to execute from the World Wide Web. These settings generally allow anyone to read and execute your programs while letting you read, execute, and write (that is, modify) your programs. (Changing the permissions for a file is discussed in Chapter Two.) For now, you might simply ask your ISP if they require certain security access permissions to be set.

☆ *How much disk space does the ISP give you for publishing?* Check the amount of disk space that your ISP provides for each account. Although Perl programs rarely require large amounts of disk space, your HTML documents and Web graphics might consume much more disk space. You don't want to be in the middle of your site's development and run out of disk space.

☆ *What will be the Web address of your final pages once they are posted on the ISP's Web server?* If you have not already asked, question your ISP about the Web addresses for your HTML pages and CGI applications.

☆ *Does the ISP support FTP and/or Telnet access?* You can develop CGI/Perl programs with an ISP's Web server in one of two ways (Figure 1.4). First, you can do your CGI/Perl development on a PC and then use an **FTP** program to copy your pages to your Web server so as to run them. You can use FTP to copy files to and from your server. Alternatively, you can do your CGI/Perl development directly on your Web server using Telnet. You can use **Telnet** to connect to a Web server over the Internet to run commands, create files, and develop software.

Writing programs on your PC means that every time you change a program, you must use FTP to copy it back and forth between the PC and Web server. Using Telnet to develop your programs on the Web server means that you must understand more about navigating and working on the server. Developing programs on the Web server is probably faster, but it does require more knowledge about working with the Web server. Also, because of security concerns, Telnet access to the Web server is sometimes not allowed.

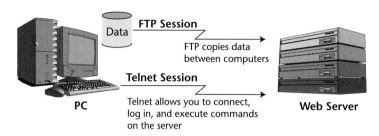

Figure 1.4 FTP is used to copy data to and from another computer. Telnet is used to actually log into another machine.

☆ **TIP   Using the Internet to Find an ISP**

Several sites on the Internet list Internet service providers. One large site is located at `http://thelist.internet.com`.

Once you obtain a client machine with Internet access and find an ISP, you are ready to start programming CGI programs with Perl.

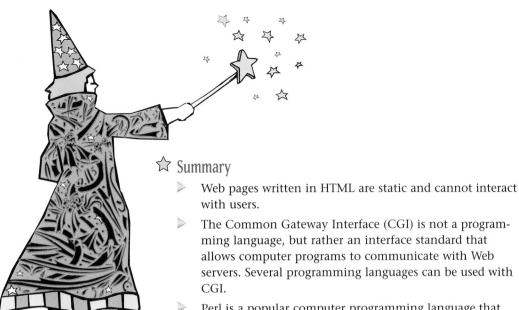

☆ Summary

⯈ Web pages written in HTML are static and cannot interact with users.

⯈ The Common Gateway Interface (CGI) is not a programming language, but rather an interface standard that allows computer programs to communicate with Web servers. Several programming languages can be used with CGI.

⯈ Perl is a popular computer programming language that can be used for developing CGI programs.

⯈ You can install Perl and your own Web server software on your PC or workstation.

⯈ If you use an Internet service provider's Web server, you need to find out several things about its services before you can start executing Perl programs. For example, not all ISPs allow subscribers to develop and execute their own CGI programs.

☆ Online References

Background about the Perl Language and Free Downloads of Perl
`http://www.perl.com`

Timeline History of the Perl Language
`http://www.perl.org/press/history.html`

NCSA Site with Documentation on the Origins of CGI
`http://hoohoo.ncsa.uiuc.edu/`

General Discussion of Alternative Web Application Programming Environments such as Perl, ASP, and PHP
`http://hotwired.lycos.com/webmonkey/programming/`

Apache Web Server Open Software Site with Free Downloads
`http://www.apache.org`

☆ Review Questions

1. What is the difference between CGI and Perl?

2. What is the difference between Telnet and FTP? Why do some ISPs not allow Telnet access?

3. How are a Web application program and a non-Web application program similar? How are they different?

4. List the steps involved when a Web browser requests a static Web page.

11

5. List the steps involved when a Web browser requests that a Web application start and then displays the application's result.

6. Which four features of Perl led to its popularity?

7. What is a Web server? List two functions that it performs.

8. Why do some Internet service providers not allow CGI Web application program development on their Web servers?

☆ Hands-On Exercises

1. Go to the Internet and search for Internet service providers. (You can also look at the Web site `http://thelist.internet.com`.)
    (a) Find at least one ISP that allows you to develop and execute your own programs. Does it allow Telnet access, FTP access, or both?
    (b) Find an ISP that will host Web pages but does *not* support Perl programs. What reasons does the ISP give for not allowing Perl programs to be developed with its site?
    (c) How much do these sites charge?

2. Go to the Internet and search for the terms *CGI* and *free*. What sort of applications can you find? Which ones are written in Perl?

3. Go to the Apache Web site `http://www.apache.org`. What is the purpose of the Apache organization? Who does the development of the Web server software? Which computer platforms are supported?

4. Go to the Perl Web site `http://www.perl.com`. Who supports and continues Perl development? Why is the language available for free? What is the most current version of Perl?

CHAPTER TWO

GETTING STARTED

O nce you have found an Internet service provider (ISP) and have answered the questions listed in Chapter One ("Introduction"), you are ready to start developing your first CGI/Perl program. This chapter describes the steps needed to get started on programming CGI/Perl. By the time you reach the end of the chapter, you will have entered and run two small programs that will help you understand the CGI/Perl development process and the procedure for generating HTML documents from CGI/Perl.

Chapter Objectives

☆ Set up an ISP account, if necessary

☆ Describe the steps needed to develop Perl programs using your ISP account

☆ Describe the steps needed to change Perl programs

☆ Learn how to create and run basic CGI/Perl programs

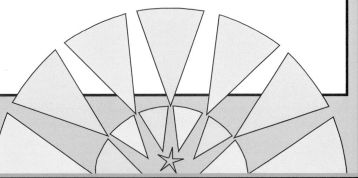

◎◎ Is Your Web Server Account Ready to Go?

Whether you are running your own Web server or using an ISP's Web server, you need to figure out certain things before you can start writing your first program. In particular, you may need to do some administrative account configuration or install the FTP or Telnet software on your PC. Whether you need to take these steps depends on how your Web server is configured and whether you already have the FTP and Telnet software you need.

These administrative tasks are described below:

☆ *Getting the appropriate FTP or Telnet software.* If you are using FTP or Telnet to access your Web server, you may need to install such software on your PC.

☆ *Connecting to the Web server.* If you are using FTP or Telnet to access your Web server, you need to know how to connect to the Web server.

☆ *Setting up your directories.* Your Web server account may not be set up correctly, so it's a good idea to check out the directories there.

☆ *Getting the location of the Perl interpreter.* You will need the location of Perl on your Web server to run CGI/Perl applications.

Each of these administrative steps is described in detail next.

☆ **SHORTCUT   Working with Your Own Web Server**

For the purposes of this chapter, the steps necessary to use Telnet and FTP to connect to a UNIX Web server are shown. If you are running a different Web server, some exceptions to these steps are noted. You need to consult your Web Server documentation for details on how to work with it.

☆ **WARNING   SSH instead of Telnet**

Some ISPs do not allow Telnet access to their sites, but instead permit you to use a special secure connection program called SSH to log in. I use an SSH Telnet program with my Web server called *Absolute Telnet*. Once configured properly, it operates like most every other Telnet program.

Do You Have the Necessary Telnet or FTP Software?

If you are running Windows on a PC (and your ISP permits Telnet access), you can use Microsoft's Telnet for Windows to access your Web server. You can also find many Telnet programs for purchase or for free on the Internet. (Try searching for *Telnet* on your favorite Internet search site.)

If you plan to use FTP, you may need to obtain and install an FTP program on your PC. Several FTP programs are also available for free and for purchase over the Internet. The examples in this book use an FTP program called *WS_FTP Pro*. A popular "lite" version of this program is also available for free over the Internet.

Getting Connected with Telnet and FTP

As indicated earlier, you may be using either Telnet or FTP to access your Web server. The following sections explain how to connect to a Web server, first using Telnet and then using FTP.

Connecting with Telnet

To connect to your Web server with Telnet, follow these steps:

1. *Connect to the Internet.* If you are not already connected, you need to connect to the Internet.

2. *Start Telnet.* On a Windows PC you can often start Microsoft Telnet for Windows by clicking `Start`, `Run`, and entering `telnet`.

3. *Connect to your Web server with Telnet.* If everything works correctly, you will see an initial Telnet screen. Use that screen to connect to your Web server. In Figure 2.1, Absolute Telnet is used to connect to a Web server called `condor.depaul.edu`.

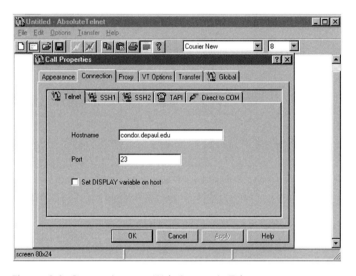

Figure 2.1 Connecting to a Web Server via Telnet

4. *Log into the server.* If a connection is established, then you will see an initial login prompt asking for your user ID and password (see the top of Figure 2.2). Use that screen to enter the user ID and password that you obtained from your ISP. Be careful when entering these, as UNIX is case sensitive. For example, the user ID *dlash* is not the same as *Dlash*.

If you have correctly entered your user ID and password, the bottom of Figure 2.2 shows the output you will receive. If you wish to end your session enter the command `logout`.

Connecting with FTP

If you are using FTP to connect to your Web server, then follow these steps to establish an FTP connection:

1. *Connect to the Internet.* If you are not already connected, you need to access the Internet.

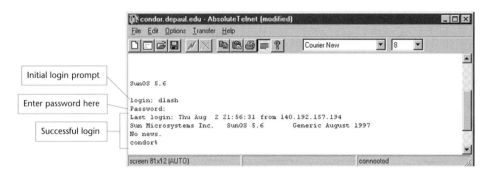

Initial login prompt

Enter password here

Successful login

Figure 2.2 A Successful Telnet Login

2. *Start FTP.* Start your FTP software. This software may be installed in a variety of places. You can often find it on a Windows PC by clicking `Start`, `Find`, `Files` or `Folders`. Enter `ftp` in the box labeled `Named` and click `Find Now`.

3. *Connect to your Web server with FTP.* Use the initial FTP screen to connect to your Web server. Figure 2.3 shows an initial connection screen. On this screen I entered my host name (`www.aw.com`), my userid (`perlpgm`), and a password (asterisks).

Once you are connected via FTP to your Web server, you will see a screen similar to Figure 2.4. The files and directories on your PC are shown on the left side of this screen. The files and directories on your Web server are shown on the right side.

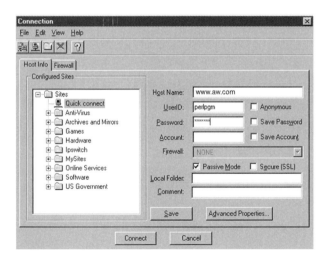

Figure 2.3 An Initial FTP Login Screen

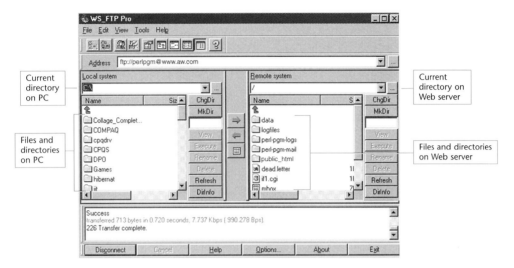

Figure 2.4 Initial FTP Screen after Logging In via FTP

Are the Required Directories Set Up Correctly?

After connecting to your Web server, you should verify that you have the directories required to store your Perl programs on the Web server. Your Web server probably has certain rules governing where your HTML pages and Perl programs must reside. For example, HTML pages are often kept in a directory called `public_html` and CGI/Perl programs in a directory called `cgi-bin`. However, many other directory name configurations are possible.

It makes good sense for you to log into your Web server and verify that the required directories exist. The remainder of this section first describes some elements of the UNIX file system and then describes some ways to navigate a UNIX file system with Telnet and FTP.

A Little about a UNIX Web Server's Directories and Files

Most UNIX Web server systems enable multiple users to store files on them. When your user account is initially created on the UNIX system, a **home** directory is also created for you in which you can store your files. All files and directories you store will be stored under your home directory. My home directory on my ISP's UNIX Web server is `/home/perlpgm`. (See Figure 2.5.) Also, in Figure 2.5, you can see that `jsmith` has a home directory at `/home/jsmith`. Other directories, such as `/bin`, `/usr`, and `/etc` are UNIX system directories that hold application programs (such as the Perl interpreter program) and system programs and files needed to run the UNIX system and Web server software.

☆ **TIP**   **Home Directories on a Web Server**

Most UNIX Web servers are configured to set your initial directory to your home directory when you successfully connect with either Telnet or FTP.

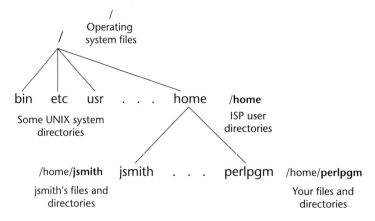

Figure 2.5 High-Level UNIX Server Directories

Within my home directory (that is, `/home/perlpgm`), my ISP's Web server has specific rules mandating where my HTML and Web application program files can reside. For example, all of my HTML files need to be placed in a directory called `public_html`. (See Figure 2.6.) My home page must be created inside `public_html` and must be saved in a file called `index.html`. All of my Web application programs must reside within the `cgi-bin` directory (that is, `/home/perlpgm/public_html/cgi-bin`). Note another aspect of Figure 2.6: It shows that I also created a directory called `/home/perlpgm/data` that is located on my Web server but is not accessible from the Internet (because it is not found under `/home/perlpgm/public_html`).

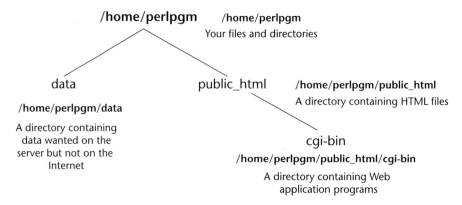

Figure 2.6 Directories on my ISP's Web Server Needed for my HTML Documents and Web Application Programs

☆ **WARNING** **Your Actual Directories May Be Different**

The directories in which you place your CGI/Perl programs and HTML files may vary on different Web server systems. Likewise, the directories in which you store your HTML documents and CGI/Perl programs may be different. The directory configuration on a Windows-based Web server is also different. Check with your ISP (or Web server documentation) if you are not sure where to store your HTML files and CGI program files.

Navigating UNIX Directories with Telnet

Using Telnet, you can navigate the directories on your UNIX file server with three basic UNIX commands:

Command	Command's Effect
pwd	**P**rints the **W**orking **D**irectory. Outputs the directory path of the current directory.
ls	**Li**S**ts the files and directories in the current directory.
cd dir_name	**C**hanges the **D**irectory to the directory named dir_name. Changes the current directory to the one you specify. (Note that you can navigate up one directory by executing cd .. —that is, cd followed by two periods.)

Figure 2.7 shows the output of using these three commands to navigate my Web server after logging in with Absolute Telnet. It shows the output of a pwd command, then ls, then cd, then pwd, and finally ls again.

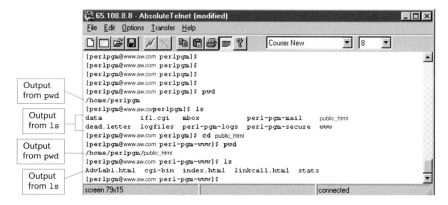

Figure 2.7 Navigating My Web Server with Unix commands in a Telnet Session

☆ **TIP**   **Additional UNIX Commands**

Appendix A shows some additional UNIX commands that you may find useful.

Navigating UNIX Directories with FTP

You can also navigate your files and directories using FTP. Once connected, you can navigate directories and files by double-clicking the folder's icon. In addition, you can navigate up one level by double-clicking the up arrow icon. Figure 2.8 shows the results of using FTP to navigate to `/home/perlpgm/public_html` on my Web server and `C:\temp` on my PC.

To copy files from your PC to your Web server, you can change directories on your Web server (on the right side of the screen shown in Figure 2.8, labeled *Remote system*) to the directory in which you want to store your files. You can then copy your files by highlighting the file on your PC side (on the left side of Figure 2.8, labeled *Local system*) by single-clicking it, and then hitting the right arrow ⮕ in the middle of the FTP window.

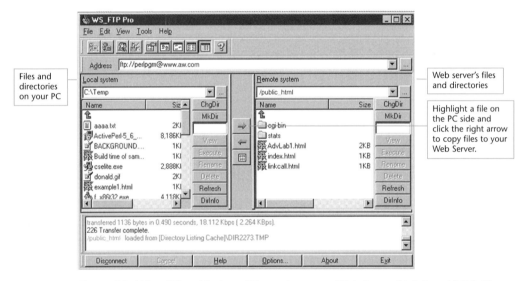

Figure 2.8 Using FTP to Navigate Directories on my Web Server (right) and PC (left)

Where Is Perl?

Another piece of information you need before you can begin to write Perl programs is the location of the **Perl interpreter**. The Perl interpreter is a computer program that translates Perl program commands into a set of commands that are more understandable to a computer. It will also run your Perl programs and generate any output. The Perl interpreter's command name is simply `perl`. The interpreter can be installed in any of several places on a Web server, so you need a way to find it.

If you use FTP access to the Web server, you will need to ask the ISP where the Perl interpreter is installed (or search its Web site to find this information). However, if your ISP allows Telnet access and operates a UNIX Web server, finding Perl yourself is not difficult. Simply connect to the Web server with Telnet, enter your user ID and password to log in, and then enter the following at the command prompt:

```
which perl
```

Another possible command is

```
where is perl
```

Figure 2.9 shows a Telnet session in which the user connects to a Web server and runs the `which perl` command. The Web server should respond with the full path to Perl. The **full path to Perl** is the set of directories containing the Perl command. In Figure 2.9, the full path name to Perl is `/usr/bin/perl`. If you detect more than one copy of Perl, you may need to ask your ISP about any differences between them and seek recommendations about which one to use.

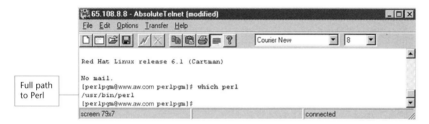

Figure 2.9 The Output of the `which perl` Command from a Web Server

Whether you get the location of Perl from your ISP, or use Telnet and the `which perl` command to obtain it, you should jot down the full path to Perl. You will need this information when you start developing programs.

☆ **TIP   Perl Location on a PC**

If you download the version of Perl from `http://www.perl.com` and install it on your PC, the Perl command is often installed in `C:\Perl\bin\Perl`.

☆ **TIP   How to Determine Your Version of Perl**

If you can Telnet into your Web server, or if Perl is installed on your PC, then you can determine the version of Perl installed by executing the following command: `perl -v`. Perl will respond by indicating the version of Perl installed and providing some other information.

◎◎ Starting Your Program Development Process

Each time you develop and run a program, you follow the same basic set of steps:

1. *Create a program file and copy (or save) it into the correct directory.* You will use an editor application to create your initial program. You must then put your program in a certain directory to make it work over the Internet.

2. *Change your program's access permissions.* Set the security permissions to make your program accessible over the Internet.

3. *Check your program's syntax.* Verify that all of your program statements are valid.

4. *Run your program.* Start your program to execute the commands in your Perl program and generate any desired results.

The following sections describe these steps in more detail.

Create Your Program File

Editors are computer applications that enable you to create, change, and save files. On Microsoft Windows, Notepad is a simple editor that works well for Perl development. (Several other Windows-based editors are available as well.) On UNIX systems, the Pico, Vi, and Emacs editors are popular choices. This section describes the use of **Pico** on a UNIX Web server, as it is the easiest of the UNIX editors to learn how to use.

☆**TIP**   **Using a Windows-Based Editor**

If you plan to use a Windows-based editor (such as Notepad), you must save your programs on the PC and then use a program such as FTP to transfer the files to the Web server. That is, start Notepad, enter your program, save it on your PC, and then use FTP to copy it to your Web server.

To use Pico on a UNIX Web server, first start a Telnet session to the Web server and log in (as described earlier in this chapter). Once connected, enter the command to start the Pico editor:

```
pico
```

If everything is working correctly, you should see an initial Pico editor window similar to that shown in Figure 2.10.

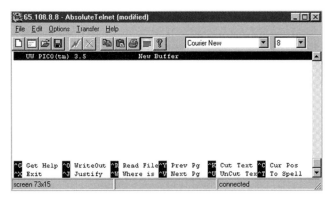

Figure 2.10 The Initial Pico Editor Screen

☆ **SHORTCUT**   **Some Pico Editor Commands**

Within Pico, press <kbd>Ctrl</kbd>-<kbd>X</kbd> (hold the <kbd>Ctrl</kbd> key down and press <kbd>X</kbd>) to exit the editor, <kbd>Ctrl</kbd>-<kbd>O</kbd> to write the edit session to a file, and <kbd>Ctrl</kbd>-<kbd>R</kbd> to read in a file.

Creating Your First Program

After you start the editor, you are ready to create a program. For your first program, let's keep things simple. Using your editor, enter the following code as shown in Figure 2.11 (the line numbers here are for reference only; do not use them in your program!):

```
1.  #!/usr/bin/perl
2.  # This program prints out a simple message
3.  print "Steady Plodding Brings Prosperity\n";
```

☆ Line 1 gives the full path name to the Perl interpreter. It must consist of a pound sign (#), followed by an exclamation point (!), followed by the Perl interpreter path name. You must enter this information without any spaces between the pound sign, exclamation point, and path name to Perl, as shown in line 1.

☆ Line 2 is a comment line. Comments, which always start with a pound sign (#), describe what the program or particular statement does. Comments do not affect the execution of a program, but they can be invaluable in a more complex program when you are trying to understand how it works.

☆ **TIP**   **Comment Usage**

Comments can also be used after the semicolon in a Perl statement. Thus line 3 could also be written as follows:

```
print "Steady plodding brings prosperity\n"; # This line prints a message
```

☆ Line 3 uses the Perl `print` command. This command outputs the text within the quotation marks when your program runs. Be careful to enter the line exactly as shown above, making sure that it ends with a semicolon (;).

Figure 2.11 Using Pico on my Web Server to Enter a Program

When you finish entering this code, save your program. Some ISPs require that you save your file with a special suffix or extension such as `.cgi` or `.pl`. For example, you might need to use a `.cgi` extension for CGI programs on your Web server, as in `simple1.cgi`. If you are using Telnet to connect to your Web server, you might be able to save your file directly in the required directory or folder: On my Web server I need to save the file into the following directory path:

```
/home/perlpgm/public_html/cgi-bin/simple1.cgi
```

Here, the name of the program is `simple1.cgi`. It is being stored in the `cgi-bin` directory, which is located within the `public_html` directory in my home directory.

☆ **TIP**   **Saving Your Programs into Place**

There are many ways to save your program into the right place. For example, if you develop your program on a Windows-based system, you might use FTP to connect to the Web server, navigate to the proper directory, and then copy your program into the desired location. If you use Telnet to connect to a UNIX Web server, you could use the three UNIX commands described earlier to navigate to the proper directory and then edit and save your program directly in the necessary directory. The important thing is to get a copy of your CGI/Perl program into the appropriate directory as required by your ISP.

Change the Program's Permissions

If you are using a UNIX Web server, you will likely need to set certain **access permissions** to your files after saving them on the Web server or copying them to the Web server with FTP. UNIX access permissions are used to define the access rights of your files. You can set the read permissions (that is, define whether the file can be read), the write permissions (that is, define whether the file can be changed), or the execute permissions (that is, define whether the file can be executed as a program.) You can set these access permissions for your user ID, for your user ID's group (that is, a set of user IDs that want to share data), and for everyone else.

The following shows how to change file access permissions on a UNIX Web server using Telnet and FTP.

Setting Permissions with Telnet on a UNIX Web Server

On a UNIX server with Telnet access, you can change your program's permissions by using the UNIX `chmod` command. In Figure 2.12, the `chmod` command is used to change the access permissions of a file to enable it to execute over the Internet.

As you can see in Figure 2.12, you specify two things for the `chmod` command: a three-digit number and a name of a file.

Figure 2.12 General Format of the UNIX chmod Command

The three-digit number really consists of three separate numbers. The first digit on the left sets your personal access permissions to the file—for example, read, write, or execute access permission. The second digit sets access permissions for your work group (usually your group includes only you, unless you define a group of users with whom you want to share your files). The final digit specifies the permissions for any other users on the system. Some common settings for each of these digits are shown below:

Digit	Permissions Meaning
7	Gives read, write, or execute access to the file
6	Gives read or write access to the file, but not execute access
5	Gives read or execute access to the file, but not write access
4	Gives read access to the file, but not write or execute access

The following examples illustrate access permission settings for the UNIX chmod command:

☆ **chmod 777 simple1.cgi** enables the end user, members of his or her work group, and anyone else to read, write, or execute the file simple1.cgi. This setting is usually not a good idea, because it allows anyone to change the file.

☆ **chmod 755 simple1.cgi** means that you can read, write, or execute the file simple1.cgi, but everyone else can only read or execute it.

☆ **chmod 644 simple1.cgi** means that you can read or write the file simple1.cgi, but everyone else can only read it. This setting is useful for data input files and log files. (Data input files and log files are covered in Chapter 7.)

☆ **TIP**   **Alternative Ways to Execute chmod**

You could also execute the chmod command by first changing to the directory containing the file and then executing the chmod command. For example, I could use the following commands to first change into my cgi-bin directory (from my home directory) and then run the chmod command on the file, as shown here:

```
cd public_html/cgi-bin
chmod 755 simple1.cgi
```

Setting Permissions with FTP on a UNIX Web Server

Setting permissions with FTP is somewhat easier than using Telnet. As with Telnet, you can use FTP to set read, write, and execute access permissions for you, your group, and everyone else. To set permissions with FTP, follow these steps:

1. Log into the Web server using the FTP command.

2. Navigate to the appropriate directories on the Web server.

3. Select the file you want to change on your Web server, then right-click it. A drop-down menu will appear. Select FTP commands, and then chmod. Figure 2.13 shows the window that then appears, enabling you to change the access permissions.

4. Select the desired read, write, and execute access permissions for your user ID, your group, and anyone else.

☆ **TIP**   **More on Permissions**

You may want to review the "Setting Permissions with Telnet on a UNIX Web Server" section for more information on the various permission settings.

Check and Correct Your Program's Syntax

Computer languages have a very specific set of rules or grammar that define valid statements. The process of **syntax checking** verifies that program statements are grammatically correct as specified by the program language grammar. For example, Perl grammar requires each line of code to end with a semicolon. If a line of a Perl program was missing this semicolon, it would have a **syntax error**. It is good practice to check the syntax of your programs before attempting to run them. Checking this syntax is akin to checking the spelling and grammar of a document before asking someone else to read it! If you skip this step, it may create confusion.

Starting Your Program Development Process

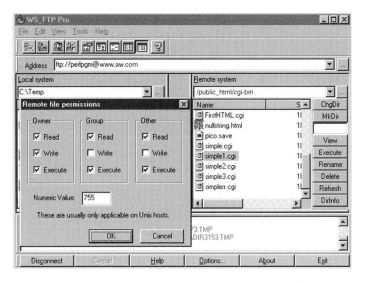

Figure 2.13 Setting Permissions Using the FTP Command

To check your program's syntax on a Web server with Telnet access, establish a Telnet session, navigate to the directory that contains the file, and then enter `perl -c filename`, where `filename` is the program file whose syntax you want to check. As an example, the following code changes the directory (from my home directory) and checks the syntax of a program file called `simple1.cgi`:

```
cd public_html/cgi-bin
perl -c simple1.cgi
```

You could also specify the full path to the file as follows:

```
perl -c /home/perlpgm/public_html/cgi-bin/simple1.cgi
```

If your program contains no syntax errors, the command will let you know by returning `syntax OK`. That is, it will respond with the following message:

```
simple1.cgi syntax OK
```

☆**WARNING** **Checking Syntax without Telnet Access**

If you cannot Telnet into your Web server, you may not have a method for checking the syntax of your Perl applications before running them. In this case, it may make sense to download a copy of Perl, install it directly on your PC, and then check the syntax of your programs there.

If your program does contain syntax errors, don't panic! Instead, realize that when you enter commands with incorrect syntax, the syntax checker can merely guess at the true nature of the problem. Sometimes, the errors identified by the syntax checker are only clues as to what is wrong. For example, if you accidentally include only one quotation mark in a `print` statement (and forget the other quotation mark), it may confuse the syntax checker, especially when you have many `print` statements. When your program contains a syntax error, you need to revise it to correct the error, save the program again, and then recheck it. For large programs, you might have to repeat this process several times to remove all of the syntax errors.

The top screen in Figure 2.14 shows a Pico editor window of program containing a syntax error. Notice that the last line is missing a quotation mark before the semicolon. The correct line should read as follows:

```
print "Steady Plodding Brings Prosperity\n";
```

The bottom screen in Figure 2.14 shows the output after checking the syntax of the file with the `perl  -c` command. Note that the output points to line 4 and indicates that a quotation mark is missing.

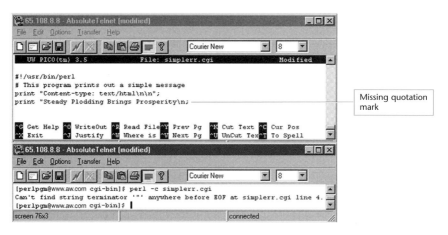

Figure 2.14 A Program with Illegal Syntax

☆**TIP**   **Dealing with Multiple Syntax Errors**

When the `perl  -c` command identifies multiple syntax errors, try to fix the first error reported by the syntax checker. Don't try to correct too many errors at once. It is usually better to fix only the first or second error and then recheck the program's syntax.

Running Your Program

There are at least two different ways to run your Perl programs:

☆ *Directly on a Web server or PC without a browser:* You can start your programs either on the Web server if you have Telnet access or on your PC if you have Perl installed.

☆ *Using your browser over the Internet.* You can start your programs by using a Web browser over the Internet and have your results display in the browser window.

Running Your Program Directly on the Web Server or PC without a Browser

Perl programs can run perfectly well without the use of a browser and Internet connection. Many Perl programs perform all sorts of tasks that don't require results to be output to the Internet. For example, a system administrator may run a Perl program that checks how well the Web server is performing. Another Perl program might by used to clean old files off a computer disk.

For our purposes, it is useful to know that you can run programs either on your PC (if you have Perl installed) or directly on a Web server via a Telnet session. Running Perl on your PC or Web server directly can be helpful when you are trying to get your programs to work. For example, when you try to start a program from your browser, you might receive an error message. If you can execute your program on the Web server (without using the browser), you can sometimes narrow down the possibilities as to the source of the problem.

If you have a UNIX Web server and can Telnet into it, you can start the program given in the previous section by entering the following command:

```
/home/perlpgm/public_html/cgi-bin/simple1.cgi
```

You can also run the program directly from the `cgi-bin` directory by changing the directory via the UNIX `cd` command (described earlier in this chapter). The following changes the directory into my `cgi-bin` on my Web server (from my home directory) and executes the program `simple1.cgi`:

```
cd public_html/cgi-bin
./simple1.cgi
```

Figure 2.15 shows the result of executing `simple1.cgi` in this way.

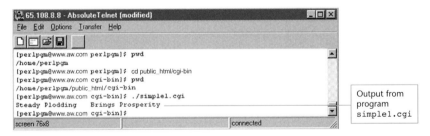

Figure 2.15 The Output of Your First Program Executed Directly on the Web Server

If Perl is installed on your PC, you can run your script there as well. Follow these two steps to run your program on a Windows-based PC:

1. *Open an MS-DOS prompt window.* Click `Start`, `Run` and then enter `command`.

2. *Run the program.* At the MS-DOS prompt, enter the location of Perl, followed by the location of your program:

```
C:\Perl\bin\Perl C:\temp\simple1.pl
```

Often you can omit the full path for Perl and simply enter the following:

```
Perl C:\temp\simple1.pl
```

☆ **SHORTCUT**   **Using cd on a Windows-Based Machine**

On a Windows-based PC, you can use the cd command while running in MS-DOS mode to change to the directory containing your program file. For example:

```
cd C:\temp
Perl simple1.pl
```

Getting Ready to Run Your Program over the Internet

Another way to start a Perl program is to use a browser over the Internet. Because this book focuses on Web programming, we will typically use this method to run our programs. To run your programs using a browser over the Internet, you need to add the following line to the example program:

```
print "Content-type: text/html\n\n";
```

Adding this line is critical if you want to use a browser to execute your Perl program. This line, which is sometimes called the **MIME content-type** line, tells the browser to expect output of type text or HTML from the CGI/Perl program. Be careful to enter this line *exactly* as shown above (including the double \n characters). If you misspell a word, forget a colon, or leave off a \n, your browser will not be able to start your program. This line should also be the first print statement in your program, appearing immediately after the code identifying the location of Perl (omit the line numbers when inputting this code):

```
1. #!/usr/bin/perl
2. print "Content-type: text/html\n\n";
3. # This program prints out a simple message
4. print "Steady Plodding Brings Prosperity\n";
```

To change your program, you must change your existing program file. You should follow the same basic steps every time you change your program file:

1. *Edit the program.* Start the editor (such as Pico, Vi, Emacs, or Notepad) and open your file.

2. *Change the program.* In our example, you are adding the MIME content-type as the second line.

3. *Save the file.* If you are developing the program on a Web server, then save the file to the proper directory on the server. If you are developing the program on your PC, then save the file there and use FTP to copy it back to the server.

4. *Check the program's syntax.* Run the perl -c *filename* command.

5. *Run the program.* You can run your program with or without your browser to test it (even with the MIME content-type line).

Running Your Program over the Internet

Once you have added the MIME Content-type line to your program and saved the revised program on the Web server, you are ready to test it over the Internet. To run your program over the Internet, follow these steps:

1. *Connect to the Internet.* If you dial in remotely, you will need to connect to the Internet.

2. *Start your browser.* You can use almost any browser program, including Netscape or Internet Explorer.

3. *Enter the URL or Web address to your file.* If you store your files in a `cgi-bin` directory under your `public_html` directory, then the address to your program (named `simple1.cgi`) might be `http://yourwebsite.com/cgi-bin/simple1.cgi`.

   You might need to check with your ISP to figure out the correct Web site address. For my Web server, I saved the program shown above in a file called `simple2.cgi` in my `cgi-bin` directory on the Web server, so it can be executed by accessing the following Web address:

   `http://www.aw.com/~perlpgm/cgi-bin/simple2.cgi`

   Figure 2.16 shows this program's output when started from a browser.

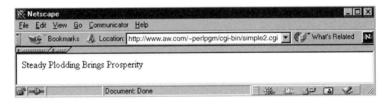

Figure 2.16 Output of Running the Example Program from a Browser Window

Dealing with Problems

Unfortunately, when you run your programs with a browser, you may not always receive the most informative error messages. Many Web servers redirect the errors from CGI programs into a separate error log located on the server. As a result, you receive a generic, cryptic message when you run a program with an error from a Web browser. For this reason, you may need to run your program without the browser when possible to help eliminate these errors.

Two common messages that you might see are **Internal Server Error** (Figure 2.17) and **500 Server Error**. When you receive either of these messages, here are some things to check:

☆ *Verify that the program syntax is correct.* The Perl interpreter should indicate that your program is free of syntax errors. (Use the `perl -c` command described eariler.)

☆ *Verify your program's access permission.* Make sure that the permissions set for the program and directories are correct.

☆ *Verify that you saved your file with the proper extension.* As mentioned earlier, your files may need to be saved with a `.cgi` or some other extension.

☆ *Verify that your program is stored in the correct directory.* As noted previously, you may need to store your programs in a special directory (such as `cgi-bin` inside the `public_html` directory).

☆ *Verify that you have the correct Web address to your program.* Double-check the accuracy of the Web address you entered in your browser.

☆ *Confirm that the first line of your program gives the correct location of the Perl interpreter.* Verify that you entered the location of the Perl interpreter correctly.

☆ *Confirm the accuracy of your MIME Content-type line.* Double-check the MIME Content-type line, making sure that it is the first `print` statement in your program, that it has the proper upper- and lower-case characters, and that you have not omitted any words.

Figure 2.17 An Internal Server Error

Generating HTML Statements from Perl Programs

Now that you have seen how to create and change a simple program, let's create an HTML document from a CGI/Perl program. This process is possible because of the way Web servers, CGI applications, and Web browsers work together. Using the CGI standard, the HTML document output from your CGI/Perl program is provided as input to your browser. The browser displays this HTML document just like any other HTML file.

As an example, consider the following CGI/Perl program. It uses `print` statements to output the HTML tags needed to create an HTML document. Figure 2.18 shows the output of this program if you saved it on your Web server, set the permissions properly, and used your browser to start the program. (Note that the line numbers are included only for reference purposes. Do not use them in your program!)

```
1.  #!/usr/bin/perl
2.  print "Content-type: text/html\n\n";
3.  print "<HTML> <HEAD> <TITLE> Example </TITLE>
          </HEAD>";
4.  print "<BODY>";
5.  print "<B><Font Size=5>This is a Test </FONT></B>";
6.  print "A very Interesting test";
7.  print "</BODY></HTML>";
```

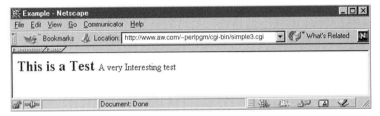

Figure 2.18 Generating a Simple HTML Document from a Perl Program

☆ Line 1: Defines the location of the Perl interpreter

☆ Line 2: The Mime Content-type line that notifies the Browser to expect text or HTML output

☆ Lines 3-7: Generates a simple HTML document

☆ **TIP**   **Using \n**

The characters \n, when used within a `print` statement, cause Perl to output a new line. While HTML documents ignore this instruction (you must use the <BR> tag to insert a line break in HTML), this code is useful for creating HTML document sources that are more *readable*. The source for your HTML documents will then look as if you typed them in an editor such as Notepad, rather than appearing on only one line.

Using Perl to generate HTML directly to your browser and creating HTML from your programs is easy. Although this example is very simple, you will see in the next chapter how this facility helps you to create dynamic Web pages.

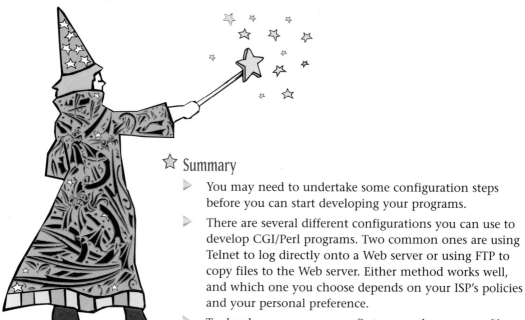

☆ Summary

- ▷ You may need to undertake some configuration steps before you can start developing your programs.

- ▷ There are several different configurations you can use to develop CGI/Perl programs. Two common ones are using Telnet to log directly onto a Web server or using FTP to copy files to the Web server. Either method works well, and which one you choose depends on your ISP's policies and your personal preference.

- ▷ To develop a program, you first create the program file with an editor, then enter your program, set the permissions, check the program's syntax, and finally run the program.

- ▷ Two statements are required in your CGI/Perl programs. The first line should identify the location of the Perl interpreter. The second line should specify the MIME Content-type.

- ▷ You can generate text output and HTML output from your Perl programs by using `print` statements.

☆ Online References

History of Telnet and FTP
`http://www.zakon.org/robert/internet/timeline/`

HTML Primer and FAQs about CGI
`http://www.htmlhelp.com/`

Home Page for the World Wide Web Consortium (Information on the HTML Standard and HTML Tutorials)
`http://www.w3.org/MarkUp/`

Primers on HTML
`http://www.htmlgoodies.com/html4-ref/`

Links to Tutorials on Perl and HTML; Downloadable Files and FAQs for FTP and Telnet Software.
`http://www.help.com`

Perl Information and Downloadable Versions
`http://www.perl.com`

☆ Review Questions

1. What is a home directory? How do you create one and what do you store there?

2. What are the three commands described in this chapter that enable you to navigate UNIX directories, and what does each command do?

3. What are the three access permissions that you can set on a UNIX Web server? For whom can you set them? What is a good access permission setting for your CGI/Perl programs?

4. What are the basic steps that you will follow each time you develop and run a program?

5. What is the purpose of checking a program's syntax? How can you syntax check your Perl programs?

6. What should be the first line of your CGI/Perl programs? What are two ways to execute such programs?

7. What is a MIME Content-type line? What does it do?

8. List at least five things you should check if running your program produces an Internal Server Error or 500 Server Error. Why aren't these errors more informative?

9. According to the text, in which directory must I store my HTML files on my Web server? What is my home directory? In which directory must I store my CGI/Perl files?

10. What are the basic steps you need to perform every time you change a program file?

☆ Hands-On Exercises

1. Modify the program in Figure 2.11 to include the following code:

```
print "Steady plodding brings prosperity.\n";
print "Hasty speculation leads to poverity.";
```

Notice the addition of \n in the first line. What happens when you view the source in the browser? Try adding an additional \n in line 1. That is, add the following code:

```
print "Steady plodding brings prosperity.\n\n";
print "Hasty speculation leads to ruin.";
```

View the source again from the browser. What is the difference?

2. Modify the program in Figure 2.14. Remove the Mime content-type line (the second line). Try running the program over the Internet. What happens? Restore the line and run the program again.

3. The following program includes some syntax errors. Input this program into a file, check its syntax, and fix the errors. When you are finished, it should correctly display the document over the Internet.

```
1. #!/usr/bin/perl
2. Print "Content-type: text/html\n\n";
3. Print <HTML><HEAD><TITLE> Example </TITLE></HEAD>";
4. Print "This is an example of a program with
        syntax";
5. Print "errors. If you correct the errors, you can"
6. Print "get your program to work.</BODY></HTML>";
```

4. Create a CGI/Perl program that outputs the following HTML document. Save your program on your Web server and view it over the Internet.

```
<HTML> <HEAD> <TITLE> More On Perl </TITLE></HEAD>
<BODY BACKGROUND="BLUE">
<H1> More On Perl </H1>

Many people who work with the <I>UNIX system</I>
appreciate the various features of the Perl
language. <BR><BR> Perl has features that combines
many of the UNIX utility programs such as:
<UL>
<LI> sed
<LI> grep
<LI> awk
</UL></BODY></HTML>
```

5. Run the program created in Exercise 4 directly on your Web server or your PC.

6. Create a CGI/Perl program that outputs the following HTML document. Save your program on your Web server and view it over the Internet.

```
<HTML> <HEAD> <TITLE> The Perl Language
</TITLE></HEAD>
<BODY>
<B><Font Size=5>T</FONT></B>he Perl language was first
    developed in 1987. Since then its use has grown
    rapidly. One use of Perl is to develop <I>Web
    application programs</I>.
</BODY></HTML>
```

7. Create a Perl program that outputs an HTML document that looks like the following. Give it a yellow background and a title of *My Preferences*.

```
Here are three things I like:
1. Baseball
2. Hot dogs
3. Apple pie
```

CHAPTER THREE

THE PERL BASICS

Now that you know how to connect to your Web server and create simple programs, you're ready to learn more about the Perl language. This chapter explains how to use Perl *variables*, *conditional statements*, and *functions*. Understanding their use will allow you to better understand how Perl programs work. It will also lay a foundation for more advanced topics such as working with Web forms and dynamic Web page creation.

Chapter Objectives

⭐ Describe Perl scalar variables for numerical and string data

⭐ Describe Perl conditional statements

⭐ Learn how to use Perl functions

⭐ Use a function to send data to your program

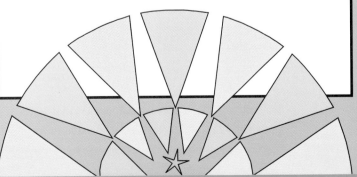

◎◎ Using Scalar Variables

Variables are a basic programming construct used in computer programs. They allow you to store and access data in computer memory. In Perl, variables that hold a singular item such as a number (for example, 1, 1239.12, or –123) or a character string (for example, "apple," " John Smith," or "address") are called *scalar variables*. Variables that hold a set of items (such as a set of numbers) are called *list variables*. For now, we will concentrate on scalar variables. (List variables are covered in Chapter Five.)

In your Perl programs, you can create and use your own scalar variables. To assign a value to a scalar variable, you place the variable's *name* on the left side of an equals sign (=) and the *value* on the right side of the equals sign. That value will be then stored, or saved, into computer memory. The following Perl statements use two variables: $x and $months.

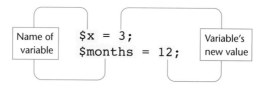

Note that each Perl statement ends with a semicolon (;). Also, note that the first statement assigns the value 3 to the variable $x and the second statement assigns the value 12 to the variable $months. These assignments represent the *current* values of $x and $months.

New values can also be assigned to variables. For example, consider the following Perl statements:

```
$X = 60;
$Weeks = 4;
$X = $Weeks;
```

This example uses two variables ($X and $Weeks). At the end of these three lines, $X has a value of 4 and $Weeks has a value of 4.

☆**WARNING** Variable Name Case

Perl variables are case sensitive, so $i and $I are considered different variable names. Likewise, $tripCounter and $Tripcounter are considered different variable names.

You can select just about any set of characters for a variable name in Perl, as long as you adhere to the following rules:

☆ Perl variable names must have a dollar sign ($) as the first character.

☆ The second character of the variable must be a letter or underscore (_).

☆ The variable name must contain fewer than 251 characters.

Thus $baseball, $_sum, $X, $Numb_of_bricks, $num_houses, and $counter1 are all valid Perl variable names. Conversely, $123go, $1counter, and counter are not valid choices.

☆ **TIP**   **Use Descriptive Variable Names**

Try to select variable names that describe how the variables are used. For example, $counter might be used as a variable that counts something. Avoid nondescriptive variable names such as $g, $o, or $k1. The idea is to use variable names in a way that makes your program easier to understand.

☆ **WARNING**   **Using Variables without a Value**

Unlike some other programming languages, Perl allows you to use a variable on the right side of an equals sign even if *no value has been assigned yet!* Perl will not issue an error message in such a case. Instead, it will assign a null value (or no value). As this assignment usually is *not* desirable, you should ensure that your variables are explicitly assigned values before you use them. You can also detect such errors by using the command perl -w to identify improper usage of variables in your program. For example, the following statement will run a program called program1.cgi and issue warnings:

```
perl -w program1.cgi
```

Combining Variables and the print Statement

In Chapter Two , you learned that you can use a print statement to output text. You can also use a print statement to output a variable's value. To output a variable's value, you place the variable name inside the double quotes of the print statement. That is, to print out the value of $x, you write the following:

> Enclose print string in double quotes

```
print "The value of x= $x";
```

Consider the following example program and browser output in Figure 3.1, which show how to initialize variables (lines 3–4) and output their values (lines 5–6). (Do not enter the numbers at the start of each line.)

```
1. #!/usr/bin/perl
2. print "Content-type: text/html\n\n";
3. $x = 3;
4. $y = 5;          Assign 3 and 5 to $x and $y
5. print "The value of x is $x. ";
6. print "The value of y= $y.";
```

Figure 3.1 The Output of the `printexample.cgi` Script

In this program:

☆ Lines 1–2 print the location of Perl and the MIME Content-type line.

☆ Lines 3–4 assign the value 3 to the variable `$x` and the value 5 to the variable `$y`.

☆ Lines 5–6 use `print` statements to output the values of `$x` and `$y`. Note that double quotation marks are used in the `print` statements.

◉ Operating on Variables

So far, we have assigned values to variables. You can also create Perl expressions to manipulate data values. To do so, you use *operators* such as a plus sign (+) for addition and a minus sign (−) for subtraction. For example, consider the following Perl program and its output, as shown in Figure 3.2.

```
1.  #!/usr/bin/perl
2.  print "Content-type: text/html\n\n";
3.  $x = 3 + 4;
4.  $y = 5 + $x;        Assign 7 and 12 to $x and $y
5.  print "The value of x is $x but y= $y";
```

Figure 3.2 The Output of a Simple Expression Program

In this program:

☆ Line 3 assigns the value 7 to the variable `$x`.

☆ Line 4 assigns 12 to `$y` (that is, 5 plus the value of `$x`).

☆ Line 5 creates the output `The value of x is 7 but y= 12`.

Addition is just one operation that you can do in Perl. Table 3.1 lists several other Perl operators and gives an example of each operator's use.

Table 3.1 Selected Perl Expression Operators

Operator	Effect	Example	Result
+	Adds two items	`$x = 2 + 2;`	$x is assigned 4
−	Subtraction	`$y = 3;` `$y = $y - 1;`	$y is assigned 2
/	Division	`$y = 14 / 2;`	$y is assigned 7
*	Multiplication	`$z = 4;` `$y = $z * 4;`	$y is assigned 16
**	Exponent	`$y = 2;` `$z = 4 ** $y;`	$z is assigned 16
%	Remainder	`$y = 14 % 3;`	$y is assigned 2

Expressions like those given in Table 3.1 can be used to manipulate data values in your programs. As an example, Figure 3.3 shows a complete program and output that uses some of these operations.

```
1. #!/usr/bin/perl
2. print "Content-type: text/html\n\n";
3. $cubed = 3 ** 3;————————————————————  Assign 27 to $cubed
4. $onemore = $cubed + 1;————————————————  Assign 28 to $onemore
5. $cubed = $cubed + $onemore;———————————  Assign 55 to $cubed
6. $remain = $onemore % 3;——————————————  Assign 1 to $remain
7. print "The value of cubed is $cubed onemore=
   $onemore ";
8. print "The value of remain= $remain";
```

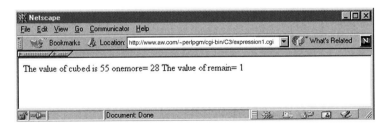

The value of cubed is 55 onemore= 28 The value of remain= 1

Figure 3.3 A Program Using Perl Expression Operators

In this program:

☆ Lines 1–2 identify the location of the Perl interpreter and output the MIME Content-type line.

☆ Lines 3–6 implement small expressions that affect the variables $cubed, $onemore, and $remain.

☆**TIP**   **Using White Space in Programs**

Perl ignores extra blank lines and spaces between characters. For example,

```
$x = 5 +                    1;
$x = 5 + 1;
$x = 5 +
              1;
```

are all legal statements (and all evaluate to 6). The middle statement is easier to read, however. Whenever you use "white space" (that is, blank spaces and lines), your goal should be to increase your program's *readability*.

Writing Complex Expressions

The previous examples used one operator in each Perl statement. When you combine multiple operators into a single statement, then **operator precedence rules** are needed to define the order in which the operators are evaluated. For example, consider the following expression:

```
$x = 5 + 2 * 6;
```

The value of $x is either 42 or 17, depending on whether you evaluate the addition or the multiplication first. Because Perl evaluates multiplication operations before addition operations, this expression evaluates to 17. Perl follows these precedence rules:

☆ First, it evaluates operators within parentheses.

☆ Next, it evaluates exponential operators.

☆ Next, it evaluates multiplication and division operators.

☆ Finally, it evaluates addition and subtraction operators.

To see how these precedence rules work, consider the Perl statements shown below. The first two equations are equivalent, and both evaluate to 82. The first statement uses the precedence rules given above, and the second clarifies these rules by using parentheses. The third statement uses parentheses to set a different order for operator evaluation, and it evaluates to 19.

```
$X = 100 - 3 ** 2 * 2;
$Y = 100 - ((3 ** 2) * 2);
$Z = 100 - ( 3 ** (2 * 2) );
```

More on Mixing Variables with HTML Output

In the section "Combining Variables and the `print` Statement," we saw how to output a variable's value; in Chapter Two, we saw how to output HTML. The following program shows an example of a Perl program that computes some simple expressions while creating a small HTML document. Notice that lines 5–7 evaluate three expressions. Lines 9–10 output the variables `$tot_day` and `$num_months` within HTML statements.

```perl
1. #!/usr/bin/perl
2. print "Content-type: text/html\n\n";
3. print "<HTML><HEAD><TITLE> Example </TITLE></HEAD>";
4. print "<BODY><FONT COLOR=BLUE SIZE=5>";
5. $num_week = 8;
6. $total_day = $num_week * 7;        ⎯⎯⎯ Assign 56 to $total_day
7. $num_months = $num_week / 4;       ⎯⎯⎯ Assign 2 to $num_months
8. print "Number of days are $total_day </FONT>";
9. print "<HR>The total number of months=$num_months";
10. print "</BODY></HTML>";
```

Figure 3.4 Printing Out Variable Values Mixed with HTML Tags

In this program:

☆ Lines 3–4 output the tags needed to start an HTML document and set an initial font size and color.

☆ Line 6 assigns 7*8 (= 56) to the variable `$totalDay`.

☆ Line 7 sets `$numMonths` equal to 8/4 (= 2).

☆ Lines 8–9 output the HTML tags to produce the output shown in Figure 3.4. They also output the values of `$total_day` and `$num_months`.

Operating on Variables

> ☆**TIP**   **View Browser Source**
>
> When you create an HTML document from a CGI/Perl program, you may find it useful to "view the source" of the HTML generated by your program. It can sometimes give you clues about why the program's output does not look right. To view the HTML source from Netscape or Internet Explorer, click View, Source.

String Variables

So far, we have discussed the use of scalar variables with numerical values. As mentioned previously, however, variables can also be assigned character string values. Character strings are used in programs to hold data such as customer names, addresses, product names, and descriptions. Consider the following example:

```
$letters="abc";
$fruit="apple";
```

Enclose string values in quotation marks

Here the variable `$letters` is assigned the character string "abc" and the variable `$fruit` is assigned "apple".

Unlike with numerical variables, you cannot add, subtract, divide, or multiply string variables. On the other hand, string variables have their own operations that you can perform. Two common operators used with such variables are the concatenate operator and the repeat operator:

The concatenate operator is used to join two strings together and takes the form of a period ("."). The following program segment illustrates its use:

```
$FirstName = "Bull";
$LastName = "and Bear";
$FullName1 = $FirstName . $LastName;
$FullName2 = $FirstName . " " . $LastName;
print "FullName1=$FullName1 and Fullname2=$FullName2";
```

Concatenation operator

This program segment would output the following:

```
FullName1=Bulland Bear and FullName2=Bull and Bear
```

The repeat operator is used when you want to repeat a string a specified number of times. It is specified by the following sequence:

```
$varname x 3
```

> ☆**SHORTCUT**   **Another Way to Concatenate Strings**
>
> You can also use double quotation marks to create concatenation directly, as in the following example:
>
> ```
> $Fullname2 = "$FirstName $LastName";
> ```
>
> This statement has the same effect as
>
> ```
> $Fullname2 = $FirstName . " " . $LastName;
> ```

Here $varname is the variable's name and x   3 means "repeat the string within $varname three times." The following program segment illustrates the use of the repeat operator:

```
$score = "Goal!";
$lots_of_scores = $score x 3;
print "lots_of_scores=$lots_of_scores";
```

This program segment would output the following:

```
lots_of_scores=Goal!Goal!Goal!
```

The following program and Figure 3.5 demonstrate the use of these two string operators.

```
 1. #!/usr/bin/perl
 2. print "Content-type: text/html\n\n";
 3. print "<HTML> <HEAD> <TITLE> String Example </TITLE>
        </HEAD>";
 4. print "<BODY>";
 5. $first = "John";
 6. $last = "Smith";
 7. $name = $first . $last;        Concatenate $first with $last
 8. $triple = $name x 3;           Repeat $name three times
 9. print "<BR> name=$name";
10. print "<BR> triple = $triple";
11. print "</BODY></HTML>";
```

Figure 3.5 Output of String Operator Examples

In this program:

☆ Lines 1–4 identify the location of Perl, outputs the MIME Content-type line, and output the HTML tags needed to start an HTML document.

☆ Line 7 assigns to $name the values $first and $last concatenated together.

☆ Line 8 assigns to $triple the variable $name repeated three times.

☆ Lines 9–10 output the contents of the variables $name and $triple.

Conditional Statements

☆ **TIP**   **Using Functions to Manipulate String Values**

There are other ways to manipulate string variables (and numerical variables) and work with their values. We will look at some of Perl's built-in functions that accomplish this task later in this chapter.

◎◎ Conditional Statements

Now that we've learned about using variables in Perl, let's look at a group of statements known as *conditional statements*. Conditional statements provide a mechanism for programs to test for certain variable values and then react differently depending on the value found. In real life, we often use conditional statements. For example, consider the following driving directions:

> *Get on Interstate 90 East at Elm Street and go east toward the city. If you encounter construction delays at mile marker 10, get off the expressway at this exit and take Roosevelt Road all the way into the city. Otherwise, stay on I-90 until you reach the city.*

In this example, there are two possible ways to reach the city depending on whether the driver finds construction under way at mile marker 10. In the first route, the driver encounters construction at mile marker 10 and gets off at Roosevelt Road. In the second route, the driver takes I-90 all the way into the city (that is, there is no construction at mile marker 10).

Perl provides three conditional clauses that enable programs to test for different conditions and react differently based on the results of that test: `if` statements, `elsif` clauses, and `else` clauses.

☆ An **if statement** is used to specify a test condition and set of statements to execute when a test condition is *true*. It can be used by itself or with `elsif` or `else` clauses. It has the following general format:

```
if ( test condition ) {
    one or more statements
}
```

It is described in more detail later in the subsection "The `if` Statement."

☆ An **elsif clause** is used with an `if` statement and specifies an additional test condition to check when the previous test conditions are *false*. It also gives one or more statements to execute when its test condition is *true*. It has the following general format:

```
if ( test condition ) {
    one or more statements
}
elsif ( test condition ) {
    one or more statements
}
```

It is described in more detail later in the subsection "The `elsif` Clause."

☆ An **else** clause is used with an `if` statement and possibly an `elsif` clause. It specifies a set of statements to execute when one or more test conditions are *false*. It has the following general format:

```
if ( test condition) {
    one or more statements
} else {
    one or more statements
}
```

It is described in more detail later in the subsection "The `else` Clause."

The if Statement

As mentioned earlier, the `if` statement specifies a *test condition* and set of statements to execute when the test condition is *true*. A test condition uses a special *test expression* enclosed in parentheses within an `if` statement. When the test expression evaluates to *true*, then one or more additional statements within the required curly brackets (`{ ... }`) are executed. When the test expression is *false*, then the program skips these statements. Regardless of whether the condition is *true* or *false*, any statements after the curly brackets (`{ ... }`) are executed. Figure 3.6 shows an example of an `if` statement.

```
if ( $aver > 69 ) {                    Enclose test condition in parentheses
    $Grade="Pass";                     Execute these statements when
    print "Grade=$Grade";              $aver is greater than 69.
}
print "Your average was $aver";        Statement(s) to execute
                                       regardless of test condition
```

Figure 3.6 An Example Perl if Statement

☆**TIP**   Semicolon Use with an **if** Statement

No semicolon appears at the end of the `if` statement itself. Instead, curly brackets (`{ ... }`) indicate a *statement block*. A statement block can consist of one or more statements. Each statement within the `if` statement block uses semicolons when they are normally required.

Numerical Test Operators

Test expressions use *test operators* to test conditions. Test operators work much like expression operators except test operators evaluate conditions. For example, the `if` statement in Figure 3.6 uses the greater than (>) operator to test whether `$aver` is greater than 69. Only when the value of `$aver` is greater than 69 will the statements within the curly brackets be executed.

Perl uses one set of test operators for testing conditions with numerical variables and another set for testing conditions involving string variables. Table 3.2 lists the numerical test operators and illustrates their use.

Table 3.2 Perl Numerical Test Operators

Numerical Test Operator	Effect	Example	Result
==	Equal to	```if ($x == 6){ $x = $y + 1; $y = $x + 1; }```	Execute the second and third statements if the value of $x *is equal* to 6.
!=	Not equal to	```if ($x !- $y) { $x = 5 + 1; }```	Execute the second statement if the value of $x *is not equal* to the value of $y.
<	Less than	```if ($x < 100) { $y = 5; }```	Execute the second statement if the value of $x *is less than* 100.
>	Greater than	```if ($x > 51) { print "OK"; }```	Execute the second statement if the value of $x *is greater than* 51.
>=	Greater than or equal	```if (16 >= $x) { print "x=$x"; }```	Execute the second statement if 16 *is greater than or equal to* the value of $x.
<=	Less than or equal to	```if ($x <= $y) { print "y=$y"; print "x=$x"; }```	Execute the second and third statements if the value of $x *is less than or equal to* the value of $y.

☆WARNING Using "==" and "="

The conditional test operator for equal to is ==; the assignment operator is =. Be careful not to confuse these two operators, because it may produce unexpected results. For example, if ($x = $y) does not test whether $x is equal to $y. Rather, it assigns $x to $y and is always *true*.

The following program includes an `if` statement and tests the value of $grade to determine whether it is greater than 89. The output is shown in Figure 3.7.

```
1. #!/usr/bin/perl
2. print "Content-type: text/html\n\n";
3. print "<HTML> <HEAD> <TITLE> String Example </TITLE>
         </HEAD>";
4. print "<BODY>";
```

```
5. $grade = 92;                Test whether $grade is greater than 89
6. if ( $grade > 89 ) {
7.    print "<FONT COLOR=BLUE>Hey you got an A.</FONT>
             <BR> ";
8. }
9. print "Your actual score was $grade";
10. print "</BODY></HTML>";
```

Figure 3.7 Output of the `if` Program Example

In this program:

☆ Lines 1–2 identify the location of Perl and define the MIME Content-type line.

☆ Lines 3–4 output the commands needed to start an HTML document.

☆ Line 5 assigns the value `92` to the variable `$grade`.

☆ Line 6 tests whether `$grade` is greater than `89`. Because it is, line 7 will execute and print `Hey you got an A`.

☆ Line 9 outputs `Your actual score was 92`.

Note that line 9 will execute regardless of the test in line 6. To illustrate this point, Table 3.3 shows some different values for `$grade` from line 5 and the resulting output.

Table 3.3 Output Resulting from Various Inputs to $grade

Line 5	Output
$grade=92;	Hey you got an A. Your actual score was 92
$grade=89;	Your actual score was 89
$grade=40;	Your actual score was 40
$grade=1100;	Hey you got an A. Your actual score was 1100
$grade=-50;	Your actual score was -50

> ☆ **TIP**   **Indent Lines of a Statement Block**
>
> It is considered good practice to indent the lines within a block of statements within curly brackets ({ ... }). This formatting can greatly improve the readability of the program. Conversely, coding lines 6–8 of the preceding example in the following manner would *not* be considered good practice:
>
> ```
> if  ($grade > 89) {
> print "<FONT COLOR=BLUE>Hey you got an A.</FONT><BR> ";
> }
> ```

String Test Operators

In addition to the numerical test operators, Perl supports a set of string test operators. These operators are used to compare string variable values using the ASCII (pronounced "ask-kee") code values. ASCII stands for American Standard Code for Information Interchange. It provides a standard, numerical way to represent characters on a computer. With the ASCII standard, every letter, number, and symbol is translated into a code number. For example, the character "A" is ASCII code 65, and the character "a" is ASCII code 97. Therefore, ASCII "A" is less than ASCII "a". Under the ASCII standard, numbers have lower ASCII code values than do letters, and uppercase letters have lower ASCII code values than do lowercase letters. Letters and numbers are coded in order, so that the character "a" is less than "b", "C" is less than "D", and "1" is less than "9".

Table 3.4 describes the Perl string test operators and offers examples of their use.

Table 3.4 Perl String Comparison Test Operators

String Test Operator	Effect	Example	Result

eq	Equal to	`$name="Nelson";`
		`if ($name eq "Nelson"){`
		`   print "Got Nelson";`
		`}`
			Prints `Got Nelson` because $name *is equal to* "Nelson".

ne	Not equal to	`$alert="Smoke";`
		`if ( $alert ne "fire" ){`
		`   print "$alert NE fire";`
		`   $ok = $ok + 1;`
		`}`
			Prints `Smoke NE fire` and then executes fourth line, because $alert *is not equal to* "fire".

lt	Less than	`if ( "auto" lt "car" ) {`
		`   print "Before car";`
		`}`
			Prints `Before car` because "auto" *is less than* "car".

gt	Greater than	`if ("Jones" gt "Smith" ){`
		`   print "After Smith";`
		`}`
			Prints nothing because "Jones" is not *greater than* "Smith".

Table 3.4 Perl String Comparison Test Operators (*continued*)

String Test Operator	Effect	Example	Result
ge	Greater than or equal to	```if ("WSOX" ge "Cubs"){ print "Sox Win"; }```	Prints Sox Win because "WSOX" *is greater than or equal to* "Cubs".
le	Less than or equal to	```$Name = "Bob"; if ("Bob" le $Name) { print "Got Bob"; }```	Prints Got Bob because "Bob" *is less than or equal to* $Name.

☆**WARNING** Be Careful Using Numerical and String Operators

If you accidentally mix the test operators and test numerical variables when using the string condition operators, your program will likely be errored. For example,

```
$X=50; $Y=150; if  ( $X lt $Y ) {
```

will evaluate to *false* because ASCII "5" is a higher code number than ASCII "1"!

The elsif Clause

As mentioned earlier, the `elsif` clause is always used with the `if` statement. It specifies an additional test condition to check when all of the previous test conditions are *false*. When its condition is *true*, the `elsif` clause gives one or more statements to execute.

Figure 3.8 shows a partial program example of using an `elsif` clause with an `if` statement. In this example, the `elsif` clause will be tested only if `$name` is not equal to "Joe". When `$name` is not equal "Joe", then the `elsif` clause is executed to check whether `$name` is equal to "Jane". Regardless of these tests, the last `print` statement is executed.

```
$found = 0;
if ( $name eq "Joe" ) {
    print "Got Name of Joe";          Execute these statements
    $found = 1;                        when if condition is true
}
elsif ( $name eq "Jane" ) {
    print "Got Name of Jane";         Execute these statements when elsif
    $found = 1;                        condition is true but if statement is false
}
print "Name=$name and found=$found\n";   Execute this statement regardless
                                          of the previous test conditions
```

Figure 3.8 An Example `if-elsif` Clause

To further demonstrate the `elsif` clause, consider the following program, which enhances the example from Figure 3.7:

```
1.  #!/usr/bin/perl
2.  print "Content-type: text/html\n\n";
3.  $grade = 92;
4.  if ( $grade > 100 ) {
5.      print "Illegal Grade > 100 ";
6.  }
7.  elsif ( $grade > 89 ){
8.      print "Hey you got an A ";
9.  }
10. print "Your actual grade was $grade";
```

> Test whether $grade is greater than 89 only when line 4 is *false*

> Executes regardless of tests on lines 4 and 7

In this example, line 4 first tests whether `$grade` is illegal—that is, greater than 100. If `$grade` is not greater than 100, then line 7 checks whether it is greater than 89. Table 3.5 gives several possible values for statement 3 and output when the program is run from a browser.

Table 3.5 Output Resulting from Various Inputs to $grade (First Revision)

Line 3	Output
$grade=92;	Hey you got an A Your actual grade was 92
$grade=89;	Your actual grade was 89
$grade=40;	Your actual grade was 40
$grade=1100;	Illegal Grade > 100 Your actual grade was 1100
$grade=-50;	Your actual grade was -50

Note that the grade program still does not work correctly when the value of `$grade` is less than 0. (A grade of –50 should be illegal.) One way to fix this problem is to add another `elsif` test condition that checks whether `$grade` is less than 0. For example, you could change the program as follows:

```
1.  #!/usr/bin/perl
2.  print "Content-type: text/html\n\n";
3.  $grade = 92;
4.  if ( $grade >= 100 ) {
5.      print "Illegal Grade > 100 ";
6.  }
7.  elsif ( $grade < 0 ) {
8.      print "illegal grade < 0 ";
9.  }
10. elsif ( $grade > 89 ){
11.     print "Hey you got an A ";
12. }
13. print "Your actual grade was $grade";
```

> Test for $grades less than 0

In this program, lines 7–9 include a test to determine whether the value of $grade is illegal because it is less than 0. Table 3.6 shows the output with various values for line 3.

Table 3.6 Output Resulting from Various Inputs to $grade (Second Revision)

Line 3	Output
$grade=92;	Hey you got an A Your actual grade was 92
$grade=89;	Your actual grade was 89
$grade=40;	Your actual grade was 40
$grade=1100;	Illegal Grade > 100 Your actual grade was 1100
$grade=-50;	illegal grade < 0 Your actual grade was -50

The else Clause

The else clause is used to specify a set of statements that execute when all other test conditions in an if block are *false*. It must be used with at least one if statement, but it can also be used with an if followed by one or several elsif statements. Figure 3.9 shows an example using an else clause.

```
if ( $name eq "Joe" ) {
    print "Got Name of Joe";
}
elsif ( $name eq "Jane" ) {
    print "Got Name of Jane";
} else {
    print "Could not validate Name=$name";
}
```

One or more statements to execute when test condition is *true*

One or more statements to execute when test condition is *true* but the previous test condition is *false*

One or more statements to execute when all the previous test conditions are *false*

Figure 3.9 An Example of an else Clause

In Figure 3.9, the else clause is used with an if statement. In this case, the statement print "Could not validate Name=$name" will be executed when $name is not equal to "Jane" or "Joe".

Now let's use the else clause to continue to improve the example from Figure 3.7. Suppose we want this program to output a different message when the value of $grade is valid but less than 90. You might code the example using an else clause as follows:

```
1. #!/usr/bin/perl
2. print "Content-type: text/html\n\n";
3. $grade = 92;
4. if ( $grade >= 100 ) {
5.      print "Illegal Grade > 100";
6. }
```

```
 7. elsif ( $grade < 0 ) {
 8.      print "illegal grade < 0";
 9. }
10. elsif ( $grade > 89 ){
11.      print "Hey you got an A";
12. }
13. else {
14.      print "Sorry you did not get an A";
15. }
```

> Executes only when the tests in lines 4, 7, and 10 are all false

This program adds another `else` clause on lines 13–15. Line 14 executes when the tests of `$grade` on lines 4, 7, and 10 are all *false* (that is, when `$grade` is between 0 and 90). Table 3.7 shows the output of this program with different values of line 3 when run from a browser.

Table 3.7 Output Resulting from Various Inputs to $grade (Third Revision)

Line 3	Output
`$grade=92;`	`Hey you got an A`
`$grade=89;`	`Sorry you did not get an A`
`$grade=40;`	`Sorry you did not get an A`
`$grade=1100;`	`Illegal Grade > 100`
`$grade=-50;`	`illegal grade < 0`

◎◎ Using Perl Functions

In the "Using Scalar Variables" section earlier in this chapter, we discussed several operators that help manipulate data. For example, the addition operator can be used to add two variables (`$x + $y`). Like many other languages, Perl includes built-in functions that provide powerful additional capabilities to enhance your programs. Functions generally work much like operators, except that most (but not all) accept one or more *arguments*. Arguments are input values into functions. They are specified in the following general format:

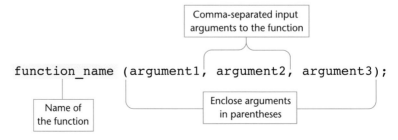

```
function_name (argument1, argument2, argument3);
```

Comma-separated input arguments to the function

Name of the function

Enclose arguments in parentheses

This section discusses several functions in more detail as examples of how Perl functions work, including the following:

☆ *Some basic Perl functions*—the square root, absolute value, length, and random number generation functions.

☆ *The* `print` *function*—more details about the capabilities of the `print` function.

☆ *The* `param` *function*—use this function to receive input into your programs.

Basic Perl Functions

Perl supports several functions that you may find useful in writing your own programs. Although Perl functions are described throughout this book, the following Perl functions may help you understand the idea underlying functions and recognize how they work with arguments.

☆ **sqrt()** The square root function accepts a single numerical argument as input. It returns to your program the square root of the argument passed in. For example,

```
$x=25;
$y=sqrt($x);
print  "x=$x y=$y and finally ", sqrt(144);
```

would output the following:

```
x=25 y=5 and finally 12
```

☆ **abs()** The absolute value function takes a single numerical argument. It returns the absolute value of this argument. For example,

```
$x=-5;
$y=42;
print  abs($x), " ", abs($y);
```

would output the following output:

```
5 42
```

Note that the extra space in the `print` line (" ") is needed to provide a space between the output values.

☆ **rand()** The rand function can be used to generate a random number from 0 to the number passed into it. It is useful for performing many tasks, such as simulating a roll of a die or displaying a random image in a document. When `int()` is used with `rand()`, it forces `rand()` to return whole numbers instead of its default fractional numbers. For example,

```
$numb = int( rand(3) );
```

returns a random number that is either a 0, 1, or 2. Here is another example of the `rand()` function:

```
$dice=int(rand(6))+1;
print "Your random dice toss is $dice";
```

The random number that is generated in this case can be a 1, 2, 3, 4, 5, or 6. Thus one possible output of this code is

```
Your random dice toss is 6
```

☆ **length()** The length function is used to work with string variables. It returns the number of characters in the string argument. For example,

```
$name = "smith";
$title = "Domestic Engineer";
print "name is ", length($name), " title is ",
    length($title), " characters long";
```

returns the following output:

```
name is 5 title is 17 characters long
```

☆ **localtime()** The local time function is typically used with the `time()` function to determine the current date and time while your program is executing. (The time() function isn't too useful by itself for our purposes. On most systems, it returns the number of seconds since January 1, 1970.) When the `time()` function is used as an argument to the `localtime()` function, the output will be a set of scalar variables that provide the current date and time information. The following shows the values returned by `localtime(time)`:

```
($sec, $min, $hr, $day, $mon, $yr, $wkday,
$DayNumOfYr, $TZ   ) = localtime(time);
```

For example,

```
($sec, $min, $hr, $day, $mon, $yr, $wkday,
    $DayNumOfYr, $TZ ) = localtime(time);
print "Time is $hr:$min:$sec Date=$mon/$day/$yr ";
print "Wkday=$wkday DayNumbOfYear=$DayNumOfYr $TZ=$TZ";
```

would produce the following example output:

```
Time is 21:12:58 Date=7/15/101 Wkday=3
    DayNumbOfYear=226 1=1
```

Normally, programs make a few adjustments to the output of `localtime()` because `localtime()` starts counting months from 0 rather than 1 (that is, 0 for January, 1 for February, 2 for March, and so on) and because it outputs the years since 1900. The following code shows a common use of `localtime()` to get date information:

```
($sec, $min, $hr, $day, $mon, $yr,
    $wkday, $DayNumOfYr, $TZ  ) = localtime(time);
$yr=$yr+1900;————————| Add 1900 to get current year |
$mon = $mon + 1;————————| Add 1 to $mon to get current month |
print "Time is $hr:$min:$sec Date=$mon/$day/$yr ";
print "Wkday=$wkday DayNumbOfYear=$DayNumOfYr $TZ=$TZ";
```

The output of this program segment would look like the following:

```
Time is 21:29:58 Date=8/15/2001 Wkday=3
    DayNumbOfYear=226 1=1
```

☆ **WARNING** **Be Careful of the Arguments That You Pass to Functions**

If you mix up your input to Perl functions and pass in a string value instead of a numerical value (or pass a numerical value when the function expects a string value), you won't receive an error message. The output will likely be erroneous, however.

The print Function

You have already been using the `print` function, although you probably don't know about its different output forms. For example, you can enclose your output statements in parentheses or omit them completely. (In most of this book, we do not use the parentheses in the `print` function.)You can also use single or double quotation marks to enclose the output. When you use double quotation marks, Perl searches through the string and outputs the value of any variables. For example,

```
$x = 10;
print ("Mom, please send $x dollars");
```

would output the following message:

```
Mom, please send 10 dollars
```

If you want the actual variable name (and not its value) to be output, then use single quotation marks. For example,

```
$x = 10;
print ( 'Mom, please send $x dollars');
```

would output the following message:

```
Mom, please send $x dollars
```

The preceding examples had only one argument (or input value) to the `print` function. You can also use commas to separate several arguments to the `print` function. For example, the following code sends three arguments to the `print` function for output:

```
$x=5;
print ('Send $bucks', " need $x. No make that ",
    5*$x);
```

This print statement request would output the following message:

```
Send $bucks need 5. No make that 25
```

Notice that each argument in the preceding example is used slightly different-ly—that is, the first argument used single quotation marks, the second argument used double quotation marks, and the third argument used no quotation marks. Also, notice that the last argument output the result of the `5*$x` operation. You can use this method to output operations and even other functions directly.

> ☆**TIP**   **Generating HTML Tags Using `print`**
>
> Using single or double quotation marks in `print` statements can be important when gen-erating HTML tags that need double quotation marks, as in the following example:
>
> ```
> print '<FONT COLOR="BLUE">';
> ```
>
> Sometimes you want to output the value of a variable inside an HTML tag that also requires double quotation marks. You can use the backslash ("\") character to signal that the double quotation marks themselves should be output, as in the following example:
>
> ```
> $color="BLUE";
> print "<FONT COLOR=\"$color\">";
> ```

The param Function

So far our programs have been fairly limited. That is, they can generate HTML pages, but they cannot dynamically respond to user input. For example, in the grade example given in the "The `else` Clause" section (with output in Table 3.7), the program always uses the same value for `$grade`. Whenever the program needs to work on a new `$grade` value, it must be changed.

Most programs receive some sort of input. For example, a Web application may get data from a Web form, a database, or even a regular file on the Web server. This section looks at the `param()` function, which offers a way to receive input into your programs. It will also describe ways to send data to your programs from a Web address without the complexities involved in creating HTML forms. (Creating HTML forms and receiving input from them are described in Chapter 4.)

Where Is param?

The `param()` function is available within the `CGI.pm` Perl library, which we will use extensively. A Perl library comprises a collection of functions available to your program once the program connects to it. The functions within `CGI.pm` were cre-ated by Lincoln Stein for his own Web development use. They have been incorpo-rated into the standard Perl library since the advent of Perl version 5.003.

Before you can use any of the `CGI.pm` functions, you need to connect to the library. You can use the following line of code to do so. It should appear at the beginning of your program (after the code identifying the location of Perl).

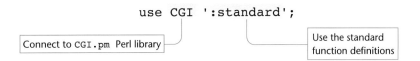

This line requests that the functions within `CGI.pm` be made available to your program using the *standard* functional mode. We will use the standard mode throughout this book; the alternative, object-oriented method is beyond the scope of our discussion.

☆**TIP**   **Perl Modules**

The `CGI.pm` module is one of several Perl modules that are available. Some of the other modules include functions that can generate graphics from Perl, work with dates, and work with databases. Some modules are not part of the standard Perl release, but can be installed as needed (usually by your Web server administrator). See the Perl language Web site at `http://www.perl.com` for more details.

Using param

As previously mentioned, your program can use the `param()` function to receive input variable values. Input variables into CGI/Perl application programs are called **CGI variables**. Their values are received into your program through your Web server as input from a Web browser.

To use `param()` in your program, you provide the CGI variable name as an argument to `param()`. The function will then return the CGI variable's value. The following is an example statement using the `CGI.pm param()` function:

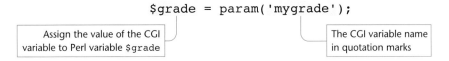

This statement requests that `param()` fetch the value of the CGI variable `mygrade` and assign its value to the Perl variable `$grade`. The CGI variable `mygrade` and its value should have been defined when your program was called (usually from a Web page).

☆**WARNING** **Specifying CGI Variable Names**

You do not use a dollar sign ("$") in front of the name of a CGI variable. For our purposes, we will use CGI variables only as arguments to the `param()` function to obtain a CGI variable's value.

The Perl program in Figure 3.10 looks for a CGI variable named `mygrade` and prints out the variable's value when it is received.

```
1. #!/usr/bin/perl
2. use CGI ':standard';
3. print "Content-type: text/html\n\n";
4. $grade = param('mygrade');
5. print ("Got a Grade = $grade");
```

> Assigns the value of the CGI variable mygrade to $grade

Figure 3.10 A Simple Program That Outputs Its Input Value

Sending Arguments to Your Web Pages

As previously mentioned, data are often provided to CGI/Perl application programs through a Web form. We will look at Web forms in more detail in Chapter Four. For now, however, we will use a Web address or URL from an Internet-connected browser to send CGI variables to our programs. Suppose you saved the program in Figure 3.10 in the following location:

```
http://www.aw.com/~perlpgm/cgi-bin/C3/param1.cgi
```

You can pass your CGI/Perl program arguments by appending a question mark ("?"), followed by the argument name, the equals sign ("="), and a value. For example, the following line sends the argument named `mygrade` with a value of 75 to the program `param1.cgi`:

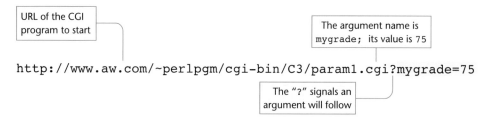

URL of the CGI program to start

The argument name is mygrade; its value is 75

```
http://www.aw.com/~perlpgm/cgi-bin/C3/param1.cgi?mygrade=75
```

The "?" signals an argument will follow

If you entered this Web address in a browser, Figure 3.11 shows the output that you would receive.

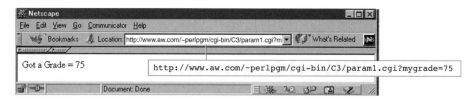

Figure 3.11 Output from Sending an Argument to the Program in Figure 3.10

When you have more than one argument to pass, you can append the additional arguments with an ampersand ("&") followed by the argument name, an equal sign ("="), and a value. For example, the following line sends the argument grade with a value of 45 and the argument name with a value of tom. In this example, the program param1.cgi is expecting only one CGI variable called mygrade, so the other argument called name will be ignored.

```
http://www.aw.com/~perlpgm/cgi-bin/C3/param1.cgi?
    mygrade=45&name="tom"
```

☆ **WARNING** **Argument Names Must Match**

The argument name in the receiving CGI/Perl program and the argument name in the sending URL Web address must match. For example, imagine that you have the following calling Web address:

```
http://www.mysite.com/cgi-bin/gradepgm.cgi?counter=23
```

The CGI/Perl program must include counter inside the call to param as follows to receive this argument:

```
$x = param('counter');
```

As another example, consider the following program, which is an adaptation of the grade program developed in "The else Clause" section. This version uses CGI variable mygrd and myname as arguments with values received via the param() function. Figure 3.12 shows two different calls to the program using two sets of options. The top screen results when the arguments ?myname=tom&mygrd=75 are sent. The bottom screen results when the arguments myname= lori&mygrd=95 are sent.

```
 1. #!/usr/bin/perl
 2. use CGI ':standard';
 3. print "Content-type: text/html\n\n";
 4. print '<HTML><BODY><TITLE>Grade</TITLE></HEAD>
          <BODY>';
 5. $grade = param('mygrd');
 6. $name = param('myname');
 7. print '<FONT size="4" color="red">';
 8. if ( $grade >= 100 ) {
 9.    print 'Illegal Grade > 100';
10. } elsif ( $grade < 0 ) {
11.    print 'illegal grade < 0';
12. } elsif ( $grade >= 90 ){
13.    print 'Hey you got an A';
14. } else {
15.    print 'Sorry you did not get an A';
16. }
17. print '<BR><FONT COLOR="blue">';
18. print "$name, your grade was $grade";
19. print '</FONT></FONT></BODY></HTML>';
```

> Gets the values of the CGI variables mygrd and myname; assigns them to $grade and $name

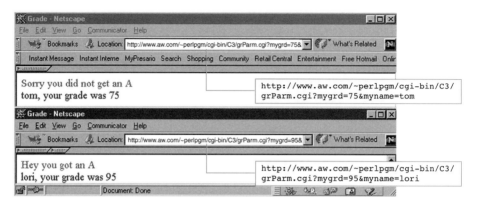

Figure 3.12 Two Calls to the Same Perl Program with Different Arguments

In this program:

☆ Lines 1–4 identify the location of Perl, output the MIME Content-type line, connect to the `CGI.pm` library, and output the tags needed to start an HTML document.

☆ Lines 5–6 get the input variables using the `CGI.pm` function `param` with `$grade` and `$name` to receive the argument values.

☆ Lines 7–16 set up an initial font (line 7) and then test the value of `$grade` against several possible values.

☆ Lines 17–19 change the font to blue and output the final message.

☆ **TIP**   **Testing for Null Values**

When you receive input data from the Web, it is useful to test whether an input variable has any value at all. Perl provides a simple method to perform this kind of testing. In the following example code, the first `if` condition evaluates to *true* if $name has any value. The `else` condition will execute if $name has no value.

```
$name = param( 'uname' ) ;
if ($name) {
    statement(s) to execute when $name has a value
} else {
    statement(s) to execute when $name has no value
}
```

Using Perl Functions

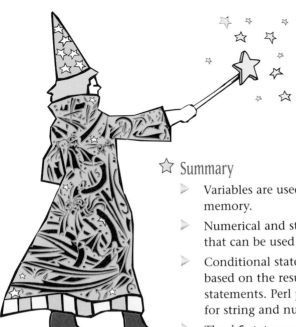

☆ Summary

▷ Variables are used to store and access data in computer memory.

▷ Numerical and string variables have unique operations that can be used to manipulate their values.

▷ Conditional statements are used to test for conditions and, based on the results of the test, execute specific program statements. Perl provides different test condition operators for string and numerical variables.

▷ The `if` statement can be used by itself and is a basic way of testing conditions. The `elsif` clause can be used with the `if` statement to provide another test condition when the original `if` statement is *false*. An `else` clause provides statements that execute when all other `if` and `elsif` conditions are *false*.

▷ Many built-in Perl functions can prove useful to your programs. These functions, which include `print()`, `sqrt()`, and `length()`, can be used directly in programs when needed. Arguments are sent to these functions inside the parentheses.

▷ The `param()` function is found in a special `CGI.pm` library. You need to connect to this library before you can use it. The `param()` function is useful for receiving arguments into your program. Arguments can be sent to your program from the address or location box of a Web browser connected to the Internet.

☆ Online References

Perl Software Download
`http://www.perl.com`

ASCII Reference Chart and Discussion
`http://www.jimprice.com/jim-asc.htm`

Lincoln Stein's Discussion of the Functions in the `CGI.pm` Module
`http://stein.cshl.org/WWW/software/CGI/cgi_docs.html`

Perl documentation site with information on statements, functions, modules, and much more
`http://perldoc.com`

Articles about Perl
`http://perl.about.com`

☆ Review Questions

1. Which of the following are not valid Perl variable names:

   `$1st_counter, $x1, $soccer, $TimeCounter, squared?`

   Why are they invalid?

2. What are the operator precedence rules in Perl? What would be the values of `$x` and `$y` after executing the following statements:

   ```
   $x = 15 + 12 / 2 - 1;
   $y = (12 + 12) / 2 + 2;
   ```

3. Which three types of conditional clauses were described in this chapter. Which is the only one that can be used by itself?

4. Which test operator is used to test whether one of two string variables is greater than the other? What test operator is used to test whether one of two numerical variables is greater than the other?

5. What would be the output of the following line of Perl code:

   `print int(rand(5));`

6. Suppose line 5 in the program that produced Figure 3.7 was deleted entirely. What will be the output of the program?

7. Write a Perl statement that outputs the following line. (Make sure that you output the value of the variable `$name`.)

   `$name was "deleted" from our database`

8. Show how you can send a value of `yellow` for a CGI variable named `color` to a program at an example URL of `http://www.pgmsite.com/cgi-bin/colortest.cgi`.

9. What line of Perl code is required to connect to the `CGI.pm` library?

☆ Hands-On Exercises

1. Write programs that calculate the following equations. Print out your results as HTML documents.

   (a) Calculate the volume of a cylinder using the following formula. Use $r = 4$ and $h = 12$. Use 3.14 as the value of π.

   $$V = \pi r^2 h$$

   (b) Calculate the average of four grades where `grade1` = 100, `grade2` = 75, `grade3` = 98, and `grade4` = 90.

   (c) Calculate the distance between two points using the Pythagorean theorem. Use input $X_1 = 2$, $X_2 = 2$, $Y_1 = 2$, and $Y_2 = 4$.

   $$\sqrt{(x_2 - x_1)^2 + (y_2 - y_1)^2}$$

2. Modify the program used to produce Figure 3.3 to test the value of `remain`. If its value is even, print the message "`even remainder`"; if its value is odd, print the message "`odd remainder`". Generate your output in HTML.

3. Modify the third revision of the grade program (found in "The `else` Clause" section) to include additional tests. If `$grade` is:
   (a) Between 90 and 100 inclusive, print "`You got an A`".
   (b) Between 80 and 89 inclusive, print "`You got a B`".
   (c) Between 70 and 79 inclusive, print "`You got a C`".
   (d) Between 60 and 69 inclusive, print "`You got a D`".
   (e) Less than 60, print "`You failed`".

4. Create a program that accepts grade values as arguments based on Exercise 1(b). Call the routine with the following values, and print the results in an HTML document.
   (a) `grade1` = 100, `grade2` = 75, `grade3` = 98, `grade4` = 90
   (b) `grade1` = 75, `grade2` = 85, `grade3` = 95, `grade4` = 100
   (c) `grade1` = 50, `grade2` = 60, `grade3` = 70, `grade4` = 100

5. Modify the program you created in Exercise 1(a) to accept the values for *r* and *h* as arguments. Test your program with the following input values:
   (a) *r* = 4, *h* = 12
   (b) *r* = 10, *h* = 10
   (c) *r* = 3, *h* = 1

6. Modify the program you created in Exercise 3 to accept one argument, called `$grade`. Call the program with the following values and print the results in an HTML document.
   (a) `$grade` = 70
   (b) `$grade` = 100
   (c) `$grade` = 150
   (d) `$grade` = 50
   (e) `$grade` = –150

7. Write a program that accepts two arguments as input: `totdebt` and `income`.
   (a) If the total debt is less than 15% of income, print an HTML document in *green* font and font size = 4 that says `Credit is approved`; output the total debt, total income, and debt as a percentage of total income.
   (b) If total debt is between 15% and 30% of income, print an HTML document in *yellow* font and font size = 4 that says `Credit is borderline`; output the total debt, total income, and debt as a percentage of total income.
   (c) If total debt is more than 30% of income, generate an HTML document in *red* font and font size = 4 that says `Credit is NOT APPROVED`; output the total debt, total income, and debt as a percentage of total income.

Test your program with the following values. Make sure your program works appropriately for each set.

(a) `totdebt` = 25,000, `income` = 100,000
(b) `totdebt` = 7500, income = 15,000
(c) `totdebt` = 0, `income` = 50,000
(d) `totdebt` = 125,000, `income` = 50,000
(e) `totdebt` = 0, `income` = 0
(f) `totdebt` = –50, `income` = –100

CHAPTER FOUR

WORKING WITH THE WEB

Chapter Three introduced you to some basic Perl statements and functions. In that chapter, the `param()` function (from the `CGI.pm` Perl module) was described as a way to receive input from the Web. This chapter explores other functions within that library and describes how to use HTML forms to send input values to your programs.

Chapter Objectives

☆ Describe the basic functions within the `CGI.pm` library that can generate HTML tags

☆ Learn the different formats of the `CGI.pm` function syntax

☆ Understand how to use forms to send data to CGI/Perl programs

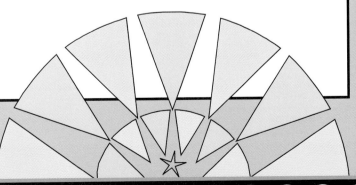

◎◎ Generating HTML Documents with CGI.pm

So far, when we have generated HTML from Perl, we have used the `print` function to output the HTML tags. Although using `print` statements to output HTML tags works well, the `CGI.pm` module provides several functions that can be used to concisely output HTML tags. (The `CGI.pm` module was introduced in Chapter Three.) As an example, look at the following lines:

```
$mypage='It is a New Day';
print "<HTML><HEAD><TITLE> $mypage </TITLE></HEAD><BODY>";
```

This code would generate the following HTML tags, which start an HTML document:

```
<HTML><HEAD><TITLE> It is a New Day </TITLE></HEAD>
<BODY>
```

You can output the same HTML by using the `CGI.pm` `start_html` function as follows:

```
$mypage='It is a New Day';
print start_html("$mypage");
```

Below is an example that shows three basic `CGI.pm` functions that generate HTML:

☆ **header**—to create the MIME Content-type line in line 3

☆ **start_html**—to create the starting HTML tags in line 4

☆ **end_html**—to create the ending HTML tags in line 7

When you use these functions with a `print` statement, the HTML tags are output directly. In Figure 4.1, the output of the program appears in the top screen and the resultant HTML is shown on the bottom screen.

```
1. #!/usr/bin/perl
2. use CGI ':standard';
3. print header;─────────────── Generate MIME Content-type line
4. print start_html;─────────────── Generate starting HTML tags
5. print '<FONT size=4 color="blue">';
6. print 'Welcome <I>humans</I> to my site</FONT>';
7. print end_html;─────── Generate ending HTML tags
```

Figure 4.1 Output of a Simple HTML Document Using `CGI.pm` Functions

In the preceding program:

☆ Line 1 identifies the location of Perl.

☆ Line 2 connects to the `CGI.pm` library.

☆ Line 3 uses the `header` function to output the MIME Content-type line. That is, it outputs `Content-type: text/html\n\n`.

☆ Line 4 uses `start_html` to output the HTML tags needed to start a document. That is, it outputs `<HTML><HEAD><TITLE></TITLE></HEAD> <BODY>`.

☆ Line 5 sets the font size and color for the document, and line 6 prints the message `Welcome humans to my site`.

☆ Line 7 uses `end_html` to output the closing HTML tags—that is, `</BODY></HTML>`.

☆**TIP**   **Using CGI.pm functions**

This example also shows that you can mix `CGI.pm` functions (lines 3, 4, and 7) and the long-hand style of creating HTML tags (lines 5 and 6). This use is perfectly acceptable. Use the `CGI.pm` functions that best improve the readability of your programs.

The Basic Formats of CGI.pm Functions

The functions within the `CGI.pm` library accept a variety of syntactic formats (that is, rules stating what makes a valid statement). Using some of these functions can become quite complicated—for example, using `CGI.pm` functions to create HTML tags for tables and lists. Here, we will stick with three basic sets of syntax for `CGI.pm` functions. This discussion will not describe *all* of the `CGI.pm` functions, but it will cover some of the most useful ones. These three basic syntax formats are as follows:

☆ *No argument format*—functions that can be used without any arguments

☆ *Positional argument format*—functions that can accept comma-separated arguments within parentheses

☆ *Name-value argument format*—functions that accept parameters submitted as name-and-value pairs

Each of these syntax formats is described below, along with examples of its use.

No Argument Format

`CGI.pm` has several functions that work without arguments. For example, the program that creates Figure 4.1 uses `header`, `start_html`, and `end_html`. When you use `CGI.pm` functions that support no arguments, you can place the function name directly within a `print` statement (as in Figure 4.1). You can also use several `CGI.pm` functions within a single `print` statement.

For example, the code shown in Figure 4.2 will output the HTML tags to start an HTML document, then output <BR>, then <BR>, and finally <HR>. Thus the output of this line would be

`<HTML><HEAD><TITLE></TITLE></HEAD><BODY><BR><BR><HR>`

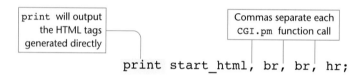

Figure 4.2 Format of a `print` Statement with Multiple Single-Argument `CGI.pm` Functions

As noted earlier, `CGI.pm` supports several functions that can work with no arguments. (Some of them also accept arguments using the positional or multiargument style; these functions will be described later in this chapter.) Table 4.1 lists some of the no-argument `CGI.pm` functions.

☆ **TIP**   **Depreciated HTML Tags**

Some of these tags, such as `<B>` , `<I>`, and `<FONT>`, are depreciated in the most recent HTML standards. They are provided here because they are still supported by the `CGI.pm` module and most HTML-compliant browsers, and they will likely be supported for years to come.

Table 4.1 Selected No-Argument CGI.pm Functions

CGI.pm Function	Example of Use	Example Output
header—generate the MIME Content-type line	print header;	Content-type:text/html\n\n
start_html—generate tags needed to start an HTML document (In this format, the document has no title.)	print start_html;	<HTML><HEAD><TITLE></TITLE></HEAD><BODY>
br—output tag	print br;	
hr—generate horizontal rule tag	print hr;	<HR>
end_html—generate tags to end an HTML document	print end_html;	</BODY></HTML>

Positional Argument Format

Some **CGI.pm** functions allow you to specify multiple arguments to them based on the position of the argument in the calling statement. The easiest functions to use are the ones that accept one argument. Figure 4.3 presents an example of this format.

Generate <H1>...</H1> tags

Argument used as a string to include in the <H1>....</H1> tags

```
print h1('Hello World');
```

Figure 4.3 Positional Argument CGI.pm Format

Table 4.2 lists several **CGI.pm** functions that support positional arguments.

Table 4.2 Selected Positional Argument CGI.pm Functions

CGI.pm Functions	Example of Use	Example Output
start_html()— generates the tags needed to start an HTML document. If a positional argument is used it becomes the document title.	start_html('My Page');	<HTML><HEAD><TITLE> My Page </TITLE></HEAD><BODY>
h1()—generates the header level 1 tags. (Note that h1(), h2(), h3(), and h4() work the same way for level 1, 2, 3,and 4 headers, respectively.)	print h1('Hello There');	<H1>Hello There</H1>
strong()—prints the argument in strong font.	print strong('Now');	<STRONG>Now</STRONG>
p()—creates a paragraph.	print p('Time to move');	<P>Time to move</P>
b()—prints the argument in bold.	print b('Exit');	<B>Exit</B>
i()—prints the argument in italics.	print i('Quickly');	<I>Quickly</I>

Several of these functions can also be concisely specified in a single `print` statement. Consider the following example:

```
print i('Please '),'come when I call you ',
    strong('immediately.');
```

This code would output the following:

```
<I>Please </I>come when I call you <STRONG> immediately.
    </STRONG>
```

The next program demonstrates the use of some CGI.pm functions with positional arguments (and some no-argument functions) to generate an HTML document. Figure 4.4 shows the output of this program.

```perl
1. #!/usr/bin/perl
2. use CGI ':standard';
3. print header, start_html('Positional Example'),
        h1('Simple Math');
4. print b('two times two='), 2*2;
5. print br, 'but ', b('four times four='), 4*4;
6. print br, 'Finally, ', b('eight times eight='), 8*8;
7. print end_html;
```

Uses Bold font for two times two= and then outputs 4.

Figure 4.4 Use of a Perl Script Including Several CGI.pm Functions to Generate HTML

Let's look at some key lines from this program in more detail:

☆ Lines 1–2 identify the location of Perl and connect to the CGI.pm library.

☆ Line 3 calls **header** (to generate the MIME Content-type line), **start_html** (to generate the starting HTML tags with a title), and then **h1** (to generate the H1 tag with `Simple Math` as the heading text).

☆ Line 4 calls **b** to make the words `two times two=` appear in a bold font. It also outputs the result of `2*2`.

☆ Lines 5-6 call **br** (<BR>) and then **b** to apply bold formatting to some text, before outputting the results of a calculation.

☆ Line 7 calls **end_html** to output the closing HTML tags.

Name-Value Argument Format

Some CGI.pm functions allow you to specify multiple arguments in argument-name/argument-value pairs. These functions can be called with the format shown in Figure 4.5.

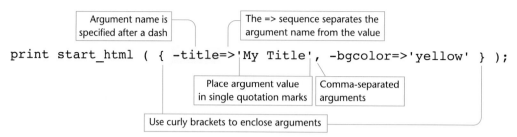

Figure 4.5 General Format of the `CGI.pm` HTM-Generating Functions

This format technically specifies the arguments as a *hash array.* (Don't worry about what "hash array" means—this topic isn't covered until Chapter Six). The line in Figure 4.5 sends a title argument and background color argument to `start_html`. It generates the following output:

```
<HTML><HEAD><TITLE>My Title</TITLE></HEAD>
<BODY BGCOLOR="yellow">
```

Table 4.3 lists some name-value `CGI.pm` functions, along with examples of their usage and output.

Table 4.3 Selected Name-Value Argument `CGI.pm` Functions

`CGI.pm` Function	Example of Usage	Example Output

start_html— generates tags to start HTML documents	`print start_html({`
	`-title=>'my title',`
	`-bgcolor=>'red' });`
		`<HTML><HEAD><TITLE>my`
		`title</TITLE></HEAD>`
		`<BODY BGCOLOR="RED">`

img—inserts an image	`print img({`
	`-src=>'myfile.gif',`
	`-alt=>'picture'});`
		`<IMG SRC="myfile.gif"`
		`alt="picture">`

a—establishes links	`print a({ -href=>`
	`'http://www.mysite.`
	`com'}, 'Click Here');`
		`<A HREF=`
		`"http://www.mysite.`
		`com"> Click Here </A>`

font()—creates `<FONT>...</FONT>` tags that can set font color, size, and type	`print font( {`
	`-color=>'BLUE',`
	`-size=>'4'},`
	`'Lean, and mean.');`
		`<FONT SIZE="4"`
		`COLOR="BLUE">Lean,`
		`and mean. </FONT>`

The following Perl program connects to the CGI.pm library and then uses the start_html function with the name-value argument format. Figure 4.6 shows the output from this program.

```
1. #!/usr/bin/perl
2. use CGI ':standard';
3. print header;
4. print start_html({-title=>'New Day ',
       -bgcolor=>'yellow'});
5. print 'Welcome One And ', i('All');
6. print end_html;
```

Name-value format
for start_html

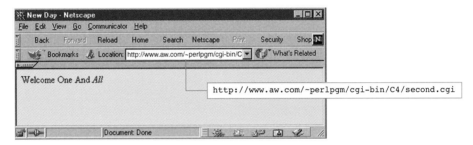

Figure 4.6 An HTML Document Created with CGI.pm Functions

In this code:

☆ Lines 1–2 identify the location of Perl and connects to the CGI.pm library.

☆ Line 3 print the MIME Content-type line.

☆ Line 4 outputs the tags needed to start an HTML document with title New Day in the <TITLE> tag and bgcolor=Yellow in the <BODY> tag.

☆ Line 5 prints the message Welcome One And All.

☆ Line 6 uses end_html to generate the closing </BODY> and </HTML> tags.

☆**TIP   More Information on CGI.pm Functions**

In general, I recommend using the CGI.pm functions that take no arguments or positional arguments. They are the easiest to use, and they help minimize your code and improve its readability to the greatest extent. Much more detail on the functions contained in the CGI.pm module can be found at http://stein.cshl.org/WWW/software/CGI/cgi_docs.html or in Lincoln Stein's book, *Official Guide to Programming with CGI.pm.*

Getting Input Data from HTML Forms

In Chapter Three, we covered the process of sending arguments to CGI/Perl programs from Web addresses through a browser. A more common method to start CGI/Perl programs and pass them arguments is to use **HTML forms**. HTML forms allow you to take advantage of methods such as **text areas**, **check boxes**, **selection lists**, and **radio buttons** to create and input data into your programs. The remainder of this chapter discusses the use of HTML forms to send data to CGI/Perl programs.

In the discussion presented here, we will focus on the creation of HTML forms by explicitly using HTML form tags from a CGI/Perl program. `CGI.pm` functions are available for each of these tags, although most of them use more complex argument formats.

Starting and Ending Forms

HTML forms are created by using the HTML `<FORM>` and `</FORM>` tags. Within these tags, you place various HTML form elements, such as text areas, check boxes, and radio buttons. The following demonstrates the use of the HTML `<FORM>` and `</FORM>` tags.

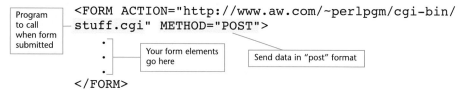

```
<FORM ACTION="http://www.aw.com/~perlpgm/cgi-bin/
stuff.cgi" METHOD="POST">
    •
    •
    •
</FORM>
```

Program to call when form submitted

Your form elements go here

Send data in "post" format

The `<FORM>` tag has two primary arguments:

☆ **ACTION=** You need this option to start your CGI/Perl programs. It specifies the Web address or URL of the CGI program to start when the form is submitted. In the preceding code, the form URL is `http://www.aw.com/~perlpgm/cgi-bin/stuff.cgi`.

☆ **SHORTCUT** **Sending E-Mail from an HTML Form**

Another action setting, the `mailto` option, sends your request via e-mail to an e-mail address:

```
<FORM ACTION="mailto:handle@handle.com" METHOD="POST">
```

The e-mail you receive from this line of code is not formatted very attractively. Most Web applications first send the form to a program, and then forward it to a database or mailbox. This book will not use this `ACTION=` option. Chapter Eight describes how to send e-mail from a CGI/Perl application.

METHOD= This argument is set to either `post` or `get`. It defines the argu-ment format that will be used to send data to the CGI/Perl program. The `get` method appends the form arguments to the end of the Web address (as we saw in "The `param` Function" section in Chapter Three). The `post` method sends the data as part of the body of the HTML document. Because the `get` method may limit the amount of data you can send, we will use `post` exclusively in our programs here.

From your CGI/Perl programs, you can output these tags using the `print` statement as follows:

```
#!/usr/bin/perl
use CGI ':standard';
print header, start_html('Sample Form');
print '<FORM
       ACTION=" http://www.aw.com/~perlpgm/cgi-bin/
          stuff.cgi"
       METHOD="POST">';
```

```
·
·        ┌──────────────────────────────────┐
·  ──────┤ Perl statements that output      │
·        │ FORM elements go here            │
         └──────────────────────────────────┘
print '</FORM>';
```

Form Buttons

Perhaps the most basic HTML form elements are form buttons. Form buttons enable you to submit the form or erase all input (and start again). When you sub-mit the form, it is sent to the location specified in the `ACTION=` argument of the `<FORM>` tag. Submit buttons have the following formats in HTML:

```
<INPUT TYPE="SUBMIT" VALUE="Click To Submit">
<INPUT TYPE="RESET"  VALUE="Clear and Restart">
```

You can use the following Perl statements to output a form and reset buttons in your programs:

```
print '<INPUT TYPE="SUBMIT" VALUE="Click To Submit">';
print '<INPUT TYPE="RESET"  VALUE="Clear and Restart">';
```

This code creates a submit button and a reset button. The reset button is labeled "Click to Submit," and the reset button is labeled "Erase and Restart."

☆**SHORTCUT** **Another Argument for the Submit Button Form Element**

The submit button also has a `NAME=` argument, which is most commonly used when you have multiple submit buttons on a form and want to determine in the receiving program which button the user clicked. (The section "Setting Up Input Text Areas" describes how to receive name-value arguments from forms.)

Getting Input Data from HTML Forms

To see a more complete example, consider the following listing and output in Figure 4.7. This program creates two buttons: a submit button and a reset button. When the form is submitted, it executes the program that created Figure 4.1. The top portion of Figure 4.7 shows the output form from the code below. The bottom portion of Figure 4.7 shows what happens when the form is submitted.

```
1. #!/usr/bin/perl
2. use CGI ':standard';
3. print header, start_html('A First Form');
4. print '<FORM
        ACTION-"http://www.aw.com/~perlpgm/cgi-bin/C4/
        first.cgi"
        METHOD="POST">';
5. print br, '<INPUT TYPE="SUBMIT"
   VALUE="Click To Submit">';
6. print '<INPUT TYPE="RESET"
   VALUE="Erase and Restart">';
7. print '</FORM>', end_html;
```

Program to execute when form is submitted

Output submit and reset buttons

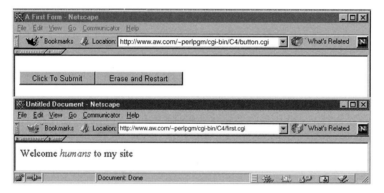

Figure 4.7 Output Form from the Preceding Listing (top) and Output When the Form Is Submitted (bottom)

In this program:

☆ Lines 1–3 identify the location of Perl, connect to the Perl `CGI.pm` library, print the MIME Content-type header, and create the starting HTML tags.

☆ Line 4 starts the `FORM` tag and sets the `ACTION` argument. Here, the action is set to start the program that generates Figure 4.1 when submitted.

☆ Lines 5–6 create the submit and reset buttons.

☆ Line 7 outputs the closing `FORM` and HTML document tags.

Setting Up Input Text Areas

So far, the forms we have created can only start a CGI/Perl program. When you learn to use other form elements, you will be able to pass in user input as arguments to your CGI/Perl programs.

The following line of HTML code demonstrates the use of an *input text area*:

| CGI variable name | | Text area box size | Maximum number of characters allowed |

```
<INPUT TEXT TYPE="text" SIZE="15" MAXLENGTH="20"
       NAME="color">
```

In a CGI/Perl program, you can output this form element as follows:

```
print '<INPUT TEXT TYPE="text" SIZE="15" MAXLENGTH="20"
       NAME="color">';
```

This code creates a text box that is 15 characters wide and can hold a maximum of 20 input characters. The NAME attribute sets a CGI variable called `color` that will be available to your form-processing programs. The value of `color` will be whatever the end user inputs into the text box.

When you want to get input from text boxes, use the `param` function as you did in Chapter Three, "The `param` Function," to get input arguments. The key is to ensure that the argument set with the NAME= argument matches the argument passed to the `param` function. Figure 4.8 shows the relationship between the calling HTML form and the receiving Perl program. In the figure, you can see how the FORM tags identify which CGI/Perl program is started and how arguments are sent and received.

Calling HTML Form

URL of program to which to send form output

```
<FORM ACTION="http://www.aw.com/~perlpgm/cgi-bin/form1Rcv.cgi"
      METHOD="POST">
<INPUT TYPE="text" SIZE="15" MAXLENGTH="20" NAME="color">
      .
      .
      .
</FORM>
```

Name of argument from text box is `color`

Receiving CGI/Perl Program

```
#!/usr/bin/perl
use CGI ".standard";
print header;
print start_html("Color my Text");
$userColor=param("color");
      .
      .
      .
```

Get the value of CGI variable `color`

Figure 4.8 How CGI/Perl Programs Are Called and Receive Arguments from HTML Forms

Suppose you use the following CGI/Perl program to generate a form with an input box, a submit button, and a reset button:

```
1. #!/usr/bin/perl
2. use CGI ':standard';
3. print header, start_html;
4. print '<FORM
          ACTION="http://www.aw.com/~perlpgm/cgi-bin/C4/
          form1Rcv.cgi"
          METHOD="POST" >';
5. print 'Enter A Color';
6. print '<INPUT TEXT TYPE="TEXT" SIZE="15"
          NAME="color">';
7. print br, '<INPUT TYPE=SUBMIT
          VALUE="Click To Submit">';
8. print '<INPUT TYPE=RESET VALUE="Erase and Restart">';
9. print '</FORM>', end_html;
```

Lines 2–4 annotations: *Program to call when form is submitted* (points to line 4). *Sets CGI variable named color* (points to line 6).

In this program:

★ Line 4 sets the action to call a program at `http://www.aw.com/~perlpgm/cgi-bin/C4/form1Rcv.cgi` when the program is submitted.

★ Lines 5–6 print the output `Enter A Color` and then create a text box. They also create a CGI variable named `color` that will be set to whatever the end user enters in the text box.

★ Lines 7–8 create the submit and reset buttons.

Now suppose that the Perl program shown below is placed on a Web server at `http://www.aw.com/~perlpgm/cgi-bin/C4/form1Rcv.cgi`. This program will start when the user clicks the submit button on the form created in the preceding program. In the following code:

★ Line 5 receives the input value using the `param` function and assigns it to `$userColor`.

★ Line 6 uses the input color value to change the color of its text.

Figure 4.9 shows the output of the form generation program (top) and the form-parsing program (bottom).

```
1. #!/usr/bin/perl
2. use CGI ':standard';
3. print header;
4. print start_html("Color my Text");
5. $userColor = param('color');
6. print "<FONT SIZE=4 COLOR=$userColor>";
7. print 'Welcome to my World';
8. print '</FONT>', end_html;
```

Line 5 annotation: *Puts the value of the CGI variable color into $userColor*. Line 6–8 annotation: *Uses $userColor to set the FONT color*.

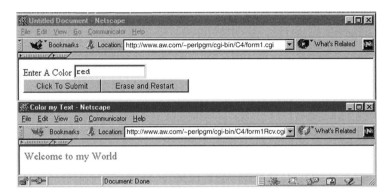

Figure 4.9 The HTML Form Created and Result When red Is Input and Submitted

Where Is the Form Validation?

While the previous form-parsing program is useful for showing how fields can be set in a text box and sent to another Perl program, it does have a serious drawback: It does not check for valid user input and uses whatever the user enters in line 6. Typically, form-parsing programs should check any user input for validity. (A little paranoia goes a long way toward making better programs!) Chapter Seven discusses ways to verify forms using regular expressions.

Sending Passwords

HTML supports creating text boxes as password areas instead of viewable text. Letters entered within a password box are viewed as asterisks ("*") instead of the text being typed. To create a password box, you set `TYPE="password"` with the `INPUT` form element tag. The other arguments to password text boxes work much like text areas. For example, the HTML for a password box shown below:

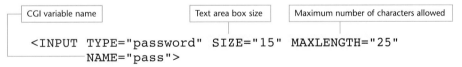

```
<INPUT TYPE="password" SIZE="15" MAXLENGTH="25"
        NAME="pass">
```

This line of code creates a password text box that is 15 characters long, and it sets a CGI variable called `pass` to the value entered by the end user. The following code demonstrates how to create the same password box in a CGI/Perl program:

```
print '<INPUT TYPE="password" MAXLENGTH="25" SIZE="15"
        NAME="pass">';
```

☆WARNING **Password Boxes Are Not Secure**

The HTML password box is not a secure method for transmitting passwords. When the user submits the form, any data input is sent in clear text (nonencrypted), just like any other HTML form field. Someone with network access could, therefore, potentially read the password being transferred. For this reason, most Web sites do not use this approach to receive and transmit passwords.

Let's look at an example that uses password text boxes. Suppose the following CGI/Perl program was used to generate the HTML password form shown in Figure 4.10:

```
1. #!/usr/bin/perl
2. use CGI ":standard";
3. print header;
4. print start_html("Color my Text");
5. print '<FORM
           ACTION="http://www.aw.com/~perlpgm/cgi-bin/C4/
           checkpass.cgi" METHOD="POST">';
6. print '<FONT COLOR="BLUE" SIZE=4>
           Enter password to see message <BR>';
7. print '<INPUT TYPE="password" SIZE="15"
           NAME="passwd">';        Sets the CGI variable named passwd
8. print br, '<INPUT TYPE=SUBMIT VALUE="Click To
           Submit">';
9. print '<INPUT TYPE=RESET VALUE="Erase and
           Restart">';
10. print '</FORM>', end_html;
```

In this program:

☆ Line 5 sends the submitted output to `http://www.aw.com/~perlpgm/cgi-bin/C4/checkpass.cgi`.

☆ Line 7 sets the password text box with a CGI variable called `passwd`. Its value will consist of whatever text the end user enters into this box.

The next program is used to verify the password that is input and is located at `http://www.aw.com/~perlpgm/cgi-bin/C4/checkpass.cgi`. Note that the program receives the password field in line 4 and then checks it against the password `PerlOK` in line 5.

```
1. #!/usr/bin/perl
2. use CGI ":standard";
3. print header; start_html('Check Pass');
4. $password=param('passwd');        Gets the value of CGI variable passwd
5. if ( $password eq 'PerlOK' ) {    Compare $password with PerlOK
6.    print 'You got the password do not tell anyone';
7. } else {
8.    print 'Sorry you do not know the password';
9.    print br, "You entered $password";
10. }
11. print end_html;
```

In this program:

☆ Line 4 receives the value of the CGI variable `passwd` into the variable `$password`.

☆ Lines 5–10 compare this value with `PerlOK` (the secret password!). If the user-entered password matches the secret password, then one message is output (line 6). Otherwise, a message is output notifying the end user that he or she entered the wrong password (lines 8–9).

Figure 4.10 shows the form generated with a password field (top), the output of the password-checking program when the password is invalid (middle), and the output when it is valid (bottom).

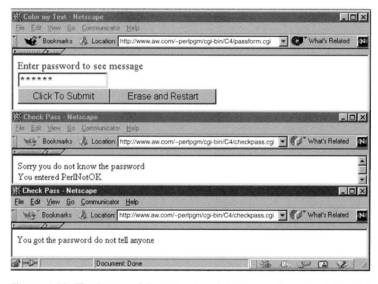

Figure 4.10 The Password Form (top) and Output with an Invalid (middle) and Valid (bottom) Password Guess

Text Areas

Text areas are very similar to text boxes, except that with text areas you can create multicolumn and multirow text input areas. The following HTML code creates a text area containing 6 rows and 50 columns. The word `Green` is the default text and will appear automatically in the text area when the form starts. The CGI variable named `color` will be sent to the form-processing program to get whatever text the end user enters into this box.

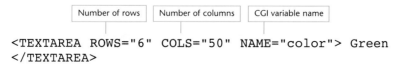

```
<TEXTAREA ROWS="6" COLS="50" NAME="color"> Green
</TEXTAREA>
```

The following code illustrates how to output this text area from a CGI/Perl program:

```
print '<TEXTAREA ROWS="6" COLS="50" NAME="color">';
print 'Green </TEXTAREA>';
```

Figure 4.11 shows an example using the text area.

Check Boxes

Check boxes are small boxes on a form that create a check mark when the user clicks them. The following HTML lines create two independent check boxes; that is, both values can be selected. When the user clicks on the check box created in the first line, the CGI variable `yesBall` will have the value `yes` in the receiving form-processing script. The second line causes the box labeled `Fish?` to be prechecked. If it is checked, the CGI variable `yesFish` will have the value `yes`.

| Label next to check box | CGI variable name | CGI variable value when clicked |

```
<INPUT TYPE="checkbox" NAME="yesBall" VALUE="yes">
            Play Baseball?
<INPUT TYPE="checkbox" NAME="yesFish" VALUE="yes"
            CHECKED> Fish?
```

You could create an equivalent set of text boxes within a CGI/Perl program as follows:

```
print '<INPUT TYPE="checkbox" NAME="yesBall" VALUE="yes">
            Play Baseball?';
print '<INPUT TYPE="checkbox" NAME="yesFish" VALUE="yes"
            CHECKED> Fish?';
```

Sometimes you might want to create a set of check boxes that use the same name argument. Using such check boxes would enable the user to check multiple boxes simultaneously, although the value received by the program would be a comma-separated list of all items checked. For example, if the first and third items in the following check boxes were checked, the form-processing program would receive a CGI variable called `summer` with two values: `bball`, `travel`.

☆ SHORTCUT   **Receiving Check Box Data**

If input from multiple check boxes within the same check box group are sent, your receiving program will receive the data as a comma-separated list. This topic is discussed in more detail in Chapter Five.

```
<INPUT TYPE="checkbox" NAME="summer" VALUE="bball">
            Play Baseball?
<INPUT TYPE="checkbox" NAME="summer" VALUE="fish"
            CHECKED> Fish?
<INPUT TYPE="checkbox" NAME="summer" VALUE="travel">
            Travel?
```

The following program creates a form containing both check boxes and text areas. When the form is submitted, it executes the program found at `http://www.aw.com/~perlpgm/cgi-bin/C4/form2Rcv.cgi` and produces the form shown in Figure 4.11.

```perl
1.  #!/usr/bin/perl
2.  use CGI ':standard';
3.  print header, start_html('Checkbox and Textarea');
4.  print '<FORM ACTION="http://www.aw.com/~perlpgm/
        cgi-bin/C4/form2Rcv.cgi" METHOD="POST">';
5.  print 'What do you eat? <BR>';
6.  print '<INPUT TYPE="checkbox" NAME="eat"
            VALUE="veggies"> Vegetables?';
7.  print '<INPUT TYPE="checkbox" NAME="eat"
            VALUE="meat"> Meat?';
8.  print '<INPUT TYPE="checkbox" NAME="eat"
            VALUE="any" checked> Anything not moving?';
9.  print '<BR> Any comments?<BR>';
10. print '<TEXTAREA ROWS="5" COLS="50"
            NAME="comments">';
11. print 'Put Comments Here </TEXTAREA>';
12. print br, br;
13. print br, '<INPUT TYPE=SUBMIT VALUE="Click To
            Submit">';
14. print '<INPUT TYPE=RESET VALUE="Erase and
            Restart">';
15. print '</FORM>', end_html;
```

Create check box group *(annotation for lines 6–8)*

Create text area *(annotation for line 10)*

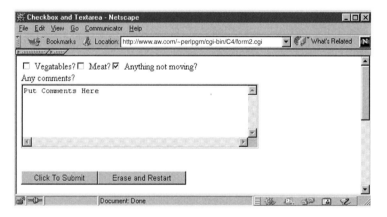

Figure 4.11 Example Illustrating the Use of Check Boxes and Text Areas

In this program:

☆ Line 4 starts the form and indicates that the submitted form should be sent to `http://www.aw.com/~perlpgm/cgi-bin/C4/form2Rcv.cgi`. This program (not shown) will output the values of the CGI variables `eat` and `comments`.

☆ Lines 6–8 create the check box group. They create a CGI variable called `eat` that can receive multiple values (comma separated) depending on which check boxes are checked by the end user.

☆ Line 10 creates a text area consisting of 5 rows, with each row being 50 columns wide. Any end-user input to the text area is assigned to the CGI variable named `comments`.

☆ Lines 13–14 create submit and reset buttons.

Radio Buttons

Radio buttons are small circles that operate similarly to check boxes, except that only one button within the group can be selected at any given time. As with check boxes, the `NAME` argument sets the CGI variable name. The `NAME` argument must be the same for all radio buttons that you want to operate together as a group. The `VALUE` argument sets the CGI variable value that will be available to the form-processing script.

Here is a set of HTML statements that create radio buttons:

```
              Label next to radio button          CGI variable name    CGI variable value

<INPUT  TYPE="radio"  NAME="summer"  VALUE="bball">
              Play Baseball?
<INPUT  TYPE="radio"  NAME="summer"  VALUE="fish"  checked >
              Fish?
<INPUT  TYPE="radio"  NAME="summer"  VALUE="travel">  Travel?
```

In a CGI/Perl program, the following code creates an equivalent set of radio buttons:

```
print '<INPUT TYPE="radio"  NAME="summer"  VALUE="bball">
          Play Baseball?';
print '<INPUT TYPE="radio"  NAME="summer"  VALUE="fish"
          checked > Fish?';
print '<INPUT TYPE="radio"  NAME="summer"  VALUE="travel">
          Travel?';
```

Figure 4.12 shows an example involving the use of radio buttons.

Selection Lists

A selection list creates a box with a scrolling list of one or more items that can be highlighted and selected by the user. The HTML `<OPTION>` tag defines each list option that will be displayed. The `SIZE` tag defines how many options will be displayed without scrolling. The MULTIPLE tag allows more than one list item to be selected simultaneously. The actual text that is displayed is returned to the form-processing script through the CGI variable specified in the NAME argument.

The following HTML code creates a selection list:

| CGI variable name | Viewable window size | More than one can be selected |

```
<SELECT NAME="Accommodations" SIZE=2 MULTIPLE>
<OPTION> A fine hotel
<OPTION SELECTED> A cheap motel!
<OPTION> A tent in the parking lot
<OPTION> Just give me a sleeping bag checked
</SELECT>
```

List items that the user can select

This HTML code would create four options formatted in a scrolling list. Only two of these options would be displayed at the same time, and the end user could select more than one option at a time. If more than one option is selected, the selections would be sent to the form-processing program as a comma-separated list. (Use of comma-separated lists by a receiving CGP/Perl program is covered in Chapter Five.)

Once again, you can use the print function to output the equivalent HTML from your CGI/Perl program:

```
print '<SELECT NAME=" Accommodations" SIZE=2 MULTIPLE>';
print '<OPTION> A fine hotel ';
print '<OPTION SELECTED> A cheap motel!';
print '<OPTION> A tent in the parking lot ';
print '<OPTION> Just give me a sleeping bag checked';
print '</SELECT>';
```

The following program demonstrates the use of radio buttons and scrolling lists. Its output is shown in Figure 4.12.

```
1. #!/usr/bin/perl
2. use CGI ':standard';
3. print header, start_html;
4. print '<FORM
          ACTION="http://www.aw.com/~perlpgm/cgi-bin/
                  C4/radioRcv.cgi"
          METHOD="POST">';
5. print "What do you want to do this summer?<BR>";
6. print '<INPUT TYPE="radio" NAME="summer"
          VALUE="bball"> Play Baseball?';
7. print '<INPUT TYPE="radio" NAME="summer"
          VALUE="fish" checked > Fish?';
8. print '<INPUT TYPE="radio" NAME="summer"
          VALUE="travel"> Travel? ';
9. print "<BR> Where would you like to stay?<BR>";
```

Create radio buttons

```
10. print '<SELECT NAME="Accommodations" SIZE=2>';
11. print '<OPTION> A fine hotel';
12. print '<OPTION SELECTED> A cheap motel!';
13. print '<OPTION> A tent in the parking lot';
14. print '<OPTION> Just give me a sleeping bag';
15. print '</SELECT>';
16. print br, br, '<INPUT TYPE=SUBMIT
           VALUE="Submit it">';
17. print '<INPUT TYPE=RESET VALUE="Erase It">';
18. print '</FORM>', end_html;
```

— Create selection list

Figure 4.12 A Form Created with Radio Buttons and Selection Lists

In this program:

☆ Line 4 identifies the location of the CGI program that will be called when the form is submitted to `http://www.aw.com/~perlpgm/cgi-bin/C4/radioRcv.cgi`. This program (not shown) will output the values of the CGI variables `summer` and `Accommodations`.

☆ Lines 6–8 define three radio buttons that set the CGI variable named `summer` to have one of three values: `bball`, `fish`, or `travel`.

☆ Lines 10–15 create a selection list that defines a CGI variable named `accommodations` that will have one of four values: `A fine hotel`, `A cheap motel!`, `A tent in the parking lot`, or `Just give me a sleeping bag`.

Hidden Fields

Hidden fields are not displayed on the form. They are typically used by form-processing applications that use multiple form screens to store values. By storing values in hidden fields, your application can "remember" things between screens. Hidden fields are useful for multiple form applications like those described in Chapter Eight. For completeness, we present their HTML format now.

The following line shows an example of an HTML format for hidden fields. It assigns the value `Likes chocolate` to the CGI variable `preference`.

CGI variable name

```
<INPUT TYPE="hidden" NAME="preference"
      VALUE="Likes chocolate">
```

CGI variable value

You can output the preceding HTML line by using the `print` function as follows:

```
print '<INPUT TYPE="hidden" NAME="preference"
      VALUE="Likes chocolate">';
```

Testing Input Using CGI.pm Debug Mode

Testing without a browser can sometimes help troubleshoot problems when you send and receive CGI variables with CGI/Perl. If you can execute Telnet commands on the Web server (or have Perl installed on your PC), you can test your scripts before executing them with a browser. `CGI.pm` enables you to enter CGI variables and values from a command line. For example, to start and send an argument to the password program from Figure 4.10, you can execute the following code:

```
perl checkpass.cgi passwd=PerlOK
```
Sets the CGI variable passwd to the value `PerlOK`

If the variable's value needs to include blank spaces, you can enclose the CGI variable name and value in quotation marks:

```
perl checkpass.cgi 'passwd=Perl Not OK'
```
Sets the CGI variable passwd to the value `Perl Not OK`

Figure 4.13 shows the result of executing the password-checking program from Figure 4.10 using two different input methods. The first method enters `PerlOK` as a password. The second method enters `Perl No Good` as a password. As you can see, a different HTML document is generated in each case.

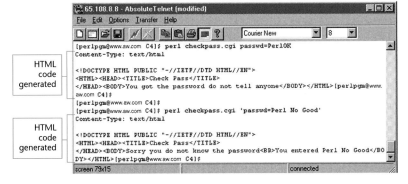

Figure 4.13 Output of Running `checkpass.cgi` with Two Sets of Debug Input

☆SHORTCUT   Using CGI.pm in Offline Mode

If you do not specify any arguments when you start your script on a Web server and use `CGI.pm` (for example, `perl checkpass`), then `CGI.pm` will enter an *offline mode* (and wait for input). It does so to enable you to enter the name-value pair for each CGI variable used by your script (for example, `passwd=PerlOK`). After you enter each CGI variable and value on a UNIX Web server, press Ctrl-D (that is, press both the Ctrl key and the D key simultaneously) to exit the input mode and run your script. On a Windows system, exit the input mode by pressing Ctrl-Z.

☆TIP   Testing Scripts Via the Internet

You can also test your scripts with a Web browser over the Internet by specifying the input arguments in a Web address, as in the following example:

```
http://www.aw.com/~perlpgm/cgi-bin/C4/checkpass.cgi?
passwd=PerlOK
```

See Chapter Three, "The `param` Function," for more details.

☆ Summary

⯈ Several functions found in the `CGI.pm` library can be used to generate HTML tags. You must explicitly connect to the `CGI.pm` library before you can use these functions.

⯈ HTML forms are the method most commonly used to start and pass data to CGI/Perl programs. The `ACTION` argument within the `<FORM>` tag indicates which CGI application to start when the form is submitted.

⯈ The individual form elements set name-value pairs used to send parameters to the CGI/Perl application. The `NAME=` attribute defines the CGI variable name. Possible form elements include text boxes, text fields, check boxes, radio buttons, and selection lists.

⯈ You can use the `param()CGI.pm` function to receive arguments from forms. The variable name used as an argument to this function must match the `NAME=` attribute set in the form.

☆ Online References

Lincoln Stein's Site Discussing the Functions in the CGI.pm Module
`http://stein.cshl.org/WWW/software/CGI/cgi_docs.html`

HTML Information Site That Also Describes How to Create HTML Forms
`http://www.htmlgoodies.com/`

HTML Tutorial, Including Instruction of Using Forms
`http://hotwired.lycos.com/webmonkey/`

Index with CGI Informational Links
`http://best-of-web.com/computer/cgi_index.shtml`

☆ Review Questions

1. What are the three format types for `CGI.pm` functions described in this chapter?

2. Write a single Perl print statement that can create the following HTML code using `CGI.pm` functions:

   `<BR><HR><H1>Introduction </H1>`

3. What does the following HTML statement do? Write a single Perl `print` statement that can create the following HTML code using `CGI.pm` functions:

   `<HTML><HEAD><TITLE>My First Document</TITLE></HEAD>`
   `<BODY>`

4. What does the `ACTION=` argument define in an HTML `<FORM>` tag? How is it useful for programming CGI/Perl applications?

5. Which HTML argument defines the CGI variable name in each form element described in this chapter? Which `CGI.pm` function is used to receive CGI variable values?

6. What is the difference between an HTML text box and a text area?

7. The following HTML code creates two radio buttons. The end user can select only one radio button at a time. What will be the CGI variable name and value if the end user selects the second radio button and then submits the form?

```
<INPUT TYPE="radio" NAME="Q1" VALUE="Got One"> First
<INPUT TYPE="radio" NAME="Q1" VALUE="Got Two" > Second
```

8. Which CGI variable and value would be set if the end user selects the option `A fine hotel` in the program that creates Figure 4.12. If the end user selects `Travel?` from the radio buttons?

9. What does the following line of Perl code do?

```
use CGI ':standard';
```

☆ Hands-On Exercises

1. Create an HTML document that uses `CGI.pm` functions to generate HTML tags. The document should have the following characteristics:
   - ☆ A title of `A Web Page` and a yellow background color.
   - ☆ A header 1 element labeled `Testing 1 2 3`.
   - ☆ Text that uses a font size of 4 and a font color of blue.
   - ☆ A paragraph of text in the document consisting of at least five lines. Change the font size, style, and color at least once.

2. Create a form that includes a text box labeled `student name` and four text boxes labeled `grade1`, `grade2`, `grade3`, and `grade4`. When the user enters his or her name and four grades, the program should return a new Web page with the user's name and average grade. Ensure that the program reports an error message when one of the fields is omitted. Also check for illegal scores.

3. Create an admission request form for the Super-Secret Society. The form should include a name text box labeled `full name` and set of check boxes that allows the end user to select one (and only one) of the following age groups:
   - ☆ 0–18
   - ☆ 18–65
   - ☆ 65 or older

The form should also include a button to submit the form. The receiving program should do the following:

☆ Output a message indicating that the end user is too young to become a member if the option 0–18 is checked.

☆ Output a message indicating that the end user may pay standard dues if the option 18–65 is checked.

☆ Output a message indicating that the end user can receive a 10% discount on dues if the option 65 or older is checked.

4. Create an additional field on the form developed in Exercise 3 that requires the end user to enter a password. Make the password `Secret01`. Output an appropriate message if the password is incorrect.

5. Create a form that generates a simple math table. Create 10 radio buttons (labeled 0–9) to select an initial number. When the form is received, the program should output a page that creates a table containing the results of multiplying the number by the values 1–12.

6. Create a form that asks the end user to guess the value of a single die. Create a set of radio buttons labeled with the numbers 1–6. Ask the end user to enter his or her name in a text box. When this form is submitted, the receiving program should do the following:

☆ Generate a random number from 1 to 6. (See the discussion of the `rand()` function in Chapter Three.)

☆ Depending on the random number generated, display one of six die images (see the book Web site at `http://perl-pgm.com` for sample images).

☆ If the user guess matches the random number, output the end user's name and an appropriate message. If the random number does not match, output the end user's name and an appropriate message.

CHAPTER FIVE

LIST VARIABLES AND LOOPS

This chapter examines list variables, looping statements, and logical compound conditional operators. List variables enable you to group data elements into lists. In turn, these groupings allow you to work with (and operate on) data as a single list rather than as individual data elements.

You use looping statements to iterate through program statements. Program loops not only help make your programs more concise, but also help you solve some particularly thorny programming problems—in fact, some programming problems cannot be solved without them.

Finally, the chapter describes compound logical conditional operators that can be applied to conditional test statements. They enable your program to work more concisely and oft-times more clearly with programming problems requiring complex conditional tests.

◎◎ Chapter Objectives

☆ Describe how list variables work

☆ Describe four types of Perl looping statements

☆ Explain how logical conditional operators are used

◎◎ List Variables (Arrays)

Perl—and most other computer languages—offers a special type of variable called a **list variable** (or **array**). List variables can help you organize data into a list instead of requiring that you work with individual scalar variables. For example, instead of working with five scalar variables called $preference1, $preference2, $preference3, $preference4, and $preference5, you might instead use one list variable called @preference. That list variable might comprise a list of all five preference values. Organizing your data into one list variable enables your programs to do the following:

☆ *Include a flexible number of list elements.* You can add items to and delete items from lists on the fly in your program.

☆ *Examine each element more concisely.* You can use looping constructs (described in the "Looping Statements" section later in this chapter) in combination with list variables to look at and operate on each item in your list in a very concise manner.

☆ *Use special list operators and functions.* You can use Perl's built-in list operators and functions to do things such as count the number of items in your list, output your entire list, and sort your list, among other things.

The following subsections describe list variables and the various list operations you can perform on them.

Creating List Variables

Suppose that you wanted to store a set of four student names into a list variable. You could create a list variable called @students that specifies each student name as shown in Figure 5.1.

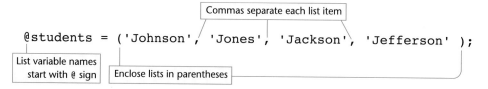

```
@students = ( 'Johnson', 'Jones', 'Jackson', 'Jefferson' );
```

Commas separate each list item

List variable names start with @ sign

Enclose lists in parentheses

Figure 5.1 Setting the Initial Value of a List Variable

The statement in Figure 5.1 creates a list variable called @students with the values 'Johnson', 'Jones', 'Jackson', and 'Jefferson'. In fact, you can create a list that consists of any scalar data. For example, you could create a list of numerical items called @grades as follows:

```
@grades    = ( 66, 75, 85, 80 );
```

This statement creates a list variable called @grades with the list elements 66, 75, 85, and 80.

Referencing List Items

Items within a list variable are referenced by a set of related scalar variables. For example, the statement in Figure 5.1 has the effect of creating a set of scalar variables called $students[0], $students[1], $students[2], and $students[3] with the following values:

```
$students[0] = "Johnson";
$students[1] = "Jones";
$students[2] = "Jackson";
$students[3] = "Jefferson";
```

☆ **WARNING** List Item Numbering

You might think the list variables in the preceding code would be numbered 1 through 4. In fact, list variables always start with item 0, so the items above are numbered from 0 to 3.

The scalar variables used to reference individual list elements consist of a *variable name* and *subscript number* pair. The subscript number is always enclosed in square brackets ([...]). For example, the following reference uses the subscript 0 and a scalar variable named $myList.

```
$mylist[0] ="baseball";
```

| Variable name | | Subscript |

Subscripts can be whole numbers, another variable, or even expressions enclosed within the square brackets. Consider the following example:

```
$i=3;
@preferences = ("ketchup ", "mustard ", "pickles ",
    "lettuce " );
print "$preferences[$i] $preferences[$i-1]
    $preferences[$i-2] $preferences[0]";
```

The output of these lines of code would be the items in the @preferences list given in reverse order. That is,

```
lettuce pickles mustard ketchup
```

You can change values in a list variable and use them in expressions just as you would other scalar variables. Consider the following example:

```
@scores = ( 75, 65, 85, 90);
$scores[3] = 95;
$average = ( $scores[0] + $scores[1] +
    $scores[2] + $scores[3] ) / 4;
```

List Variables (Arrays)

The first line creates a list variable called @scores with the initial values 75, 65, 85, and 90. The second line reassigns the fourth list item from 90 to 95 (remember that numbering goes from 0 to 3, not from 1 to 4). The third line sets $average equal to (75 + 65 + 85 + 95) / 4—that is, to 80.

☆ **SHORTCUT**   **Creating Lists on the Fly**

The format used in Figure 5.1 is not the only way to create a list. You can also create a list by simply assigning items to a list variable with the variable name/subscript form shown earlier. For example, the following code creates a list called @work with three items:

```
$work[0]="Clean garage"; $work[1]="Mow lawn"; $work[2]="Paint fence";
```

Now let's look at a complete example. The following code uses Perl's built-in rand() function, which returns a random number from 0 to the number passed into it. (This function is described in detail in Chapter Three, "Basic Perl Functions.") When another of Perl's built-in functions, int(), is used with rand(), it forces rand() to return whole numbers instead of its default fractional numbers. For example, int(rand(6)) returns a random number that is either 0, 1, 2, 3, 4, or 5.

The following code outputs a random menu item as a "special." Next, it creates a radio button for each possible menu choice. Figure 5.2 shows the output of this program.

```
 1. #!/usr/bin/perl
 2. use CGI ':standard';
 3. print header, start_html('Menu Choice');
 4. @menu = ('Meat Loaf', 'Meat Pie',                    [Create @menu
            'Minced Meat', 'Meat Surprise' );             list variable]
 5. $item = int(rand(4));              [Generate a random number from 0 to 3]
 6. print '<FORM ACTION="http://www.aw.com/~perlpgm/
            cgi-bin/C5/choice.cgi" METHOD="POST">';
 7. print "<FONT SIZE=4 > What do you want to eat for
            dinner? ";
 8. print br, "Our special is <FONT COLOR=BLUE>
            $menu[$item] </FONT>";
 9. print br, '<INPUT TYPE="RADIO" NAME="eat"
            VALUE="0">', "$menu[0]";
10. print br, '<INPUT TYPE="RADIO" NAME="eat"
            VALUE="1" checked>', "$menu[1]";          [Use list items
11. print br, '<INPUT TYPE="RADIO" NAME="eat"          as labels for
            VALUE="2">', "$menu[2]";                   radio buttons]
12. print br, '<INPUT TYPE="RADIO" NAME="eat"
            VALUE="3">', "$menu[3]";
13. print br, '<INPUT TYPE=SUBMIT VALUE="Submit">';
14. print '<INPUT TYPE=RESET></FORM>', end_html;
```

Figure 5.2 Output of the Form Example Using a List Variable

In this program:

☆ Lines 1–3 identify the location of Perl, connect to the CGI.pm module, and output the MIME Content-type line (using header) and starting HTML tags (using start_html).

☆ Line 4 sets the initial value of the list variable @menu to four separate menu choices.

☆ Line 5 uses Perl's built-in rand() function to assign a random number from 0 to 3, inclusive, to the variable $item.

☆ Line 6 creates the <FORM> HTML tag.When the user clicks the submit button, it sends the form to http://www.aw.com/~perlpgm/cgi-bin/ C5/choice.cgi.

☆ Line 7 prints the message, What do you want to eat for dinner? Line 8 uses the <FONT> tags to output Our special is and then an item from the @menu list. This menu item is selected based on the random value of $item.

☆ Lines 9–12 create the radio buttons. Because all of these buttons have the same CGI variable name (eat), only one can be selected at any time. A different list item from @menu is output as each radio button's label.

☆ Line 13 creates HTML tags to create a line break and then a submit button. Line 14 outputs the tags to create a reset button and the tags to end the form and HTML document.

☆**WARNING** **Accessing an Item beyond the End of a List Variable**

Perl will not send an error message if you try to use a subscript number that exceeds the number of elements in your list variable—for example, if you use $menu[100] with the program that creates Figure 5.2. Instead, it will simply use whatever data currently resides in that particular memory location. Of course, this tactic will not be what you intended.

Outputting the Entire List Variable

You can output all of the elements of a list variable by using the list variable in a print statement. For example,

```
@workWeek = ('Monday', 'Tuesday', 'Wednesday',
    'Thursday', 'Friday' );
print "My work week is @workWeek";
```

would output all of the elements in @workWeek separated by spaces. That is, it would output

My work week is Monday Tuesday Wednesday Thursday Friday

We will use this construct to output list values to examine the list.

☆TIP   Using Double Quotes

You must use double quotes when your goal is to output the contents of a variable in a print statement. Using single quotes will output the print string exactly as specified—not the value of any variables found in it. (See Chapter Three, "The print Function" section, for more details.)

Getting the Number of Elements in a List Variable

If you want to know the length or number of elements in a list, you can use a special operator called the **range operator**. The range operator is always set to the value of the last subscript number of your list. For example, if an array has six elements numbered from 0 to 5, the range operator would be set to 5.

The range operator has the following general format:

$$\$\#my\_list$$

Range operator starts with $ followed by #	List variable name is @my_list has a range operator $#my_list

Thus, if your list variable was called @grades, the range operator would be

$#grades

You can use this list operator to get the last items from a list. For example, the following two lines would set $last_one equal to 80:

```
@grades    = ( 66, 75, 85, 80 );
$last_one = $grades[$#grades];
```

You can also use the range operator to determine your list length. Be careful, however, because this operator is always *1 less than the total number in the list* (since list elements start counting at 0 rather than 1). Consequently, to obtain the list's true length, you add 1 to the range operator. For example, consider the following statement sequence:

```
@workWeek = ('Monday', 'Tuesday', 'Wednesday',
             'Thursday', 'Friday' );
$daysLong = $#workWeek + 1;
print "My work week  is $daysLong days long";
```

These three statements would output the following message:

```
My work week is 5 days long.
```

Now let's look at a complete example involving the range operator. Suppose the following code was used to receive the form from Figure 5.2. That is, the program that creates Figure 5.2 is set to submit its form to `http://www.aw.com/~perlpgm/cgi-bin/C5/choice.cgi`. Suppose the following program was stored at that location. The output produced by this program appears in Figure 5.3.

```
1. #!/usr/bin/perl
2. use CGI ':standard';
3. print header, start_html("Got Your Preference");
4. @menu  =  ("Meat Loaf", "Meat Pie", "Minced Meat",
             "Meat Surprise" );
5. $response = param('eat');
6. print "<FONT size=4> You Selected @menu[$response]";
7. $menuLen = $#menu + 1;
```

> Use range operator

> Output the item selected

```
8. print br, "We had $menuLen items available";
9. print br, "These items were @menu", end_html;
```

Figure 5.3 Program Output That Prints Out Array Length and Array Contents

In this program:

☆ Line 4 sets up the list variable @menu. Note that the code must include the list items in the same order as the calling program that creates Figure 5.2.

☆ Line 5 gets the CGI variable named eat that the calling program designated as an index value (that is, 0, 1, 2, or 3) into the @menu list.

☆ Line 6 prints the value of the @menu item that the user selected. This operation is possible because the value passed as a parameter is the index into the list variable @menu and the items within the @menu list variable are stored in the same order in both programs.

☆ Line 7 calculates the length of the list. (Recall that the code must add 1 because the list number starts with 0, not 1.)

☆ Lines 8–9 output the list length and the values of the @menu list items.

☆SHORTCUT   **Another Way to Get the Length of a List Variable**

You can also find the length of a list variable by assigning the list variable name to a scalar variable. For example, the following code assigns to $size the number of elements in the list variable @grades:

```
$size=@grades;
```

Adding and Removing Items from a List

Sometimes it is handy to add and remove items from a list. Perl supports two sets of functions to help you add and delete items from the front and rear of a list.

☆ **shift()** and **unshift()**: These functions add and remove elements from the *beginning* of a list. The shift() function *removes* an item from the beginning of a list. For example, you can use shift() in the following code

```
@workWeek = ('Monday', 'Tuesday', 'Wednesday',
    'Thursday', 'Friday' );
$dayOff = shift(@workWeek);
print "dayOff= $dayOff workWeek=@workWeek";
```

to output the following:

```
dayOff= Monday workWeek=Tuesday Wednesday Thursday
Friday
```

The counterpart to shift is the unshift function. The unshift function adds an element to the *beginning* of the list. For example,

```
@workWeek = ('Monday', 'Tuesday', 'Wednesday',
    'Thursday', 'Friday' );
unshift(@workWeek, "Sunday");
print  "workWeek is now =@workWeek";
```

would output the following:

```
workWeek is now =Sunday Monday Tuesday Wednesday
Thursday Friday
```

☆ **pop()** and **push()**: These functions add and remove elements from the *end* of a list. The pop() function removes an item from the *end* of the list. Here is an example of the pop() function:

```
@workWeek = ("Monday", "Tuesday", "Wednesday",
    "Thursday", "Friday" );
$dayOff = pop(@workWeek);
print "dayOff= $dayOff workWeek=@workWeek";
```

This code would output the following:

```
dayOff= Friday workWeek=Monday Tuesday Wednesday
Thursday
```

The counterpart to pop() is push(). This function adds an element to the end of an array. For example,

```
@workWeek = ('Monday', 'Tuesday', 'Wednesday',
    'Thursday', 'Friday' );
push(@workWeek, 'Saturday');
print  "workWeek is now =@workWeek";
```

would output the following:

```
workWeek is now =Monday Tuesday Wednesday Thursday
Friday Saturday
```

☆ **TIP**   **Getting an Item Off of a List**

You can use pop() and shift() to remove items from the front and back of a list variable without saving the results into a scalar variable. For example, the following code removes an item from the end of the @workWeek list variable:

```
pop(@workWeek);
```

Extracting Multiple Values from a List

So far we have accessed one item at a time from a list variable. For example,

```
@myList = ( 'hot dogs', 'ketchup', 'lettuce', 'celery');
$essentials = @myList[ 2 ];
print "essentials=$essentials";
```
Extracts third item from @myList

would output:

```
essentials=lettuce
```

Sometimes it is useful to extract multiple values from a list at once. If you use multiple subscripts (specified as comma-separated values) for a list variable, you will extract a sub-list with the matching list items. As an example, consider the following:

```
@myList = ( 'hot dogs', 'ketchup', 'lettuce', 'celery');
@essentials = @myList[ 2, 3 ];
print "essentials=@essentials";
```
Extracts third and fourth items of @myList

The output of this code is

```
essentials=lettuce celery
```

In the preceding code, the second line extracts the third and fourth list items (recall that index numbering goes from 0 to 3) from @myList. The extracted values are placed into the new list called @essentials, which the third line then outputs.

In a similar fashion, you can use a list variable as an index into another list variable. Consider the following code

```
@myList - ( 'hot dogs', 'ketchup', 'lettuce', 'celery');
@keyones = ( 0, 3 );
@essentials = @myList[ @keyones ];
print "essentials=@essentials";
```

> Extracts first and fourth items of @myList

which produces this output:

```
essentials=hot dogs celery
```

In the preceding code, the second line creates @keyones as a list containing the values 0 and 3. The third line uses @keyones to extract the first and fourth elements from the list @myList. The extracted values are put into a new list called @essentials, which the fourth line then outputs.

This ability to extract multiple items from a list variable can be very useful when handling certain HTML form elements. For example, check boxes and selection lists allow the end user to select multiple items at the same time (see Chapter Four, "Check Boxes" and "Selection Lists"). When the end user submits the form, the receiving program will receive a comma-separated list of values. If it is set up correctly, the receiving program can then determine which items were selected by extracting multiple items from a common list variable.

Let's look at an example that involves handling form elements that permit multiple selections. The following program creates such a form. If the end user selects all items on the form, the program will send to multichoice.cgi the CGI variable named countries with value "0,1,2,3". The top portion of Figure 5.4 shows the output of the form called checklist.cgi.

```
1. #!/usr/bin/perl
2. use CGI ':standard';
3. print header;
4. @menu = ('USA', 'China', 'Canada', 'Mexico' );
5. print '<FORM
          ACTION="http://www.aw.com/~perlpgm/cgi-bin/C5
                  /multichoice.cgi" METHOD="POST">';
6. print '<FONT SIZE=4 > What countries have you
          visited?';
```

> Establish list variable @menu

```
 7. print '<INPUT TYPE="checkbox"
         NAME="places" VALUE="0">', "$menu[0]";
 8. print '<INPUT TYPE="checkbox"
         NAME="places" VALUE="1" checked>',
         "$menu[1]";
 9. print '<INPUT TYPE="checkbox"
         NAME="places" VALUE="2">', "$menu[2]";
10. print '<INPUT TYPE="checkbox"
         NAME="places" VALUE="3">', "$menu[3]";
11. print br, '<INPUT TYPE=SUBMIT VALUE="Submit">';
12. print '<INPUT TYPE=RESET></FORM>', end_html;
```

Set CGI variable places to 0–3 depending on end user's selection

The following code is from the receiving program found at http://www.aw.com/~perlpgm/cgi-bin/C5/multichoice.cgi; this program creates the output shown at the bottom of Figure 5.4.

```
1. #!/usr/bin/perl
2. use CGI ':standard';
3. print header, start_html("Got Your Countries");
4. @menu = ('USA', 'China', 'Canada', 'Mexico' );
5. @response =param('places');
6. $num = $#response +1;
7. print "<FONT SIZE=4> You selected $num responses,
         @menu[@response]";
8. print "</FONT>", end_html;
```

Establish @menu list variable

Output all items selected by end user

Gets the number of items selected

Figure 5.4 Initial Screen (top) and Form-Processing Program (bottom) That Get Both Elements Selected

In the multichoice.cgi program:

☆ Line 4 creates the list variable @menu that corresponds to the list variable in the calling form program.

☆ Line 5 gets the list of items selected by the end user. This list is stored in the list variable @response using the CGI variable places.

☆ Lines 6–7 first get the total list elements (using the range operator) and then output the selected list elements from the menu preference list.

Using Lists of Lists

Some data are best represented by creating a list of lists (sometimes called a multi-dimensional list). For example, suppose you wanted to represent the data in Table 5.1, in which three different parts each have four pieces of data. These data can be represented as a list of lists as shown in Figure 5.5.

Table 5.1 Data to Be Represented as a List of Lists

Part Number	Part Name	Number Available	Price
AC1000	Hammer	122	12
AC1001	Wrench	344	5
AC1002	Hand Saw	150	10

```
Regular list variable name      Each row is comma-separated and
                                enclosed in square brackets

@Inventory = (
    ['AC1000', 'Hammer', 122, 12],
    ['AC1001', 'Wrench', 344, 5],
    ['AC1002', 'Hand Saw', 150, 10]
);

Regular parentheses on outside
```

Figure 5.5 A Multidimensional List

Items in a multidimensional list can be accessed with two subscripts, rather than the usual one subscript employed with one-dimensional lists. The first subscript indicates the row in which the item appears, and the second subscript identifies the column where it is found. In the preceding example, $Inventory[0][0] has value AC1000, $Inventory[1][0] has value AC1001, and $Inventory[2][0] has value AC1002.

The following code demonstrates how individual items can be accessed using the multidimensional list from Figure 5.5:

```
$numHammers = $Inventory[0][2];
$firstPartNo = $Inventory[0][0];
$Inventory[0][3] = 15;
print "$numHammers, $firstPartNo, $Inventory[0][3]";
```

This would output

```
122, AC1000, 15
```

☆ **TIP**   **Using Coding Style to Improve the Readability of Your Programs**

You can use scalar variables to describe the meaning of columns in a multidimensional list. For example, instead of writing

```
$item = $Inventory[0][3];
```

you can write the following:

```
$PRICE=3;
$item = $Inventory[0][$PRICE];
```

This technique can greatly improve the readability of your programs because the variable name $PRICE provides a label for the third column of the multidimensional list. (See the program that creates Figure 5.6 for another example.)

Now let's look at a small program that uses a multidimensional list to display information about products. The form associated with this program is shown at the top of Figure 5.6. The key portion of the form is the following HTML code, which creates the radio buttons and sets the CGI variable item to be a number from 0 to 3. The output is sent to `http://www.aw.com/~perlpgm/cgi-bin/C5/GetInvent.cgi`.

```
<BR><INPUT TYPE=radio NAME="item" VALUE=0 >Hammers
<BR><INPUT TYPE=radio NAME="item" VALUE=1 >Wrenches
<BR><INPUT TYPE=radio NAME="item" VALUE=2 >Hand Saws
<BR><INPUT TYPE=radio NAME="item" VALUE=3 >Screw Drivers
```

The output of the program at `http://www.aw.com/~perlpgm/cgi-bin/C5/GetInvent.cgi` appears at the bottom of Figure 5.6 and its program code is shown below.

```
1. #!/usr/bin/perl
2. use CGI ':standard';
3. print header, start_html('Inventory Answer');
4. # Inventory: PartNO, Item, Num In Stock, Price
5. $PRTNO=0; $ITEM=1; $NUM=2; $PRICE=3;          ⎤ Set scalar variables
                                                  ⎦ to column numbers
6. @Inventory =  (
     [ 'AC1000', 'Hammers', 122, 12 ],
     [ 'AC1001', 'Wrenches', 344, 5 ],           ⎤ Establish the multi-
     [ 'AC1002', 'Hand Saws', 150, 10 ],         ⎦ dimensional list
     [ 'AC1003', 'Screw Drivers', 250, 2 ]
   );
7. $pick=param('item');                          ⎯ Get end-user's selection
8. if ( $pick >= 0 && $pick <= 3 ) {
9.   print "Yes we have $Inventory[$pick][$ITEM].";
10.  print br, "In fact we have $Inventory[$pick][$NUM]
     of them.";
11.  print br, "They are $Inventory[$pick][$PRICE]
     dollars.";
```

Display items from @inventory multidimensional list

```
12. } else { "print sorry we do not have that item"; }
13. print end_html;
```

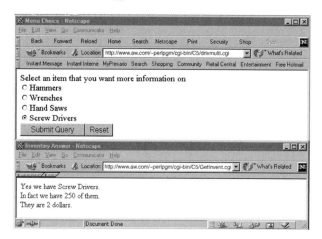

Figure 5.6 Output of the Multidimensional List Example

In this program:

☆ Line 5 sets the variables `$PRTNO`, `$ITEM`, `$NUM`, and `$PRICE` equal to values representing the various columns of the `@Inventory` multidimensional list.

☆ Line 6 sets up `@Inventory` as a multidimensional list with four rows and four columns.

☆ Lines 9–11 use `$pick` from the calling form to establish the row. This value is combined with the column values set in line 5 to get individual items from the `@Inventory` list.

◎◎ Looping Statements

Perl supports four program constructs that enable programs to repeat sections of code. By repeating sections of code with loops, you can achieve two goals:

☆ *Your programs can be much more concise.* When similar sections of statements need to be repeated in your program, you can often put them into a loop and reduce the total number of lines of code required.

☆ *You can write more flexible programs.* Loops allow you to repeat sections of your program until you reach the end of a data structure such as a list or a file (files are covered in Chapter Seven). Without a looping structure, you would need to know the number of list elements or the length of the file in advance.

To see how loops work, consider Figure 5.7. Both sections of the code in this figure seek to determine the largest value in the @grades list variable, which includes four elements. The code on the left must examine each list element (that is, $grade[0], $grade[1], $grade[2], $grade[3]) individually. The code on the right side uses the loop established in its second line to repeat the statements within the curly brackets four times. Each iteration has a different value for the variable $i and, therefore, its if statement (third line) checks whether a different list element *is greater than* $max. (The while loop used in the right-side code is described in more detail later in this chapter, in "The while Loop")

```
$max = 0;
if ( $grades[0] > $max ) {
    $max = $grades[0];
} if ( $grades[1] > $max ) {
    $max = $grades[1];
} if ( $grades[2] > $max ) {
    $max = $grades[2];
} if ( $grades[3] > $max ) {
    $max = $grades[3];
```

```
$max = 0; $i = 0;
while ( $i < 4 ) {
    if ( $grades[$i] > $max ) {
        $max = $grades[$i];
    }
    $i = $i + 1;
}
```

Each time through, the loop looks at a different list element

Without looping, you must have a separate if statement for every list element

Figure 5.7 Two Sections of Code That Look for the Maximum Value in a List Variable

Imagine how the left-side code would look if the list variable had to check 50, 100, or even 1000 elements in the list value. In the same situation, the right-side code would include the same number of lines. It would just change the value in the while statement (in line 2) from 4 to 50, 100, or 1000.

Perl supports four types of looping constructs:

☆ The for loop

☆ The foreach loop

☆ The while loop

☆ The until loop

Each type of loop is described below.

The for Loop

You use the for loop to repeat a section of code a specified number of times. This looping construct is typically employed when you know how many times a section of code should be repeated. It has the general format shown in Figure 5.8.

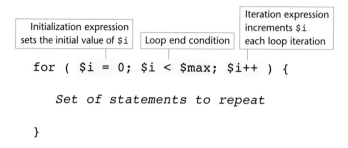

Figure 5.8 The General Format of the `for` Loop

Figure 5.8 repeats the *Set of statements to repeat* $max times. The number of repetitions of the loop is controlled by the three parts of the `for` statement.

☆ *The initialization expression* defines the initial value of a variable used to control the loop. In Figure 5.8, the variable $i is used to control the loop; it has an initial value of 0.

☆ *The loop-ending condition* defines the condition that triggers termination of the loop. The valid test conditions are the same as those from the "Conditional Statements" section in Chapter Three. The condition is evaluated during each loop iteration. When it evaluates to *false*, the loop ends. In Figure 5.8, the loop will repeat as long as $i is less than $max.

☆ *The iteration expression* is evaluated at the end of each loop iteration. In Figure 5.8, the expression $i++ means to add 1 to the value of $i during each iteration of the loop. Another common `for` loop iteration expression is $i--, which subtracts 1 from the value of $i.

☆**WARNING** Semicolon Use in **for** Statements

A semicolon (";") is required between the first two parts of the `for` statement, but not the last one, as shown in Figure 5.8.

Inside the loop, the value of $i differs during each iteration of the loop. In Figure 5.8, this variable would have a value of 0 in the first iteration, 1 in the second iteration, 2 in the third iteration, and so on.

The program below demonstrates the use of a `for` loop. Figure 5.9 shows the form that starts this script (top screen) and the output of the receiving program (bottom screen). The following HTML code is used to set up the radio buttons in the form-generating program located at http://www.aw.com/~perlpgm/cgi-bin/C5/drivfor.cgi:

```
<FONT SIZE=4 > Start loop at ?
<INPUT TYPE="radio" NAME="start" VALUE="0" CHECKED> 0
<INPUT TYPE="radio" NAME="start" VALUE="1" > 1
<INPUT TYPE="radio" NAME="start" VALUE="2" > 2
<INPUT TYPE="radio" NAME="start" VALUE="3" > 3
```

```
<BR>End loop at
  <INPUT TYPE="radio" NAME="end" VALUE="3" CHECKED> 3
  <INPUT TYPE="radio" NAME="end" VALUE="4" >   4
  <INPUT TYPE="radio" NAME="end" VALUE="5" >   5
  <INPUT TYPE="radio" NAME="end" VALUE="6" > 6
```

The key part of the HTML code that generates top screen of Figure 5.9

The form created by this HTML code sets the CGI variable `start` to have the starting loop value and the CGI variable `end` to have the ending loop value. These values are passed to the form-processing program shown below, which is located at `http://www.aw.com/~perlpgm/cgi-bin/C5/forloop.cgi`. This program creates the output shown at the bottom of Figure 5.9—that is, a table of squared and cubed values. The output starts with the value of the CGI variable `start` and ends with the value of the CGI variable `end` (set in the form element shown previously).

```perl
1.  #!/usr/bin/perl
2.  use CGI ':standard';
3.  print header, start_html('For Loop');
4.  $start = param ('start');         ┐  Get end-user selections
5.  $end = param ( 'end');
6.  print '<TABLE  BORDER=1><TH>Numb</TH><TH>Sqr</TH>
      <TH>Cubed</TH>';
7.  for ( $i = $start; $i < $end;  $i++ ) {   ┐ Loop from
                                               │ $start to
                                               │ $end times
8.      $i_sq=$i**2;
9.      $i_cubed=$i**3;
10.     print "<TR><TD> $i </TD><TD> $i_sq </TD><TD>
          $i_cubed </TR>";
11. }
12. print "</TABLE>That is the end and i=$i";
13. print  end_html;
```

Figure 5.9 An Example of a `for` Loop

In this program:

☆ Lines 4–5 use the `param()` function from the `CGI.pm` library to get the values of the CGI variables named `start` and `end`.

☆ Line 6 creates a table starting with the `<TABLE BORDER=1>` tag and the `<TH>` (table header) tags. The table headers are set to be `Numb`, `Sqr`, and `Cubed`.

☆ Lines 7–11 provide the `for` loop, which starts at `$start` and ends at `$end`. These values are input by the end user via a form. The value of `$i` is incremented during each iteration of the loop.

☆ Lines 8–9 set the values of `$i_sq` and `$i_cubed`. Because `$i` changes for each loop iteration, these values change as well.

☆ Line 10 outputs the values of `$i_sq` and `$i_cubed` inside table row (`<TR> ... </TR>`) and table data (`<TD> ... </TD>`) tags. This line creates a table row for each iteration of the `for` loop.

☆ Line 12 outputs the final value of `$i` outside the loop.

☆ **WARNING** **Check End-User Input**

The program that generates the bottom of Figure 5.9 is useful for illustrating the `for` loop, but it is not *defensive* enough for real-world use. For production use, this program should verify that any input data are valid (even though the program is controlled by radio buttons with set specific values). Such a defensive style of programming can catch errors in other forms that might call this program or guard against a future change that accidentally allows incorrect input. Chapter Seven discusses the use of regular expressions to verify form data.

The foreach Loop

The `foreach` loop is typically used to repeat a set of statements for every element in a list. It has the general format shown in Figure 5.10.

Loop scalar value receives the next list element each loop iteration	Repeat the loop once for every element in the list variable

```
foreach $item ( $items_array ) {

    Set of statements to repeat

}
```

Figure 5.10 The General Format of a `foreach` Loop

In Figure 5.10, you can see that the `foreach` loop uses a special scalar variable that gets the next list item for every loop iteration. Thus, if the list items were

```
@items_array = ("A", "B", "C");
```

then the loop variable `$item` from the loop shown in Figure 5.10 would be equal to "A" in the first iteration, "B" in the second iteration, and "C" in the third iteration.

Let's look at a full example of the use of the `foreach` loop. This program searches to see whether the user input is one of the "secret numbers" (3, 6, 9) contained in a list variable. Figure 5.11 shows the program's calling form (top screen), which is located at `http://www.aw.com/~perlpgm/cgi-bin/C5/drivforeach.cgi`. This form sets the CGI variable `guess` to a value between 0 and 9 with the following HTML radio button definition. When the user clicks the submit button, the program found at `http://www.aw.com/~perlpgm/cgi-bin/C5/foreach.cgi` begins.

```
<INPUT TYPE="radio" NAME="guess" VALUE="0" CHECKED> 0
<INPUT TYPE="radio" NAME="guess" VALUE="1" > 1
                    .
                    .
                    .
<INPUT TYPE="radio" NAME="guess" VALUE="8" > 8
<INPUT TYPE="radio" NAME="guess" VALUE="9" > 9
```

Part of the HTML code that creates the top window in Figure 5.11

The form-processing program found at location `http://www.aw.com/~perlpgm/cgi-bin/C5/foreach.cgi`, which is shown below, compares the radio button selected against the secret numbers. It also uses a new command (in line 12) called `last`. When this statement executes, it breaks out of the loop. In this program, it stops searching the loop if a matching number is found. Figure 5.11 shows the calling form (top screen), the program's execution (middle screen), and the output when the user picks 6 (middle screen) and then 8 (bottom screen).

```
1.  #!/usr/bin/perl
2.  use CGI ':standard';
3.  print header, start_html(' A foreach Example');
4.  @secretNums = ( 3, 6, 9 );     Iterate through each item
5.  $uinput = param( 'guess' );    of @secretNums
6.  $ctr=0; $found=0;
7.  foreach $item ( @secretNums ) {     $item is set to a different
8.      $ctr=$ctr+1;                     @secretNums value in
                                         each loop iteration
9.      if ( $item == $uinput ) {
10.         print "Number $item. Item found was number $ctr
                <BR>";
11.         $found=1;
12.         last;              Breaks out of
13.     }                      the loop
```

```
14.  }
15.  if ( $found ) {
16.      print "<BR> I checked $ctr item(s).";
17.  } else {
18.      print "<BR>Your guess, $uinput was NOT FOUND!
                I checked $ctr item(s).";
19.  }
```

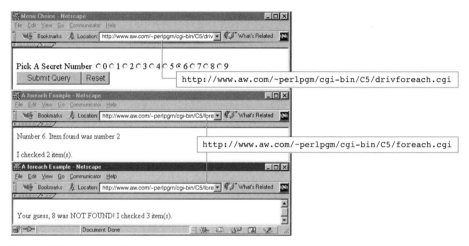

Figure 5.11 An Example of a `foreach` Loop

In this program:

☆ Line 4 sets up the `@secretNums` list variable with initial values of 3, 6, and 9.

☆ Line 5 gets the user input from the form shown at the top of Figure 5.11.

☆ Line 7 sets up the `foreach` loop that will iterate through the `@secretNums` list variable elements.

☆ Line 8 uses `$ctr` to keep track of the number of times that the loop repeats.

☆ Lines 9–13 check whether the current list element `$item` was found. If it is found, a message is output and `last` is used to quit the loop (rather than continue checking other values). The flag variable `$found` is set to 1 so that line 15 can determine that the item was found.

The while Loop

You use a `while` loop to repeat a section of code as long as a test condition remains *true*. It has the general format shown in Figure 5.12.

Condition enclosed in parentheses	Repeat as long as the conditional test is true

```
while ( $ctr < $max ) {

    Set of statements to repeat


}
```

Figure 5.12 The General Format of a while Loop

The loop shown in Figure 5.12 will repeat looping as long as the **loop end condition** is *true*. If the loop end condition is initially *false*, then the statements within the loop body will never execute.

☆**TIP**   **Infinite Loops**

If the test condition of a while loop is *always true*, then the loop will never end. Creating such an **infinite loop** is generally a bad idea. If you accidentally set up an infinite loop, you might have to exit the window that's running your program (that is, the MS-DOS window, Telnet window, or Web browser) to terminate your program.

Figure 5.13 shows a full example using a while loop. The form that starts this program is shown in the top screen; the output appears in the bottom screen. The following program generates the input shown on the bottom screen in Figure 5.13.

```
1.  #!/usr/bin/perl
2.  use CGI ':standard';
3.  print header, start_html(' A While Example');
4.  $upick=param('upick');
5.  $ctr = 1;
6.  print ( "<FONT Size=4> Numb of times to find
              $upick " );
7.  print ( '<TABLE BORDER=1> <TH> Numb <TH> Rand ' );
8.  $rnum= int(rand(10));
9.  while ( $rnum != $upick ) {
10.     print ("<TR> <TD> $ctr <TD> $rnum </TR>");
11.     $ctr = $ctr + 1;
12.     $rnum= int(rand(10));
13.  }
14.  print ("<TR> <TD> $ctr <TD> $rnum </TR>");
15.  print ('</TABLE>', br, "FOUND in $ctr times
              random=$rnum" );
```

Repeat lines 9–13 while $rnum is not the user's pick

Each iteration creates a table row

Generate next random number

Figure 5.13 An Example of a `while` Loop

In this program:

☆ Line 4 uses the **param CGI.pm** function to get the value of the CGI variable named **upick** from the calling form.

☆ Line 5 sets the initial value for **$ctr**, which counts the loop's iterations.

☆ Line 8 sets the variable **$rnum** equal to an initial random number (from 0 to 9).

☆ Line 9 loops as long as **$rnum** (the random number) is not equal to **$upick** (the input value). Line 10 prints the unsuccessful random number attempts. Line 12 gets the next random number to use in the next loop test in line 9.

☆ Line 15 outputs the final string indicating how many iterations it took to find the number selected by the end user.

The until Loop

The `until` loop operates just like the `while` loop except that it loops as long as its test condition is *false* and continues until it is *true*. If the end condition is *false* initially, however, at least one iteration still occurs. Figure 5.14 shows this loop's general format.

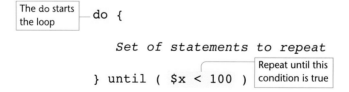

Figure 5.14 The General Format of an `until` Loop

The use of an `until` loop is very similar to the use of a `while` loop. The next example includes the program used to generate Figure 5.12, but this time created with an `until` loop instead of a `while` loop. In this case, using the `until` loop enables you to use somewhat more concise code than does using the `while` loop.

```perl
1. #!/usr/bin/perl
2. use CGI ':standard';
3. print header, start_html(' A While Example');
4. $upick=param('upick');
5. $ctr = 1;
6. print ( "<FONT Size=4> Numb of times to find
      $upick " );
7. print ( '<TABLE BORDER=1> <TH> Numb <TH> Rand ' );
8. do {
9.     $rnum= int(rand(10));           Generate next random number
10.    print ("<TR> <TD> $ctr <TD> $rnum </TR>");     Output table row
11.    $ctr = $ctr + 1;
12. } until ( $rnum == $upick );      Repeat lines 8–12 until $rnum is equal to $upick
13. print ('</TABLE>', br, "FOUND in $ctr times
    random=$rnum" );
```

In this program:

☆ Line 4 uses the `param()` CGI.pm function to get the value of the CGI variable named `upick`.

☆ In lines 8–12, the first line (line 8) starts the loop. Lines 9–11 will be executed no matter what. Line 9 generates a random number, and line 10 outputs this number. Line 12 checks whether the random number is equal to the user pick. If it is, the loop is terminated. If it is not, line 9 will execute again.

☆**TIP**   **Which Loop to Use?**

There is no rule that dictates which type of loop you should use for a particular type of programming problem. In fact, you often can solve a problem using more than one type of loop (as in the programs from the subsections "The `while` loop" and "The `until` loop"). Try to use the type of loop that is the easiest for the particular programming task at hand.

◎◎ Creating Compound Conditionals

So far, all of our test conditions have tested only one condition at a time. For example, consider the following statement, which tests a single condition—if `$x` is less than `$max`:

```perl
if ( $x < $max )
```

Sometimes, when there are several conditions to test, you can solve the programming task more concisely by using **logical conditional operators**. Logical conditional operators can be used to test more than one test condition at once when working with `if` statements, `while` loops, and `until` loops. For example, the following line of code will loop as long as `$x > $max` *and* `$found` is not equal to 'TRUE':

```
while ( $x > $max && $found ne 'TRUE' )
```

Perl supports three logical test operators that can be used with `if` and looping statements:

☆ `&&`—*the AND operator.* This operator is primarily used to create a compound test condition in `if`, `while`, or `until` statements. It enables you to create a statement like the following:

```
while ( $ctr < $max && $flag == 0 ) {
```

This statement would repeat the statements in its loop as long as `$ctr` is less than `$max` and `$flag` is equal to 0. Whenever either of these expressions is *false*, the loop will terminate.

☆ `||`—*the OR operator.* This operator is used much like the AND operator; that is, it is primarily used to create a compound test condition in `if`, `while`, or `until` statements. It enables you to create statements like the following:

```
if ( $name eq "SAM" || $name eq "MITCH" ) {
```

This statement would execute the statements within the `if` statement if `$name` is equal to either "SAM" or "MITCH".

☆ `!`—*the NOT operator.* This operator is used to test whether an expression is *false*. It can be used in a `while`, `until`, or `if` statement. Here is an example usage:

```
if ( !$FLAG == 0 )
```

This statement is *true* when `$FLAG` is anything except 0.

The following example demonstrates the use of a logical test operator. The program is called from the form shown at the top of Figure 5.15. This form permits the end user to select two numbers, which it then uses as the values for the CGI variables `pick1` and `pick2`. The receiving program (shown in the lower part of Figure 5.15) checks whether both of the selected numbers match its "combination" (1 and 7).

```
1. #!/usr/bin/perl
2. use CGI ':standard';
3. @safe = (1, 7);
4. print header, start_html('My Personal Safe');
5. $in1 = param( 'pick1' );
6. $in2 = param( 'pick2' );
```

Get both end-
user selections

```
7. if (( $in1 == $safe[0] ) && ( $in2 == $safe[1])){
8.     print "Congrats you got the combo";
9. }
10. else {
11.    print "Sorry you are wrong! ";
12.    print "You guessed $in1 and $in2 ";
13. }
14. print end_html;
```

Check whether both input values match

☆ **WARNING** **Use Compound Conditionals Carefully**

Use caution when including compound conditionals in your programs, as they can be tricky and introduce errors into a program's logic. When you use compound conditionals, it's a good idea to create test cases that test each targeted condition independently.

Figure 5.15 Output of a Program Using Logical Conditional Tests

In this program:

☆ Line 3 sets the values in the **safe** list variable to 1 and 7.

☆ Lines 5–6 get the CGI variables **pick1** and **pick2**.

☆ Lines 7–8 check whether the first input number (**$in1**) is the first list element *and* the second input number (**$in2**) is the second list element. If so, a congratulations message is output.

☆ Summary

▷ List variables offer a way to organize data in your program into one list instead of using individual scalar variables. Data elements within a list can be accessed by a common variable name, which is made up of two parts: a variable name and subscript values.

▷ Using list variables enables you to add and delete list items on the fly in your programs, use loop constructs to examine and operate on each item in your list, and utilize special list operators and functions.

▷ Perl supports a set of statements that enable you to create loops, which in turn allow you to solve some programming problems much more concisely. Loops can be especially useful for examining and operating on data organized into lists. Loop statements include the `for`, `foreach`, `while`, and `until` loops.

▷ The logical operators can be used to carry out compound tests within a conditional test statement. The logical AND operator, `&&`, evaluates to *true* when both conditions are *true*. The logical OR operator, `||`, evaluates to *true* when either condition is *true*. The logical NOT operator, `!`, evaluates to *true* when the test condition is *false*.

☆ Review Questions

1. In the list variable defined in Figure 5.1, what is the value of each of the following? `$students[1]`, `$students[8-5]`, `$students[0]`

2. What are three advantages of using loops?

3. What is the range operator? For what purpose can you use it?

4. What are four functions used to add and delete items from a list variable?

5. What is the output of the following code:
   ```
   @list1 = ( 9, 8, 7, 6, 5 );
   print "sublist=@list1[ 0, 3, 1 ]";
   ```

6. What is a multidimensional list? In Figure 5.5, what is the value of `$Inventory[2][3]` and `$Inventory[1][1]`?

7. Name four types of looping constructs. Which one can you use to repeat a set of statements for each element in a list variable?

8. What is the maximum number of times that the `while` loop used in the program that generates Figure 5.13 can iterate?

9. What are the three parts of a `for` statement? What does each part do?

10. Name the three compound conditional test operators. What does each mean?

☆ Hands-On Exercises

1. Use the `rand()` function to create an HTML page that displays one of four banner ads on a random basis. The book Web site (`http://www.aw.com/~perlpgm`) includes some sample banner items. *Hint:* Place the names of the banner files into a list variable. Use the output of the `rand()` function to select an item from the list variable, as in Figure 5.2.

2. Rewrite the program from Figure 5.9 to use a `while` or `until` looping construct rather than a `for` loop.

3. Modify the program from Figure 5.4 to change the output as follows:
   ☆ If the end user selects only North American countries (the United States, Canada, or Mexico), then create an HTML document that suggests that the user try traveling to Asia.
   ☆ If the end user selects only China, then create an HTML document that suggests that the user try traveling to North America.
   ☆ If the end user selects all four destinations, then suggest the user consider becoming a frequent flier with your airline.
   ☆ For all other entries, output the destinations that the user did *not* pick.

4. Create a multiple-choice Web-based exam that includes at least four questions with the following properties:
   ☆ Each question has at least four choices labeled "A", "B","C," and "D". (Make up the questions yourself but use the answer key shown below.)
   ☆ The answer key to the exam shown below:

Question Number	Correct Answer
1	"D"
2	"C"
3	"B"
4	"A"

   ☆ When the end user submits the form, score the questions and output the overall percentage of answers correct. In the output, indicate which answers were wrong. *Hint:* Store the answer key in a list variable.

5. Modify the program from Figure 5.15 to become a four-number combination instead of a two-number combination. Use the combination 9, 6, 3, 1 as the set of "safe" numbers.

6. Modify the program and calling form from Figure 5.6. Allow the end user to search and output all items that cost less than some specified amount. For example, if the end user entered 3, then `Screw Drivers` would be output. If the end user entered 6, then `Screw Drivers` and `Wrenches` would be output.

7. Create a simple calendar application that displays an event on a calendar for a particular month. The starting form should display the calendar shown below. It should be numbered and have the five events preset on days 4, 16, 17, 18, 19, and 20. The form should allow two operations:

(a) Add an event. Provide a text box in which the end user can define an event to add and offer a selection list of possible days. When submitted, the calendar should be updated to include the new event. (Allow no more than 15 characters for the event name.)

(b) Delete an event. Provide a text box in which the end user can define an event to delete and offer a selection list of possible days. When submitted, the calendar should be updated to eliminate the deleted event. If the event cannot be found, show an appropriate message.

Sunday	Monday	Tuesday	Wednesday	Thursday	Friday	Saturday
1	2	3	4 Holiday	5	6	7
8	9	10	11	12	13	14
15	16 Vacation	17 Vacation	18 Vacation	19 Vacation	20 Vacation	21
22	23	24	25	26	27	28
29	30					

HASH LISTS AND SUBROUTINES

This chapter covers two more features of the Perl language that are important for solving programming problems. *Hash lists* provide a different way to represent list data than do list variables. For some programming problems, hash lists can be easier to use and execute more quickly. *Subroutines* can help reduce the number of lines in your programs, provide a way to reuse programming code, and make your programs easier to understand.

Chapter Objectives

☆ Describe how to use hash lists and hash tables in Perl

☆ Learn how to use subroutines in a program

☆ Learn how to combine form generation and processing into a single program

◎◎ Hash Lists

In Chapter Five, you learned how list varibles can be used to organize related data into a single list. Perl supports another type of list variable called a **hash list** (or *associated array*). Hash lists do not store items in sequentially ordered lists in the same way as list variables. Instead, they store elements as pairs of values, with the first element being the *key* and the second being the *data* element. The key is used to look up or provide a cross-reference to the data value. Thus, instead of employing sequential subscripts to refer to data in a list, you use keys.

In some instances, hash lists offer more advantages than do list variables:

☆ *When you need to cross-reference one piece of data with another.* For example, you may have a part number and want to look up the corresponding product description. Although this kind of cross-referencing can be done with regular list variables, Perl supports some convenient functions that use hash lists for this purpose.

☆ *When you are concerned about the access time required for looking up data.* Suppose your application keeps lots of data in a list and needs to find a set of data associated with a product number (such as a product description, cost, and size). Hash lists provide much quicker access to data than do list variables (assuming that you can organize the data to be cross-referenced by a set of keys in the first place).

Using Hash Lists

Hash lists use the general format shown in Figure 6.1. As shown in this figure, the hash list variable starts with percent sign ("%") rather than the at sign ("@") used with list variable names. Also, when you create a hash list, you assign items in key/value pairs. In Figure 6.1, for example, "Jan" is the key with a value of 31, "Feb" is the key with a value of 28, "Mar" is the key with a value of 31, and so on.

```
Name of hash list variable starts with  %
              Key element 1 and data element 1        Key element 3 and data element 3
                  Key element 2 and data element 2
%months = ( "Jan", 31, "Feb", 28, "Mar", 31, "Apr", 30,
            "May", 31, "Jun", 30, "Jul", 31, "Aug", 31,
            "Sep", 30, "Oct", 31, "Nov", 30, "Dec", 31 );
```

Figure 6.1 The General Syntax for Hash Lists

When you want to access an item in the hash list, you can use the syntax shown in Figure 6.2. Note that when you access an individual item, the hash variable starts with a dollar sign ("$") because you access each item from a hash list as a scalar variable. Also, you use curly brackets (rather than the square brackets used with list variables) to specify a key. Finally, a key is specified for hash lists instead of a subscript as with list variables.

☆ SHORTCUT   Alternative Hash List Syntax

Perl also allows you to create a hash list using the => operator, which signifies that you are associating a key with a value. The hash list in Figure 6.1 could, therefore, be defined as follows:

```
%months = ( "Jan" => 31, "Feb" => 28, "Mar" => 31, "Apr" => 30,
"May" => 31, "Jun" => 30, "Jul" => 31, "Aug" => 31, "Sep" => 30,
"Oct" => 31,"Nov" => 30, "Dec" => 31 );
```

Both definition styles work equally well. For simple hash lists, this book will not use the => syntax, though it will use it for multidimensional hash lists.

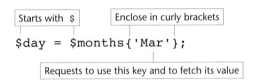

Figure 6.2 Accessing Elements in a Hash List

☆ WARNING   You Cannot Fetch Keys by Data Values

You might be tempted to use a data element to fetch a key from a hash list, as in the following example:

```
$mon = $months{ 28 };
```

This syntax is incorrect, because hash lists can fetch data values only by using keys (not the other way around).

The following program uses a hash list to calculate the number of days remaining in a month (after the end user selects a starting day and month). The form shown at the top of Figure 6.3 requests that the end user select a month and day. (The programming code to generate the top form is not provided here but is available on the book Web site (http://www.aw.com/~perlpgm). It sets the CGI variable startmon to be a three-letter month, such as "Jan", and the CGI variable startd to be a number between 1 and 31.) In line 4 of the program, the hash list definition associates each month name with the total days in that month. Figure 6.3 shows the output of this program when April 15 is selected (middle screen) and when April 31 is selected (bottom screen).

```
1. #!/usr/bin/perl
2. use CGI ':standard';
3. print header, start_html( 'Month Calc' );
4. %months = ( "Jan", 31, "Feb", 28, "Mar", 31,
       "Apr", 30, "May", 31, "Jun", 30, "Jul", 31,
       "Aug", 31, "Sep", 30,"Oct", 31, "Nov", 30,
       "Dec", 31 );
5. $startm = param('startmon');
6. $startd = param('startday');
7. $mdays=$months{ "$startm" };
```

Create a hash list

Get number of days in the month selected by the user

```
8.  if ( $startd <= $mdays ) {
9.      $daysLeft = $mdays - $startd;
10.     print "There are $daysLeft days left in
            $startm.";
11.     print  br, "$startm has $mdays total days ";
12. } else {
13.     print "Hmmm, there aren't $startd day in
            $startm";
14. }
15. print end_html;
```

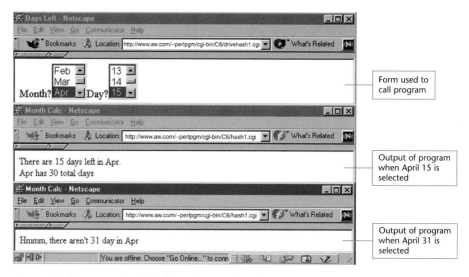

Figure 6.3 Program That Calculates the Number of Days Left in a Month

In this program:

☆ Line 4 defines the hash list of %months. It associates a month name with the number of days in that month.

☆ Lines 5–6 get the value of the input CGI variables startnum and start-day from the form shown in the top screen in Figure 6.3. The calling form sets the CGI variable startm to "Jan", "Feb", "Mar", ..., "Dec" based on the end -user's selections. In line 6, the CGI variable startday will have a value that is a number from 1 to 31 (based on the end user's selection from the calling form).

☆ Line 7 looks up the number of days in a particular month from the hash list and stores it into $mdays.

☆ Line 8 checks whether the date input is legal. For example, it is possible for the end user to enter 31 days for June in the form—a clear error. Line 8 compares the number of days in the month with the number input from the end user.

☆ Line 9 calculates the number of days left in the month when valid input is received.

☆ **WARNING** **Dealing with Leap Years**

The preceding program does not take into account whether a particular year is a leap year. Extra logic is required to detect whether February is the selected month and the current year is a leap year.

Accessing and Outputting Hash Keys and Values

Perl provides two functions that can be used to access and output hash keys and values: keys() and values().

The **keys()** function returns a list of all keys in the hash list. For example,

```
%Inventory = ( 'Nuts', 33, 'Bolts', 55, 'Screws', 12);
@keyitems = keys(%Inventory);
print "keyitems= @keyitems";
```

Because Perl outputs hash keys and values according to how they are stored internally (which is not necessarily the same order in which you stored them), one possible output order with the preceding code is

```
keyitems= Screws Bolts Nuts
```

The **values()** function returns a list of all values in the hash list. For example,

```
%Inventory = ( 'Nuts', 33, 'Bolts', 55, 'Screws', 12);
@elements = values(%Inventory);
print "elements= @elements";
```

Again, the order of the output depends on how Perl stores hash values internally. One possible output order would be

```
elements= 12 55 33
```

These functions are often used to output the contents of a hash list. For example, the following code uses the keys() function to output a key/value pair of the hash list %Inventory:

```
%Inventory = ( 'Nuts', 33, 'Bolts', 55, 'Screws', 12);
foreach $item ( (keys %Inventory) ) {
    print "Item=$item Value=$Inventory{$item} ";
}
```

In the second line, (keys %Inventory) generates a list of keys. The foreach portion of that statement then assigns each individual key to $item. The print statement can then output each key/value pair. The following is one possible output order:

```
Item=Screws Value=12 Item=Bolts Value=55 Item=Nuts
    Value=33
```

Changing, Adding, Deleting, and Verifying Hash List Items

Perl offers several hash-specific operations and functions. This section focuses on how to change, add, and delete hash elements, and how to verify whether a hash element exists.

Changing a Hash Element

You can change the value of a hash list item by giving it a new value in an assignment statement. For example,

```
%Inventory = ( 'Nuts', 33, 'Bolts', 55, 'Screws', 12);
$Inventory{'Nuts'} = 34;
```

This line changes the value of the value associated with Nuts to 34.

Adding a Hash Element

You can add items to the hash list by assigning a new key a value. For example,

```
%Inventory = ( 'Nuts', 33, 'Bolts', 55, 'Screws', 12);
$Inventory{'Nails'} = 23;
```

These lines add the key Nails with a value of 23 to the hash list.

Deleting a Hash List Item

You can delete an item from the hash list by using the delete() function. For example,

```
%Inventory = ( 'Nuts', 33, 'Bolts', 55, 'Screws', 12);
delete $Inventory{'Bolts'};
```

These lines delete the Bolts key and its value of 55 from the hash list.

Verifying an Element's Existence

You can use the exists() function to verify whether a particular key exists in the hash list. It returns *true* (1) if the key passed as an argument appears in the hash list. It returns *false* (0) if the key is not in the list. The following is an example that demonstrates the use of the exists() function:

```
%Inventory = ( 'Nuts', 33, 'Bolts', 55, 'Screws', 12);
if ( exists( $Inventory{'Nuts'} ) ) {
    print ( "Nuts are in the list" );
} else {
    print ( "No Nuts in this list" );
}
```

This code outputs Nuts are in the list.

☆**TIP**   **Changing Key Values**

You can change the value of an existing key, but you cannot change or rename a key for a particular value in the hash list. The best way to accomplish the latter goal is to delete the key/value pair and then add the new key and value.

☆**WARNING**   **Keys Are Case Sensitive**

Like most things in Perl, keys are case sensitive. Thus, if you wrote the following two lines, you would end up with four keys—Nuts, Bolts, Screws, and nuts—and would not change the value stored in conjunction with Nuts:

```
%Inventory = ( 'Nuts', 33, 'Bolts', 55, 'Screws', 12);
$Inventory{'nuts'} = 32;
```

The following program enables the end user to add an element to a hash list from an input form. The input form is shown at the top of Figure 6.4. (Its code is not shown but is available on the book Web site.) (http://www.aw.com/~perlpgm.) The middle screen shows the output when an add command is successfully executed. When the user enters an illegal command (anything other than add), the bottom screen is output.

```
1.  #!/usr/bin/perl
2.  use CGI ':standard';                            Create hash list
3.  print header, start_html( 'Inventory' );
4.  %invent = ( "Nuts", 44, "Nails", 34, "Bolts", 31 );
5.  $action = param('Action');
6.  $whatkey = param('Key');                  Check whether key
7.  $whatvalue = param('Value');              exists in the hash list
8.  if ( $action eq "Add" ) {
9.      if ( exists( $invent{ "$whatkey" } ) ) {
10.         print "Sorry already exists $whatkey <BR>";
11.     } else {                                    Add new
12.         $invent{"$whatkey"} = $whatvalue;       key/value pair
13.         print "Adding key=$whatkey val=$whatvalue
                <BR>";
14.         print "—-<BR>";                         Output entire
15.         foreach $key ( ( keys %invent ) ) {     hash list
16.             print "$invent{$key} key=$key <BR>";
17.         }
18.     }
19. } else { print "Sorry No Such Action=$action<BR>"; }
20. print end_html;
```

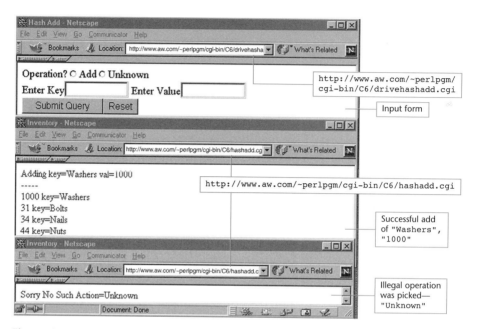

Figure 6.4 An Example Add Hash Item Program

In this program:

☆ Line 4 creates a hash list with three elements with the keys `Nuts`, `Nails`, and `Bolts`.

☆ Lines 5–7 get the `Action`, `Key`, and `Value` CGI variables.

☆ Line 8 checks whether the CGI variable `Action` is equal to "Add". This value was set by the calling form. If the value of `Action` is not "Add", then line 19 outputs an invalid command message.

☆ Line 9 checks whether the key passed in already exists. If it does not, line 12 adds the key/value pair to the list and line 13 prints them out. Lines 15–17 output the entire list.

Environmental Hash Lists

When your Perl program starts from a Web browser, a special **environmental hash list** is made available to it. This hash list comprises a set of keys and values that describe the environment state when your program was called. The key/value pairs are stored in the **%ENV** hash.

The environmental hash list can be used just like any other hash list. For example, the following line of code outputs the language setting of the end user's browser that accessed the program:

```perl
print "Language=$ENV{'HTTP_ACCEPT_LANGUAGE'}";
```

An example output from this statement might be `Language=en` for English.

Many values appear in the environmental hash list. The following are some of the more important ones.

☆ **HTTP_REFFERER.** This variable defines the URL of the Web page that the user accessed prior to accessing your page. For example, a value of `HTTP_REFFERER` might be "`http://www.mypage.com`". This variable is set when someone links to or reaches your site via the submit button. You could, for example, use it to check whether your form-processing program was called from the URL of your form-generating program. You might then elect to reject anyone accessing your form-processing program from somewhere else (to reduce the chances of someone tampering with your site.)

☆ **REQUEST_USER_AGENT.** This variable defines the browser name, browser version, and computer platform of the user who is starting your program. For example, its value might be "`Mozilla/4.7 [en] (Win 98, I)`" for Netscape. You may find this value useful if you need to output browser-specific HTML code.

☆ **HTTP_ACCEPT_LANGUAGE.** This variable defines the language that the browser is using. For example, its value might be "`en`" for English for Netscape or "`en-us`" for English for Internet Explorer.

☆ **REQUEST_METHOD.** This variable indicates whether your program was called with the `post` or with the `get` method. (Chapter Four provides more details on these methods.) You could use this variable in conjunction with other environmental variables to get form data and other arguments passed to your program. Fortunately, we can use the `param()` function within `CGI.pm` to accomplish the same goal (as described in Chapters Three and Four); for that reason, this book will not cover how to parse data with these environmental variables.

☆ **REMOTE_ADDRESS.** This variable indicates the TCP/IP address of the computer that is accessing your site. TCP/IP addresses are the physical network addresses of computers on the Internet—for example, `65.186.8.8`. The `REMOTE_ADDRESS` variable may have some value if you log information about visitors at your site.

☆ **REMOTE_HOST.** This variable is set to the domain name of the computer connecting to your Web site. It is a logical name that maps to a TCP/IP address—for example, `www.yahoo.com`. It is empty if the Web server cannot translate the TCP/IP address into a domain name.

Checking Language with Environmental Variables

The following program checks the language settings of the end user's browser that is accessing my site. Line 5 checks for 'en' and 'en-us' as the value of `HTTP_ACCEPT_LANGUAGE`. Both tests are needed because Netscape sets the variable to 'en' and Internet Explorer to 'en-us'. Figure 6.5 shows the output of this program when it is run on Internet Explorer (top screen) and on Netscape (bottom screen).

```perl
1.  #!/usr/bin/perl
2.  use CGI ':standard';
3.  print header, start_html('Check Environment');
4.  $lang=$ENV{'HTTP_ACCEPT_LANGUAGE'};
5.  if ( $lang eq 'en' || $lang eq 'en-us' ) {
6.      print "Language=$ENV{'HTTP_ACCEPT_LANGUAGE'}";
7.      print "<BR>Browser= $ENV{'HTTP_USER_AGENT'}";
8.  }
9.  else {
10.     print 'Sorry I do not speak your language';
11. }
12. print end_html;
```

Get language environmental variable

Test whether language is English

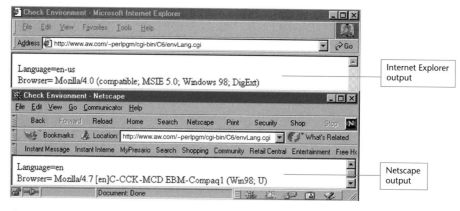

Internet Explorer output

Netscape output

Figure 6.5 Using Some CGI/Perl Special Environmental Variables

In this program:

☆ Line 4 saves the value of `HTTP_ACCEPT_LANGUAGE` into `$lang`. Line 5 checks whether it is 'en' (as set in Netscape) or 'en-us' (as set in Internet Explorer).

☆ Lines 6–7 output the values of the language and browser settings.

☆ **TIP**   **Logging Data about Visitors**

The environmental variables REQUEST_USER_AGENT, REMOTE_ADDRESS, and REMOTE_HOST can provide some useful information about visitors to your Web page and trends in end user access. It may be worth your while to log this information into a database or file (Chapter Seven covers file I/O). Be careful, however, not to rely on this data too much (for example, for security purposes), as computers can easily change domain names and TCP/IP addresses.

☆**SHORTCUT   Checking Browser Types**

You can use environmental variables to check the browser type that is accessing your site. For example, you can use the *match* and *binding* operators to search a string for a set of characters. (The match and binding operators are covered in Chapter Seven.) The following code demonstrates this idea. Here, the second statement is *true* if $browser contains the string MSIE (for Internet Explorer):

```
$browser=$ENV{'HTTP_USER_AGENT'} ;
if ( $browser =~ m/MSIE/ ) {
    print "Got Internet Explorer Browser=$browser";
} else { print "browser=$browser";}
```

Creating a Hash List of List Items

In Chapter Five, you learned how to create a list of lists—that is, a multidimensional list. You can also create hash lists of lists or hash tables. Hash tables use a key to cross-reference it with a list of values (instead of using simple key/value pairs).

For example, suppose you wanted to represent the data in Table 6.1 using a hash table. These data can be represented in a hash table as shown in Figure 6.6.

Table 6.1 Data to Be Represented with a Hash Table

Part Number	Part Name	Number Available	Price	Picture File
AC1000	Hammer	122	12	hammer.gif
AC1001	Wrench	344	5	wrench.gif
AC1002	Hand Saw	150	10	saw.gif

```
                    Part Num is key for a list of items
                          Use => to associate a key with the list
    %Inventory= (
                    AC1000=>['Hammer', 122, 12, 'hammer.gif'],
                    AC1001=>['Wrench', 344, 5, 'wrench.gif' ],
 Hash variable name  AC1002=>['Hand Saw', 150, 10, 'saw.gif' ]
           );
                          List enclosed in square brackets
```

Figure 6.6 An Example of a Statement That Creates a Hash Table

You can access items from a hash table much like you access a hash list, except you must add a subscript to identify the specific element in the hash table. In this example, $Inventory{'AC1000'}[0] is 'Hammer', $Inventory {'AC1001'}[0] is 'Wrench', and $Inventory{'AC1002'}[1] is 150.

> ☆ **TIP**   **Hash Tables and Databases**
>
> If Table 6.1 looks like a database record, it is not an accident. Hash tables are the primary method that Perl uses to work with databases. Chapter Eight discusses more about databases.

The following example demonstrates how you can access and change individual items in a hash table. The following code uses the `%Inventory` hash table defined in Figure 6.6:

```perl
$numHammers = $Inventory{'AC1000'}[1];
$Inventory{'AC1001'}[1] = $Inventory{'AC1001'}[1] + 1;
$partName =   $Inventory{'AC1002'}[0];
print "$numHammers, $partName, $Inventory{'AC1001'}[1]";
```

This code would output

```
122, Hand Saw, 345
```

> ☆ **WARNING**   **Don't Go Past the End of a List**
>
> Be careful not to use subscript numbers greater than the number of elements in your hash table—for instance, `$Inventory{'AC1000'}[20]` in the preceding example. The results will likely be some random memory location and not what you intended.

The next program demonstrates how you access elements in a hash list. It outputs a form (shown in Figure 6.7) that asks the end user to select a table element for deletion. For consistency, line 4 uses the same hash table definition as Figure 6.6, albeit with one extra row. (All of the table elements are not used, however.) Note how lines 7–11 go through each key and display the part name and number of parts available by using radio buttons. (Figure 6.8 shows the form-processing program stored at `http://www.aw.com/~perlpgm/cgi-bin/C6/GetInventHash.cgi` that actually deletes the table row. The next section, "Adding and Deleting Items from a Hash Table," discusses the deletion of hash table rows in more detail.)

```perl
1. #!/usr/bin/perl
2. use CGI ':standard';
3. print header, start_html('Menu Choice');
4. %Inventory =  (
       AC1000 => [ 'Hammers', 122, 12, 'hammer.gif'],
       AC1001 => [ 'Wrenches', 344,  5, 'wrench.gif'],
       AC1002 => [ 'Hand Saws', 150, 10, 'saw.gif'],
       AC1003 => [ 'Screw Drivers', 222, 3,
           'sdriver.gif']
   );
5. print '<FORM ACTION="http://www.aw.com/~perlpgm/
           cgi-bin/C6/GetInventHash.cgi" METHOD="POST">';
6. print '<Font size=4 > Pick an item you want to
       delete', br;
```

> Establish a hash multidimensional list

```
7.  foreach $item (keys %Inventory) {
8.      $name=$Inventory{$item}[0];
9.      $Numb=$Inventory{$item}[1];
10.     print "<INPUT TYPE=radio NAME=\"item\"
            VALUE=$item > $name - we have $Numb", br;
11.
12. }
13. print br, '<INPUT TYPE=SUBMIT VALUE="Click To
        Submit">';
14. print '<INPUT TYPE=RESET VALUE="Erase and
        Restart">';
15. print '</FORM>', end_html;
```

Create radio button with CGI variable named item to have the value of the hash key

Output the hash list

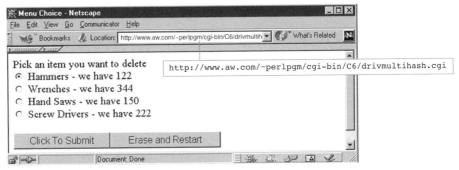

Figure 6.7 Using a Hash Table in a Form

In this program:

☆ Line 4 sets up a hash table of inventory items called %Inventory.

☆ Line 5 sends the output of the form to http://www.aw.com/~perlpgm/cgi-bin/C6/GetInventHash.cgi.

☆ Line 7 loops through each key of the hash table. Lines 8–9 access the part names and number of parts in the hash table. Line 10 creates the radio button form element containing the item name and number available.

Adding and Deleting Items from a Hash Table

When you want to add a hash table row, you must specify a key and list of items. For example, the following item adds an entry line to the %Inventory hash table (from Figure 6.6) with the key 'AC1003':

```
$Inventory{'AC1003'} = ['Screw Drivers', 222, 3,
    'sdriver.gif' ];
```

Because the exists() and delete() hash functions both work on a single key, you can specify them just as you did before. For example, the following code checks whether a key exists before deleting it:

```
if ( exists $Inventory{'AC1003'} ) {
   delete $Inventory{'AC1003'};
} else {
   print "Sorry we do not have the key";
}
```

☆ **WARNING** **Deleting a Key That Does Not Exist**

Always check whether the key exists before you try to delete it. If you try to delete a nonexistent key, Perl will *not* issue an error message or provide any indication that the key was not found (or not deleted).

The following application processes the form input from Figure 6.7 by deleting an inventory item (in this case, a hammer). The program is stored at the location `http://www.aw.com/~perlpgm/cgi-bin/C6/GetInventHash.cgi`. Its argument is a key to be deleted (in the CGI variable `item`). First, it checks whether the key exists in its hash table. Then, if the key exists, it deletes the key and data values.

```
1.  #!/usr/bin/perl
2.  use CGI ':standard';
3.  print header, start_html('Inventory Answer');
4.  %Inventory =  (
         AC1000 => [ 'Hammers', 122, 12, 'hammer.gif'],
         AC1001 => [ 'Wrenches', 344,  5, 'wrench.gif'],
         AC1002 => [ 'Hand Saws', 150, 10, 'saw.gif'],
         AC1003 => [ 'Screw Drivers', 222, 3,
            'sdriver.gif']
      );
5.  $KEY=param('item');
6.  if ( exists( $Inventory{$KEY} ) ) {
7.     delete ( $Inventory{$KEY} );
8.     foreach $item (keys %Inventory) {
9.        $Name=$Inventory{$item}[0];
10.       $Numb=$Inventory{$item}[1];
11.       $Cost=$Inventory{$item}[2];
12.       $Picture=$Inventory{$item}[3];
13.       print "$Name $Numb \$$Cost $Picture", br;
14.    }
15. } else { print "sorry we do not have that item"; }
16. print end_html;
```

Check whether the received key exists; if so, delete the record

Iterate through the remaining records and print them out

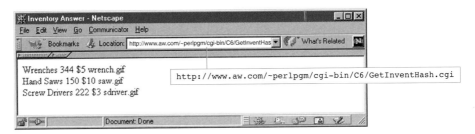

Figure 6.8 The Result of Deleting a Record

In this program:

☆ Line 4 sets up the same hash table as that used in the calling form in Figure 6.7.

☆ Line 5 gets the CGI variable `item` passed in from the program that generates Figure 6.7.

☆ Lines 6–7 first check whether the key exists and then deletes it if it exists.

☆ Lines 8–14 use a `foreach` loop to output the remaining hash table elements. Note how line 13 uses a backslash ("/") in front of the dollar size to output a dollar sign ("$").

☆**TIP**   **Using Files and Databases with Hash Tables**

Although the programs that generate Figures 6.7 and 6.8 use the same definition for the `%Inventory` hash table, the values in such a hash table would more commonly come from a file or database accessed at the start of the program (rather than being preset inside the program). Chapter Seven covers the process of reading and writing data to files. Note also that the program from Figure 6.7 would normally save the changed hash table back to a file or database.

◎◎ Using Subroutines

As you start to write more complex programs, you will find that your programs are easier to understand and maintain if you divide them into logical sections. You might also find sets of statements that are executed several times in different parts of a program. **Subroutines** provide a way for programmers to group a set of statements, set them aside, and turn them into mini-programs within a larger program. These mini-programs can be executed several times from different places in the overall program.

Creating and using subroutines offers several advantages:

☆ *Smaller overall program size.* If a set of statements will be executed more than once in the overall program, you can place these statements into a subroutine and just call them wherever needed. This approach reduces the number of lines in the program. For example, if the program calculates a long complex expression (perhaps a standard deviation) several times with different input values, then placing the expression in a subroutine will likely result in fewer lines of code.

☆ *Programs that are easier to understand and change.* Subroutines can make complex and long programs easier to understand and change. For example, consider a program that receives input from a Web form, queries a database, and generates a new Web page containing the result. Rather than writing this program as a long list of statements, you might use one subroutine that reads input from a Web form, a second subroutine that queries a database, and a third subroutine outputs the results to a Web page. With this logical division of tasks, the purpose of each section of code becomes much clearer.

☆ *Reusable program sections.* As you identify and define subroutines, you might find that some subroutines are useful to other programs. For example, you might define a subroutine that creates a common page footer for the Web pages on your site. You could then use this subroutine in several different programs that output Web pages for your site to create the common page footer.

Working with Subroutines

You can create a subroutine by placing a group of statements into the following format:

```
sub subroutine_name {
    set of statements
}
```

You always start a subroutine definition with the Perl reserved word `sub`. You use the `subroutine_name` to refer to the subroutine later. The curly brackets (`{ ... }`) define a block of statements within the subroutine. The set of statements consist of regular Perl statements that should execute each time the subroutine is called.

Suppose you want to create a subroutine that automatically prints out the HTML tags needed to output two columns of a table. You might decide to create a subroutine called `outputTableRow()` that would look like the following:

```
sub outputTableRow {
    print '<TR><TD>One</TD><TD>Two</TD></TR>';
}
```

When you are ready to execute the statements in this subroutine, you can enter the name of the subroutine preceded by an ampersand:

```
&outputTableRow;
```

Whenever you call the `outputTableRow()` subroutine by inserting an `&outputTableRow` line into your code, the three lines of the `outputTableRow()` subroutine will be executed. Figure 6.9 shows the output of using the `outputTableRow()` subroutine.

```
1.  #!/usr/bin/perl
2.  use CGI ':standard';
3.  print header, start_html( 'Subroutine Example' );
4.  print 'Here is simple table <TABLE BORDER=1>';
5.  &outputTableRow;
6.  &outputTableRow;
7.  &outputTableRow;
8.  print '</TABLE>', end_html;
9.  sub outputTableRow {
10. print '<TR><TD>One</TD><TD>Two</TD></TR>';
11. }
```

Call the
outputTableRow()
subroutine

Line executed when
outputTableRow
is called

Figure 6.9 Output of the `outputTableRow()` Subroutine

In this program:

☆ Line 4 outputs `Here is simple table:` and then `<TABLE BORDER=1>` to start the table.

☆ Lines 5–7 call the subroutine `outputTableRow()` three times, each time outputting another row of the table.

☆ Lines 9–11 output a table row with two cells, with `One` in the first cell and `Two` in the second cell.

☆**TIP**   **Use Comments at the Start of a Subroutine**

It is a good practice to place comments at the start of a subroutine that give brief description of what the subroutine does and perhaps how it is used. Recall that the pound sign ("#") precedes a comment.

Passing Arguments to Subroutines

The example in Figure 6.9 has a major limitation: The subroutine is not general enough. That is, it always outputs the same table row with One in the first cell and Two in the second cell. To place different labels in the cells, you would have to change the subroutine. One way to circumvent this limitation is to generalize the subroutine by allowing it to accept input variables for each table cell. These input variables are called **arguments to the subroutine**.

☆ **TIP**   **You Have Already Used Arguments**

Several of the Perl functions introduced earlier in this book used arguments—such as the sqrt(), length(), and rand() functions described in Chapter Three. For example, sqrt($num) takes $num as an argument. Similarly, the CGI.pm param() function accepts a CGI variable as an argument.

To send arguments to a subroutine, place the argument in parentheses when you call the subroutine. Consider the following call to outputTableRow():

```
&outputTableRow( 'A First Cell', 'A Second Cell' );
```

This line calls &outputTableRow() with the first argument set to 'A First Cell' and the second argument set to 'A Second Cell'.

Within a subroutine, you can access the arguments by using a special argument list variable called @_. With @_, a subroutine can access the arguments passed to it by using

☆ $_[0] as the variable name for the first argument,

☆ $_[1] as the variable name for the second argument,

☆ $_[2] as the variable name for the third argument,

⋮

☆ $_[n] as the variable name for the nth argument.

Thus, if the outputTableRow() subroutine was called as shown below, then $_[0] would be set to 'A First Cell' and $_[1] would be set to 'A Second Cell':

```
&outputTableRow( 'A First Cell', 'A Second Cell' );
```

Figure 6.10 shows the results of a more generalized outputTableRow() subroutine that accepts two arguments for two table cells to output. The code for this subroutine follows:

```
1. #!/usr/bin/perl
2. use CGI ':standard';
3. print header, start_html( 'Subroutine with
      arguments' );
4. print 'Here is simple table: <TABLE BORDER=1>';
```

```
 5. for ( $i=1; $i<=3; $i++ ) {
 6.    &outputTableRow( "Row $i Col 1", "Row $i Col 2");
 7. }
 8. print '</TABLE>', end_html;
 9. sub outputTableRow {
10.    print "<TR><TD>$_[0]</TD><TD>$_[1]</TD></TR>";
11. }
```

Call outputTableRow( ) with two arguments

First argument

Second argument

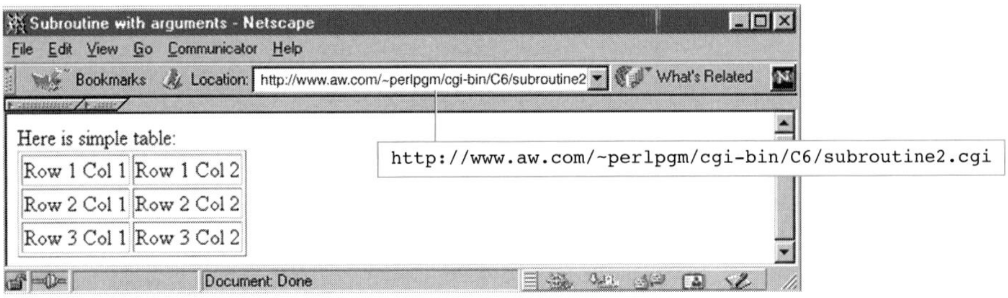

Figure 6.10 Output of the `outputTableRow( )` Example with Arguments

In this program:

☆ Lines 5–7 create a `for` loop that repeats three times. Each loop calls `outputTableRow( )` with a different set of arguments.

☆ Lines 9–11 create a new version of `outputTableRow( )` that uses the first (`$_[0]`) and second (`$_[1]`) arguments as the first and second cells, respectively, in the table row to output.

☆**TIP**   **Determining the Number of Arguments Received**

There are at least two different ways to determine the number of arguments received.

First, recall from Chapter Five, "Getting the Number of Elements in a List Variable," that the range operator is set to the last element in a list variable. Using this information, the number of arguments sent to a subroutine could be determined inside the subroutine as follows:

```
$numargs = $#_ + 1;
```

Second, you can use the @_ variable directly. For example,

```
$numargs = @_;
```

Returning Values

Subroutines can be defined so that they return values to the calling program. This approach can be a useful way for a calling program to receive the results of a computation or to determine if the computation within the subroutine completed successfully. We have already used return values from some Perl built-in functions. For example, the following code assigns the returned value of `sqrt(144)` to `$result`:

```
$result = sqrt(144);
```

Within a subroutine, you can use a statement of the form shown in Figure 6.11 to return a value to the calling program.

```
return ( $result );
```

| Scalar or list variable with a value to return |

Figure 6.11 The general format of the return statement

The effect of the `return` statement is to stop the execution of the subroutine and return the specified value to the calling program. As an example, the following code creates a simple subroutine that compares two numbers and returns the larger of the values.

```
1. sub simple_calc {
2. # PURPOSE: returns largest of 2 numbers
3. # ARGUMENTS $_[0] - 1st number, $_[1] - 2nd number
4.     if ( $_[0] > $_[1] ) {
5.         return( $_[0] );
6.     } else {
7.         return( $_[1] );
8.     }
9. }
```

Here line 5 returns the first argument ($_[0]) if it is larger. Otherwise, line 7 returns the second argument ($_[1]).

This subroutine can be called as shown below. With this code, $largest will receive the value returned.

```
$largest = &simple_calc( $num1, $num2 );
```

Now let's look at a complete program that uses a subroutine to return a value. In this case, the subroutine returns either *true* (1) or *false* value (0) as a method to determine if the subroutine found any disallowed words. The input form (shown at the top of Figure 6.12) asks the end user to provide some text input but not to use any "dirty" words (that is not to use the words mud, dirt, slime or grease). The receiving program (shown at the bottom of Figure 6.12) uses a subroutine called CheckInput() to check whether the input includes any disallowed words. Note that CheckInput() returns 1 if the input is acceptable and 0 if it is not. The middle screen in Figure 6.12 shows the output when the end user inputs a forbidden word; the bottom screen shows the output with valid input. Finally, note that line 14 uses the *match* and *binding* operators to search for any disallowed words. This line is *true* if the input data includes a word not allowed *anywhere* in the input text. (Chapter Seven discusses the match operator in more detail.)

```
1.  #!/usr/bin/perl
2.  use CGI ':standard';
3.  print header, start_html('Input Check ');
4.  @dirty=('mud', 'dirt', 'slime', 'grease');
5.  $input=param('uinput');
6.
7.  if ( &CheckInput($input ) ) {
8.      print "Input received: $input";
9.  } else {
10.     print "Sorry I cannot accept the input=$input";
11. }
12. sub CheckInput {
13.     foreach $item ( @dirty ) {
14.         if ( $_[0] =~ m/$item/ ) {
15.             print "Hey $item is not clean!", br;
16.             return 0;
17.         }
18.     }
19.     return 1;
20. }
```

Call the subroutine CheckInput(); send the end user input as an argument

Start of the CheckInput() subroutine

Use the match operator to check whether the string contains an item from @dirty

Please let us know how we are doing but, please keep it clean!

Your name is mud!

Submit Query   Reset

http://www.aw.com/~perlpgm/cgi-bin/C6/driveUinput.cgi

Calling form

Hey mud is not clean!
Sorry I cannot accept the input=Your name is mud!

Output when a dirty word is used

http://www.aw.com/~perlpgm/cgi-bin/C6/GetDirtyInput.cgi

Input received: Your doing OK.

Output when a dirty word is not used

Figure 6.12 Output of a Program That Checks for Disallowed Words

In this program:

★ Line 4 defines a list of words that are not allowed as input.

★ Line 5 gets the input from the text area set by the form generation program via the CGI variable `uinput`.

★ Line 7 checks whether the output from `CheckInput` is 0 or 1. If it is 1, then the if statement is *true* and line 8 is executed. If the value is 0, then line 10 is output.

★ Line 12 marks the beginning of the `CheckInput` subroutine.

★ Line 13 loops through each item in the list of the dirty words.

★ Line 14 uses the match operator to determine whether the input text includes one of the dirty words. If one is found, then line 15 prints out a message and the subroutine returns 0.

★ Line 19 returns 1. This statement is executed only when no dirty words are found in the input text.

Using Return Values to Combine Program Files

As you have probably realized, all of the applications introduced so far have required you to maintain two separate files. One file contains a program to generate the form, and the other file contains a program to parse the form. You can combine these two files if your program tests the return value of `param()` to determine whether the program was called with any CGI variable arguments. At least two advantages are associated with maintaining one file instead of two:

★ *With one file, it is easier to change arguments.* Every time you add a parameter to the form, you can add the corresponding `param()` call right in the same file. This is not only easier to make the change but is also less error prone.

★ *It is easier to maintain one file.* That is, combining the form-generation and form-parsing program files makes it easier to keep straight which two files are supposed to work together. This simplification can be a great convenience when you are working with numerous programs.

To combine the form-generation program and form-processing program, you must test whether the `CGI.pm param()` function has any arguments to send the program. You can test this condition as shown in Figure 6.13.

If no parameters, then this is the first time using the program. Call `create_form` to create the form.

Check whether there are any parameters

```
if ( !param() ) { create_form(); }
else { process_form(); }
```

Must be some parameters to process, so call `process_form`

Figure 6.13 Testing Whether a Program Should Create or Process a Form

The first line in Figure 6.13 checks `param()` to determine whether any arguments must be processed. If not, then this occasion is the first time the program is being executed, so it will call the `create_form()` subroutine. The `create_form()` subroutine will create the HTML tags needed to generate the HTML form. If the first line in Figure 6.13 is *false* (that is, it finds arguments to be processed), then `param()` will be able to access arguments, and the `process_form()` subroutine will be called. The `process_form()` subroutine will then read the form arguments and take action on them.

☆**TIP**   **Build Incrementally**

When you create programs by using multiple subroutines, build them incrementally—that is, one subroutine at a time. For example, to build the program from Figure 6.15, first implement the `create_form()` subroutine by using the following "stub" for `process_form()`:

```
sub process_form { return; }
```

Once `create_form()` works correctly, you can add the necessary programming statements within `process_form()`.

In the following example, form generation and form parsing have been combined into a single program. The top screen in Figure 6.14 shows the output of the `create_form()` subroutine. This subroutine essentially asks the end user for some input and sends this input back to itself at `http://www.aw.com/~perlpgm/cgi-bin/C6/subroutine4.cgi`. The bottom portion of Figure 6.14 shows the output from the `process_form()` subroutine when it receives arguments that must be processed.

```perl
1.  #!/usr/bin/perl
2.  use CGI ':standard';          Called if no arguments are received
3.  print header;
4.  if ( !param() ) {  create_form(); }
5.  else {   process_form(); }     Called if arguments are received
6.  sub create_form {              Start of the
7.  # PURPOSE: Use this to create form   create_form()
                                          subroutine
8.      print start_html( 'Create Form' );
9.      print '<FORM ACTION="http://www.aw.com/~perlpgm/
            cgi-bin/C6/subroutine4.cgi" METHOD="POST">';
10.     print "<FONT COLOR='BLUE' SIZE=5> How we doing?
            </FONT>";
11.     print '<INPUT TEXT TYPE="text" SIZE="15"
            NAME="doing" >';
12.     print br, '<INPUT TYPE=SUBMIT VALUE="Click To
            Submit">';
13.     print '<INPUT TYPE=RESET VALUE="Erase and
            Restart">';
14.     print '</FONT>', end_html;
15. }
```

```
16. sub process_form {                    Start of the process_form()
17. # Use this to process the form        subroutine
18.    print start_html( 'Received Form ');
19.    $answ=param('doing');
20.    print "<FONT COLOR='RED' SIZE=5> You Said ...
          </FONT>";
21.    print "$answ", end_html;
22. }
```

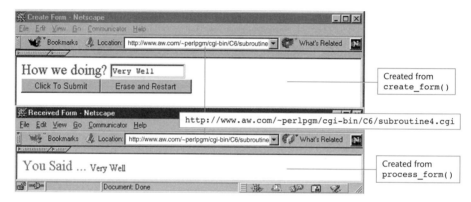

Figure 6.14 Output of the Form and Form-Handling Subroutines Within One Program

In this program:

☆ Lines 4–5 decide whether to generate an HTML form or parse the form, depending on whether **param( )** has any arguments. The code is the same as that from Figure 6.13.

☆ Lines 9–11 are part of the **create_form( )** subroutine. Line 9 creates a form-starting tag that is set to submit the form back to itself—that is, to **http://www.aw.com/~perlpgm/cgi-bin/C6/subroutine4.cgi**. Line 11 creates a **TEXT** input field to receive the end user's input.

☆ Lines 16–22 are part of the **process_form( )** subroutine. Line 19 gets the input, and then line 21 prints its value.

Using Subroutines in External Files

One goal in creating subroutines is to make the subroutines general enough to be as useful as possible. For example, the program from Figure 6.10 made the **outputTableRow( )** subroutine more useful by generalizing it with arguments. However, any program that wants to use this subroutine would need to copy it into the program file. For example, if we started another program that wanted to use **outputTableRow( )**, we would have to copy the subroutine lines into the new program. While this approach would work, a better solution would be to store the subroutine in a separate file, so that any program could subsequently call the subroutine without having to copy the lines.

Storing and using subroutines into separate files is straightforward. You simply follow these steps:

1. *Move all of the subroutine lines to a new file.* For example, we might place lines 9–11 from the program associated with Figure 6.10 into new file:

```
sub outputTableRow {
    print "<TR><TD>$_[0]</TD><TD>$_[1]</TD></TR>";
}
```

2. *Place a number 1 at the end of the new file.* This step provides a return value of 1, which helps Perl recognize that the subroutine executed successfully. For example, see the last line of the program associated with Figure 6.15, which appears later in this section.

3. *Name the subroutine file.* Usually, this file has a `.lib` suffix, which indicates that it is a library file of subroutines. For example, you might call the file `startdoc.lib`.

4. *Place the subroutine file in the same directory as the program file.* For now, we will assume that the subroutine library file and any programs that want to use it reside in the same directory.

5. *Include an additional `require` line in the calling program.* Before a program can use the subroutine library file, it must add a line that indicates where to look for that file. This line has the following format:

```
require 'library_filename';
```

As an example, imagine that you take the `outputTableRow()` subroutine (lines 9-11 from Figure 6.10) and store it in a file called `htmlhelper1.lib`. In addition, suppose that you add a new subroutine called `specialLine()`. The subroutine `specialLine()` takes two arguments: a color and message to print out. The following code shows the content of `htmlhelper1.lib`. You can also take this opportunity to add comments (lines 2–4 and 8–10) that describe the subroutine and input arguments.

```
 1. sub outputTableRow {
 2.     # PURPOSE: outputs a table row with 2 cols
 3.     # ARGUMENTS: uses $_[0] for first col
 4.     #            : uses $_[1] for second col
 5.     print "<TR><TD>$_[0]</TD><TD>$_[1]</TD></TR>";
 6. }
 7. sub specialLine {
 8.     # PURPOSE: Output a line with variable color:
 9.     # ARGUMENTS: $_[0] is the line to output
10.     #            : $_[1] is the line color.
11.     print "<B><Font COLOR=$_[1] FACE=\"Helvetica\" >
           $_[0] </FONT></B>";
12. }
13. 1
```

Line 6: Output a table row with two columns

Line 11: Output a line with color as the second argument

Line 13: Place a 1 at end of external subroutine file

To use the subroutines in the file `htmlhelp1.lib`, you could modify the program from Figure 6.10 so that it looks like the following and then save it in a file called `subroutine3.cgi`:

```
1.  #!/usr/bin/perl
2.  use CGI ':standard';
3.  require 'htmlhelper1.lib';
4.  print header, start_html('Some External
        Subroutines');
5.  &specialLine( 'Here is a simple table', 'RED' );
6.  print '<TABLE BORDER=1>';
7.  print '<TH> Num </TH> <TH> Num Cubed </TH>';
8.  for ( $i=0; $i<3; $i++ ) {
9.      &outputTableRow( $i, $i**3 );
10. }
11. print '</TABLE>', end_html;
```

Line 3 — Connect to the subroutine file

Line 6 — Output a special RED line

Line 9 — Call the subroutine three times

Figure 6.15 Output of a Program with External Subroutine Files

In this program:

☆ Line 3 uses the `require` statement to connect to the file `htmlhelper1.lib`. This file contains the external subroutines `outputTableRow()` and `specialLine()` described earlier.

☆ Line 5 calls the subroutine `specialLine()`, which is located in the external file `htmlhelper1.lib`. It outputs 'Here is a simple table' in a red color.

☆ Lines 8–10 call the `outputTableRow()` subroutine three times using a loop. These lines provide two arguments to `outputTableRow()`:`$i`, which counts the number of iterations of the loop, and `$i**3`, which is the cubed value of `$i`.

☆ Summary

▷ Hash lists store data in name/value pairs instead of sequentially ordered list variables. They can be very useful for cross-referencing data, and they allow for much faster data lookups than do list variables.

▷ Perl uses special operations for adding and deleting hash list items, checking whether hash keys exist, and getting lists of keys and values.

▷ Hash tables are lists indexed by keys. They allow you to represent related items with a common key. Using this one key, you can find the entire list of information.

▷ The environmental hash list, which is called %ENV, contains environmental variables that describe how your program was called.

▷ Subroutines allow you to group a set of statements, set them aside, and turn those grouped statements into mini-programs within a larger program. These mini-programs can be executed several times from different places in the overall program. They can also help you create smaller programs that are easier to understand, easier to modify, and reusable.

▷ Subroutines can be called anywhere from within a program as often as necessary. A program can pass them arguments that provide input data to the subroutines. Subroutines can also return values and be placed in external files so that they can be shared.

☆ Review Questions

1. Give two instances when using hash lists might be more advantageous than list variables.

2. Using the hash list defined in Figure 6.1, what would be the values of $x, $y, and $z?

   ```
   $x = $months{'Mar'}; $y = $months{'Jan'} * 2;
   $z = ( $months{'Mar'} - $months{'Feb'} );
   ```

3. What would be the output of the program from Figure 6.3 if it were called with the following input?
   (a) `startmon=Apr startday=5`
   (b) `startmon=Jul startday=4`
   (c) `startmon=XXX startday=12`

4. When are the values of the environmental hash list set? Write a `print` statement that outputs the TCP/IP address of the computer that is accessing your Web site.

5. Using the `%Inventory` multidimensional hash list defined in the program associated with Figure 6.7, what would be the values of $x, $y, and $z shown below?

```
$x = $Inventory{'AC1001'}[3];
$y = $Inventory{'AC1003'}[44-42];
$z = $Inventory{'AC1001'}[sqrt(16)-2];
```

6. What are four advantages of using subroutines?

7. What would be the variable name of the third argument received into a subroutine? The first argument? How can you determine the number of arguments passed into a subroutine?

8. List the steps needed to copy a subroutine to an external file. What line would you add to your program to connect to a set of subroutines in a file called `mysubs.lib`?

9. What are two advantages of putting both the form-generation and form-processing programs into the same program (and file)? What would the following line do if the program was called with no arguments? Four arguments?

```
if (!param() ) { build_form() }
else { handle_form() }
```

10. What would be the output from the subroutine `outputTableRow()` (from Figure 6.10) if it was called with each of the following statements?
(a) `&outputTableRow( 1, 'Happy' );`
(b) `&outputTableRow( "Time", "OUT");`
(c) `&outputTableRow( "Partial" );`

☆ Hands-On Exercises

1. Modify the program from Figure 6.3 to also allow the end user to select a year from 2001 to 2010.
   (a) If the year selected is a leap year, add an extra day to the number of days in February. Ensure that the program works correctly in these leap-year situations.
   (b) Change the program so that it calculates the number of days from the date selected by the end user to the beginning of the next new year (January 1). Correctly account for leap years.
   (c) Optional: Combine the form-generation and -processing programs from 1(b) into a single program with `create_form()` and `process_form()` parts.

2. Create a form and related form-handling program that displays the various products in inventory and the number available. Allow the end user to select an item from "inventory" and "order" 1, 10, 50, 75, or 100 of those items. If the number of items to be ordered exceeds the number available, then display an appropriate message. Otherwise, let the end user know that the "order" was accepted and display the new number of items available. You should also "verify" that the end user input is either 1, 10, 75, or 100. Use the following information as the initial "inventory," representing it in your program as a hash list.

Item Number	Available
Laptops	1
Desktops	50
Printers	76
Disk Drives	26
Modems	122

3. Modify Figure 6.8 to allow the end user to add and delete an inventory hash table row. Allow the user to add any part number (as long as it does not already exist). Make sure that the price and number available are numbers from 0 to 10,000.

4. Write a program that outputs all of the keys and values of the environmental hash list to a Web page. (*Hint:* Use the `keys()` function described in the "Accessing and Outputting Hash Keys and Values" section.)

5. Modify the program from Exercise 1(a) in Chapter Three to use a form to request input values to the formula. When the end user inputs a valid number between 0 and 100,000, output the results of the formula. Place the formula calculation into a subroutine. Use a `return` statement to return values to the calling program.

6. Generalize the `outputTableRow()` subroutine from Figure 6.10 to accept an arbitrary number of table row elements as input. (*Hint:* Use the range operator `#$_` or `@_` to determine how many elements were sent to it.) Test the program with an application that asks the end user to enter a number of rows (between 1 and 12) and number of columns (between 1 and 10.) When these data are received, populate the table to create a multiplication table. For example, if the end user asks for three columns and four rows, the program should produce the following output:

Num*1	Num*2	Num*3
1	2	3
2	4	6
3	6	9
4	8	12

7. Place the program created in Exercise 5 or 6 in Chapter Four into a single program using `create_form()` and `process_form()` subroutines.

CHAPTER SEVEN

MATCHING PATTERNS AND FILES

One strength of the Perl language is the rich set of functions and operators that it offers for matching, changing, and manipulating patterns in string variables. Working with string variables is vital for CGI/Perl programs, because form input appears as string variables to CGI/Perl programs. These functions and operators provide ways for programs to filter undesirable CGI/Perl Web input and clarify expected input with the end user.

Working with files provides a way for programs to store and retrieve data files on a Web server. Writing and reading files enables CGI/Perl applications to remember data between the times when a program executes. Using files, a program can look up product inventory data, update customer data, increment a page counter, save form comments, and perform many other tasks.

◎◎ Chapter Objectives

☆ Use Perl pattern matching and regular expressions to filter input data

☆ Work with files to enable a program to store and retrieve data

◎◎ Working with Patterns in String Variables

Many programming problems require matching, changing, or manipulating patterns in string variables. For our purposes, the most common use involves verifying fields received from form input. For example, if you are expecting a form field to provide a telephone number as input, your program needs a way to verify that the input comprises a string of seven digits. Perl provides a set of operators and functions that enable you to filter user input and notify the end user of illegal input values. This ability not only enables your program to react better to honest mistakes by the end user, but also provides a first line of defense against intentional hacking of your site.

Perl supports a rich set of pattern matching operators and functions that aid with problems in which a program needs to work with string contents. These operators and functions include the following:

☆ The **match operator** enables your program to look for patterns in strings.

☆ The **substitute operator** enables your program to change patterns in strings.

☆ The **split function** enables your program to split strings into separate variables based on a string pattern.

☆ **Regular expressions** provide a pattern matching language that can work with these operators and functions to work on string variables.

We will look at each of these operators and functions in this chapter.

The Match Operator

The match operator is used to test whether a particular pattern appears in a string. It is used with the binding operator ("=~") to see whether a variable contains a particular pattern. It is most commonly used in format shown in Figure 7.1.

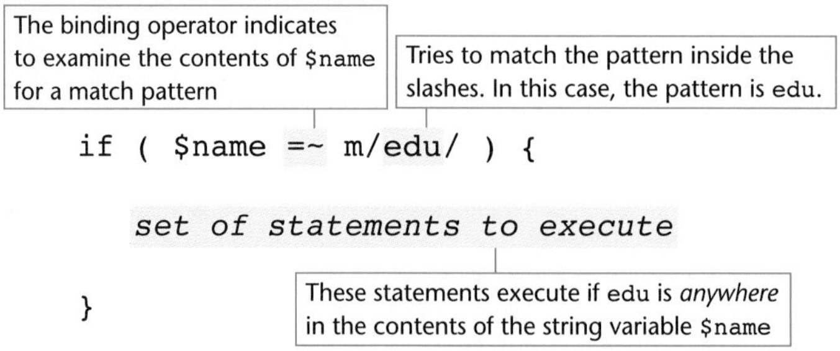

The binding operator indicates to examine the contents of $name for a match pattern

Tries to match the pattern inside the slashes. In this case, the pattern is edu.

```
if ( $name =~ m/edu/ ) {

        set of statements to execute

}
```

These statements execute if edu is *anywhere* in the contents of the string variable $name

Figure 7.1 General Format of the Match Operator

In Figure 7.1, the match operator is used to determine whether the pattern edu is in the variable $name. To further clarify how this operator works, Table 7.1 lists some possible values for $name and shows whether the first line from Figure 7.1 would be *true* or *false* in each case.

Table 7.1 Testing Pattern Matching with $name

Value of $name	Test from Figure 7.1
'www.myschool.edu'	*True* because the string contains edu
'www.myschool.com'	*False* because edu is not in the string
'I like my education'	*True* because the string contains edu
'I Like My Education'	*False* because matching is case sensitive
'I liked umbrellas'	*False* because edu is not in the string

The most common match pattern delimiter used is the slash ("/"), though other delimiters are possible. For example, both of the following statements use valid match operator syntax:

☆ if ($name =~ m!Dave!) {

☆ if ($name =~ m<Dave>) {

Both search for the pattern Dave in the variable $name.

Note that the character m is *optional* when slashes are used. Thus the following statement is also valid:

```
if ( $name =~ /Dave/ ) {
```

☆**TIP**   **The Reverse Binding Operator**

You can use the reverse binding operator, !~, to test if the pattern is *not* found in a string variable. For example, the following statement is *true* when the variable $color does not contain the pattern blue

```
if ( $color !~ m/blue/ ) {
```

The Substitution Operator

The substitution operator is similar to the match operator but also enables you to change the matched string. You can also use the substitution operator with the binding operator ("=~") to test whether a variable contains a pattern. It most commonly has the format shown in Figure 7.2.

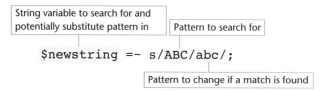

Figure 7.2 General Format of the Substitute Operator

The default behavior of the substitute operator is to substitute the *first occurrence* of the search pattern for the change pattern in the string variable. For example, the following statements use the substitute operator to change the first occurrence of t to T:

```
$name = "tom turtle";
$name =~ s/t/T/;
print "Name=$name";
```

The output of this code would be

```
Name=Tom turtle
```

You can place a g (for global substitution) at the end of the substitution expression to change all occurrences of the target pattern string in the search string. For example,

```
$name = "tom turtle";
$name =~ s/t/T/g;
print "Name=$name";
```

The output of this code would be

```
Name= Tom TurTle
```

☆ **TIP   Using Regular Expressions with Substitution**

To achieve more precision in the match patterns, you must understand Perl regular expressions (as described in the "Using Regular Expressions to Match Patterns" section later in this chapter). For example, regular expressions allow you to look for characters or numbers in specific locations in the string.

A Full Pattern Matching Example

As an example of pattern matching, consider the form shown at the top of Figure 7.3. This form requests that the end user select a command and a part number. (Its program code is not shown, but does supply values for the CGI variables command and uprod.) The receiving program (the code shown below) checks whether the command and part number are valid (even though they are started from radio buttons), ensures that the product number looks reasonable, and then looks for the product number in its list of valid product numbers. The middle screen in Figure

☆ SHORTCUT   **Using Translate**

Perl supports a similar function to substitute called `tr` (for "translate"). It is most useful for translating characters from uppercase to lowercase, and vice versa. The `tr` function allows you to specify a range of characters to translate *from* and a range of characters to translate *to*. For example, the second line in the following code translates all lowercase letters in $name to uppercase:

```
$name="smokeY";
$name =~ tr/[a-z]/[A-Z]/;
print "name=$name";
```

Would output:

```
name=SMOKEY
```

7.3 shows the output when the product number is valid. The bottom screen shows the output when invalid input is received.

```
1.  #!/usr/bin/perl
2.  use CGI ':standard';
3.  print header, start_html('Command Search');
4.  @PartNums=( 'XX1234', 'XX1892', 'XX9510');
5.  $com=param('command');
6.  $prod=param('uprod');
7.  if ($com eq "ORDER" || $com eq "RETURN") {
8.      $prod =~ s/xx/XX/g;    # switch xx to XX
9.      if ($prod =~ /XX/ ) {
10.         foreach $item ( @PartNums ) {
11.             if ( $item eq $prod ) {
12.                 print "VALIDATED command=$com
                        prodnum=$prod";
13.                 $found = 1;
14.             }
15.         }
16.         if ( $found != 1 ) {
17.             print br,"Sorry Prod Num=$prod NOT
                    FOUND";
18.         }
19.     } else {
20.         print br, "Sorry that prod num prodnum=$prod
                looks wrong";
21.     }
22. } else {
23.     print br, "Invalid command=$com did not receive
                ORDER or RETURN";
24. }
25. print end_html;
```

Check for a valid command

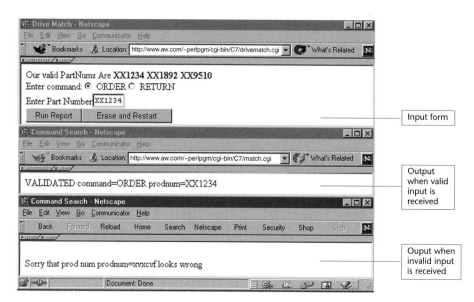

Figure 7.3 Output of a Simple Matching Program

In this program:

☆ Line 4 puts a series of valid part numbers into a list variable.

☆ Line 7 checks whether the command received is valid. It demonstrates a good defensive style of programming because it rejects illegal commands.

☆ Line 8 uses the substitute operator to change **xx** to **XX**, in case the end user made a mistake in capitalization during input of the part number.

☆ Lines 9–15 confirm that `$partnum` contains at least **XX** before continuing with the program. If it is acceptable, the program looks through each item of the list variable to see if it can find a matching valid part number. If so, it has validated the command and part number (line 12).

☆**TIP   Checking End-User Input**

Your programs should check all input received from forms via the Internet—even if end users are expected to use only your front-end form. Someone might attempt to execute your program via an URL (using question marks to specify CGI variables and values) to try out different input values. (See Chapter Three.) Alternatively, someone might build his or her own form and use it to execute your program.

Using Regular Expressions to Match Patterns

There are many other patterns that you might want to search for in an effort to validate string fields. Perl supports a powerful and complex pattern matching language called **regular expressions** to enable programs to more completely match patterns. Regular expressions make up a small language of special matching operators that can be employed to enhance Perl string pattern matching.

The Alternation Operator

You use the alternation operator (the vertical bar, "|") to look for alternative strings for matching within a pattern. This operator is used to define different alternative patterns to match (that is, you use it to indicate that the program should match one pattern OR the other). The following shows a match statement using the alternation operator (left) and some possible matches based on the contents of $address (right); this pattern matches either com or edu.

Match Statement	Possible Matching String Values for $address
if ($address =~ /com|edu/) {	"www.mysite.com", "Welcome to my site", "Time for education", "www.mysite.edu"

You use parentheses within regular expressions to specify groupings. For example, the following matches a $name value of Dave or David.

Match Statement	Possible Matching String Values for $name
if ($name =~ /Dav(e|id/) {	"Dave", "David", "Dave was here", "How long before David comes home"

The Character Class Operator

The character class operator ("[...]") is used to match *one* of the characters found between the square brackets. Below is an example matching statement (on the left) and possible matches (on the right). The matching pattern must consist of the characters Sea followed by n or t. The pattern Seant! would not match this pattern.

Match Statement	Possible Matching String Values for $name
if ($name =~ /Sea[nt]!/) {	"Sean!", "Seat!", "Here comes Sean!", "Take a seat!"

A more common use of the class operator is to specify a range of values to match. To specify a range, you use a dash ("-"). For example, [0-9] specifies a number from 0 to 9, [A-Z] specifies any capital letter from "A" to "Z", and [a-z] specifies a value from lowercase "a" to "z". For example, the following pattern matches if a number from 0 to 9 is found in $prodcode.

Match Statement	Possible Matching $prodcode Values
if ($prodcode =~ /[0-9]/) {	"apple1", "24234", "suzy44" "s1mple", "I visited 2 stores"

Because each character class matches only one character, you must use multiple character class operators to search for specific string formats. The following example looks for a pattern of two capital letters followed by a number.

Match Statement	Possible Matching $code Values	Possible Nonmatching $code Values
if ($code =~ /[A-Z] [A-Z][0-9]/) {	"AA9", "Send Product AZ9", "MY12", "BB0 was down"	"xx1", "Ab1", "AX", "A111", "X11"

When the caret symbol ("^") appears at the start of a character class (that is, within the square brackets as in "[^ ...]"), it means NOT—that is, look for a character *not* matching the pattern in the character class. The following example looks for any character *not* within the range 5–9, then a digit within the range 0–9, then a capital letter.

Match Statement	Possible Matching $code Values	Possible Nonmatching $code Values
if ($code =~ /[^5-9] [0-9][A-Z]/) {	"The AA9 is OK", "Product 44X is down", "It was 9Years ago."	"51X", "Product 81A", "AX68A"

☆ TIP   **Different Uses for the Caret Symbol**

The caret ("^") symbol has different meanings depending on how it is used. Within a character class, as in [^ ...], it means NOT. In the section "Special Character Classes," you will learn how it can be used as a character quantifier.

The following program uses both pattern matching and the alternation operator. The top screen in Figure 7.4 shows the form that calls this program (its code is not shown here); it asks for a product code and description. The product code should be of the format CODE## (that is, the word CODE followed by two digits). The description cannot contain the words "boat" or "plane". The middle screen in Figure 7.4 shows the output of the program when the end user enters "boat" as a description. The bottom screen in Figure 7.4 shows the output when a valid input is received.

```
1. #!/usr/bin/perl
2. use CGI ':standard';
3. print header, start_html('Quick Check');
4. $prodcode = param('code');
5. $description = param('description');
6. if ( $prodcode !~ m/CODE[0-9][0-9]/ ) {
```

> Matches if $prodcode does not contain CODE followed by two numbers

```
7.    print 'Sorry require CODENN product code format';
8. } elsif ( $description =~ m/(boat)|(plane)/ ) {
```

> Matches boat or plane

```
9.    print "Sorry, we do not sell boats or planes
         anymore";
10. } else {
11.    print "Thank you, we will get back to you shortly
         for $prodcode";
12. }
13. print end_html;
```

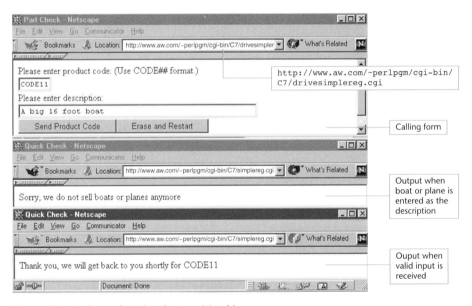

Figure 7.4 An Example Using Pattern Matching

☆ Lines 4 and 5 get the CGI variables `code` and `description` from the calling form.

☆ Line 6 checks whether the part number follows the CODE## format (that is, the word CODE followed by two digits). It uses the reverse binding operator ("`!~`"), which returns *true* if the pattern is *not* present.

☆ Line 8 uses the alternation operator to check for the presence of the patterns `boat` and `plane` in the description.

☆ Line 11 is output when the product code is valid and the description does not contain the words "boat" or "plane".

☆ **WARNING** **More Specific Regular Expression Needed**

The regular expression used in Figure 7.4 is still not specific enough. For example, input of the words `product CODE12 is my choice` would still match in line 6 of the program. The section "Setting Specific Patterns with Quantifiers" later in this chapter explains how to use character quantifiers to create even more specific regular expressions.

Special Character Classes

Perl has a set of preset character classes for matching individual items. Their use adds clarity to your regular expressions. For example, to match a single space, you can use `\s`. The two lines shown below are equivalent, but the one on the right uses the `\s` special character class and is a little easier to see and understand:

```
if ( $name =~ m/ / )                    if ($name =~ m/\s/ )
```

Table 7.2 presents some of Perl's special character classes, their meanings, and examples of their use.

Table 7.2 Selected Perl Special Character Classes

Character Class	Meaning
\s	*Matches a single space.* For example, the following matches "Apple Core", "Alle y", and "Here you go"; it does not match "Alone": `if ( $name =~ m/e\s/ ) {`
\S	*Matches any nonspace, tab, newline, return, or formfeed character.* For example, the following matches "ZT", "YT", and ";T": `if ( $part =~ m/\ST/ ) {`
\w	*Matches any word character (uppercase or lowercase letters, digits, or the underscore character).* For example, the following matches "Apple", "Time", "Part time", "time_to_go", " Time", and "1234"; it does not match "#%^&": `if ( $part =~ m/\w/ ) {`

Table 7.2 Selected Perl Special Character Classes (*continued*)

Character Class	Meaning
\W	*Matches any nonword character (not uppercase or lowercase letters, digits, or the underscore character).* For example, the following matches "A*B" and "A{B", but not "A**B", "AB*", "AB101", or "1234": `if ( $part  =~ m/A\WB/ ) {`
\d	*Matches any valid numerical digit (that is, any number 0–9).* For example, the following matches "B12abc", "The B1 product is late", "I won bingo with a B9", and "Product B00121"; it does not match "B 0", "Product BX 111", or "Be late 1": `if ( $part =~ m/B\d/ ) {`
\D	*Matches any non-numerical character (that is any character not a digit 0–9).* For example, the following matches "AB1234", "Product number 1111", "Number VG928321212", "The number_A1234", and "Product 1212"; it does not match "1212" or "PR12": `if ( $part =~ m/\D\D\d\d\d\d/) {`

Setting Specific Patterns with Quantifiers

Character quantifiers enable your Perl programs to look for very specific patterns. For example, you can use the dollar sign ("$") to ensure that a pattern matches only if the string ends with the specified pattern. Consider the following example, which searches based on whether $name ends with the characters Jones:

```
if ($name =~ /Jones$/ ) {
```

Thus "John Jones" would match but "Jones is here" would not. "Johnston and Jones" and "The guilty party is Jones" would also match.

Table 7.3 describes some of the character quantifiers used in Perl.

Table 7.3 Selected Perl Character Quantifiers

Character Quantifier	Meaning
^	*Matches when the following character starts the string.* For example, the following matches "Smith is OK", "Smithsonian", and "Smith, Black": `if ( $name =~ m/^Smith/ ) {`
$	*Matches when the preceding character ends the string.* For example, the following matches "the end", "Tend", and "Time to Bend": `if ( $part =~ m/end$/ ) {`

(*continues*)

Table 7.3 Selected Perl Character Quantifiers (*continued*)

Character Quantifier	Meaning
+	*Matches one or more occurrences of the preceding character.* For example, the following matches "AB101", "ABB101", and "ABBB101 is the right part": `if ( $part =~ m/^AB+101/ ) {`
*	*Matches zero or more occurrences of the preceding character.* For example, the following matches "AB101", "ABB101", "A101", and "A101 is broke": `if ( $part =~ m/^AB*101/) {`
.	*A wildcard symbol that matches any one character.* For example, the following matches "Stop", "Soap", "Szxp", and "Soap is good"; it does not match "Sxp": `if ( $name =~ m/^S..p/ ) {`

Building Regular Expressions That Work

As you may have figured out from the previous examples, regular expressions are very powerful—but they can also be virtually unreadable. For this reason, it is recommended that you start with a simple regular expression and then refine it incrementally. That is, build one piece at a time and test each piece as you go along.

The following example builds a regular expression that looks for a date field in the *dd/mm/yyyy* format (for example, 05/05/2002 but not 5/12/01). The steps below detail the process used to incrementally build the regular expression.

1. *Determine the precise field rules.* That is, determine what is valid input and invalid input. For example, if you want to create a text field that accepts only a date field, think through the valid and invalid rules for the field. Perhaps you might decide to allow 09/09/2002 but not 9/9/2002 or Sep/9/2002. Work through several examples as follows:

Rule	Reject These
05/05/2002—Will accept / as a separator	05 05 2002—Require slash delimiters
05/05/2002—Use a four-digit year	05/05/02—Four-digit year only

Rule	Reject These
`05/05/2001`—Contain only a date	`The date is 05/05/2002`—Only date fields allowed
	`05/05/2002 is my date`— Only date fields allowed
`05/05/2001`—Two digits for months and days	`5/05/2002`—Two-digit months only `05/5/2002`—Two-digit days only `5/5/2002`—Two-digit days and months only

2. *Get the form and form-handling programs working.* Build the form that includes the field for which you want to set a regular expression and then build the receiving subroutine or program that accepts the field. Make sure that these work before you add the regular expressions. For example, a first form-handling program might contain the following lines. Notice that the second line requires only that at least one character be entered for `$date`; no other validation is performed.

```
$date = param('udate');
if ( $date =~ m/.+/ ) {          At least one character
    print 'Valid date=', $date;
} else {
    print 'Invalid date=', $date;
}
```

3. *Start with the most specific term possible.* For example, slashes must always separate two characters (for the month), followed by two more characters (for the day), followed by four characters (for the year). Therefore, you can change the second line above to the following:

```
                Any two characters followed by slash   Any four characters
if ( $date =~ m{../../....} ) {
```

This code requires at least two characters, then /, then at least two more characters, then /, then at least four characters. Thus `12/21/1234` and `fj/12/ffff` are valid, but `1/1/11` is not. Notice that the code uses curly brackets (`{ ... }`) instead of slashes as a field separator because slashes are part of the regular expression (and the curly brackets make the expression look a little cleaner).

4. *Anchor the parts you can.* Add the `^` and `$` character quantifiers where possible. Also, add the `\d` character class to require numbers instead of any character.

```
                                    Two numbers
        Must start with two numbers    between slashes    Ends with four numbers
if ( $date =~ m{^\d\d/\d\d/\d\d\d\d$} ) {
                    Matching string separator instead of slashes
```

Now you are getting close to the end, because 01/16/2003, 09/09/2005, 01/12/1211, and 99/99/9999 are valid.

5. *Get more specific if possible.* After examining the output, note that two more rules can be added:

   (a) The first digit of the month can be only 0, 1, 2 or 3. For example, 05/55/2002 is clearly an illegal date.

   (b) Only years from this century are allowed. Because this example application does not care about dates like 05/05/1999 or 05/05/3003, it will use a regular expression to eliminate them and use only dates from the twenty-first century.

These rules are added below by specifying [0-3] in the first digit of the days field and requiring that the first digit of the year field start with 2.

Matches 0, 1, 2, or 3	Matches number 2 followed by three digits

```
if ( $date =~ m{^\d\d/[0-3]\d/2\d\d\d$} ) {
```

Now the regular expression recognizes input like 09/99/2001 and 05/05/4000 as illegal.

> ☆ **TIP**   **Regular Expression Special Variables**
>
> Using regular expressions will set several scalar variables that can help you build regular expressions. You can output these variables to view the matching and nonmatching portions of the string. The $& variable will be equal to the first piece of text that matched, $' will be the text before the match, and $' will be the text after the first match. For example,
>
> ```
> $name='*****Marty';
> if ( $name =~ m/\w/ ) {
>     print "got match at=$& ";
>     print "B4=$'after=$'";
> } else { print "Not match"; }
> ```
>
> would output the following:
>
> ```
> got match at=M B4=***** after=arty
> ```

The following program uses the regular expression developed earlier in this section to validate a date. The top of Figure 7.5 shows the form used to request a date and start this program (its code is not provided here). It sets CGI variable udate to the end user input. The middle screen shows the response when the end user enters an invalid date. The bottom screen shows the response when the end user enters a valid date.

```
1. #!/usr/bin/perl
2. use CGI ':standard';
3. print header, start_html('Date Check');
4. $date=param('udate');
```

```
 5. if ( $date =~ m{^\d\d/[0-3]\d/2\d\d\d$} ) {
 6.    print 'Valid date=', $date;
 7. } else {
 8.    print 'Invalid date=', $date;
 9. }
10. print end_html;
```

The date-checking
regular expression

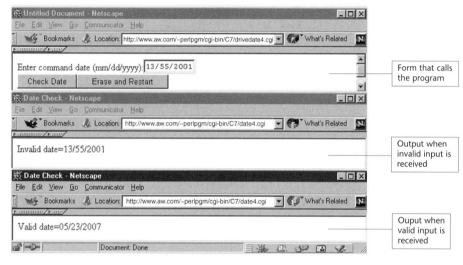

Form that calls
the program

Output when
invalid input is
received

Ouput when
valid input is
received

Figure 7.5 Program Output That Uses a Regular Expression to Validate a Date Field

☆**WARNING** **More Specific Regular Expression Needed**

The code in the preceding program still accepts dates such as 2/30/2002. Additional checking would be required to fix this problem. We will do a little more checking in the example program associated with Figure 7.7.

☆**TIP** **Incremental Regular Expression Examples**

The Web site for this book has the incremental examples (used to construct the date-checking regular expression available at http://www.aw.com/~perlpgm/cgi-bin/C7/drivedate1.cgi, http://www.aw.com/~perlpgm/cgi-bin/C7/drivedate2.cgi, and http://www.aw.com/~perlpgm/cgi-bin/C7/drivedate3.cgi.

The Split Function

You use the split function to break a string into different pieces based on the presence of a field separator. This function takes two arguments: a pattern to match (which can contain regular expressions) and a string variable to split. The string variable is split into as many pieces as there are matches for the pattern, with the results being given as a list. The split() function has the general format shown in Figure 7.6.

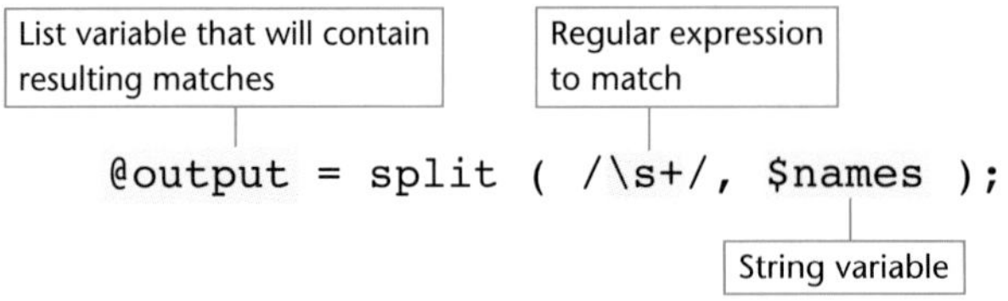

Figure 7.6 General Syntax of the Split Function

To see how the split function works, examine the following program lines:

```
$line = "Please , pass      thepepper";
@result =  split( /\s+/, $line );
```

These lines set the @result list variable to each character group separated by one or more spaces. Thus the list variable @result will contain the following values:

```
$result[0] = "Please";
$result[1] = ",";
$result[2] = "pass";
$result[3] = "thepepper";
```

In another example, the following code breaks $line into pieces using a comma (",") as a delimiter.

```
$line = "Baseball, hot dogs, apple pie";
@newline =  split( /,/, $line );
print "newline= @newline";
```

These lines will have the following output:

```
newline= Baseball  hot dogs  apple pie
```

When you know how many matches to expect, it is sometimes useful to provide a list of scalar variables that will receive the split fields, instead of a list variable. For example,

```
$line = "AA1234:Hammer:122:12";
($partno, $part, $num, $cost) =  split( /:/, $line );
print "partno= $partno part=$part num=$num cost=$cost";
```

will yield the following output:

```
partno= AA1234 part=Hammer num=122 cost=12
```

☆TIP   Using split() with Files

This example shows how to use split() to access an inventory record with a colon delimiter. This approach is often used when data are stored in files. Working with files is covered later in this chapter.

The following program uses the `split()` function and further refines the date validation program (using regular expressions) associated with Figure 7.5. In addition, it illustrates that some checking on fields may still be needed even after regular expressions are used. For example, line 7 in the program uses `split()` to break the `$date` field into `$mon`, `$day`, and `$year`. With these fields split, the program can much more specifically check these fields for validity than is possible even with regular expressions (for example, it can check whether `$month` is between 1 and 12). The top screen of Figure 7.7 shows the form that starts the program (its code is not provided here), the middle screen shows the output when the end user enters invalid input, and the bottom screen shows the output when the end user enters valid date.

```perl
1.  #!/usr/bin/perl
2.  use CGI ':standard';
3.  print header, start_html('Date Check');
4.  $date=param('udate');
5.  if ( $date =~ m{^\d\d/[0-3]\d/2\d\d\d$} ) {
6.      print 'OK from REG EXP date=', $date;
7.      ($mon, $day, $year) = split( /\//, $date );
8.      if ( $mon >= 1 && $mon <= 12 ) {
9.          if ( $day <= 31 ) {
10.             print " Valid date mon=$mon
                day=$day year=$year";
11.         } else {
12.             print " Illegal day specifed day=$day";
13.         }
14.     } else {
15.         print " Illegal month specifed mon=$mon";
16.     }
17. } else {
18.     print 'Invalid date=', $date;
19. }
```

Same regular expression as Figure 7.5

Split $date using a slash (/) as the delimiter

In this program:

☆ Line 5 use the same regular expression to check the dates as does the program from Figure 7.5.

☆ Line 7 uses the split function to split the date field. Using slashes ("/") as delimiters, it splits the `$date` string variable into `$mon`, `$day`, and `$year`. The regular expression in line 5 makes this operation possible because it verifies that the regular expression includes slashes.

☆ Line 8 checks for valid `$mon` (month) input from 1 and 12.

☆ Line 9 confirms that `$day` (day) is not greater than 31.

☆ Line 10 outputs an appropriate message if all of the input is valid.

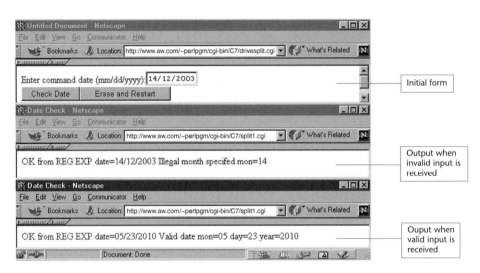

Figure 7.7 An Example Using the Split Function

◎◉ Working with Files

Although the programs we have created so far are able to accept input data from the end user, they cannot store data values in-between those times when they are started. For example, the hash table inventory example from Chapter Six (Figure 6.7) sets the same initial values for the inventory each time the program is started. When inventory items are deleted, this program does not provide a way to store the inventory value updates.

Working with files will enable your programs to store data, which can then be used at some future time. This section describes ways to work with files in your CGI/Perl programs, including opening files, closing files, and reading from and writing to files.

Using the open() Function

You use the `open()` function to connect a program to a physical file on a Web server. It has the format shown in Figure 7.8.

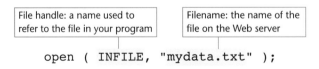

```
open ( INFILE, "mydata.txt" );
```

Figure 7.8 Format of the `open()` Function

As you can see in Figure 7.8, `open()` has two arguments: a file handle and a filename.

☆ The **file handle** is a name you pick to refer to the file to which your program connects. (It is described in depth in "Using the File Handle to Read Files" later in this chapter.) Unlike scalar variables, list variables, or hash list variables, a file handle starts with a letter or number—not with "$", "@", or "%". By Perl programming convention (and to provide a good, clear programming style), each letter in the file handle is capitalized.

☆ The **filename** is the name of the file to which your program will connect. If it resides in the same file system directory path as your program, then you need specify only the filename (and not the entire full file path). Unless otherwise specified, the file is opened as read-only. "Using the File Handle to Read Files" later in this chapter provides more details about specifying filenames.

The open() function returns 1 (*true*) when it successfully opens and connects to the specified file. It returns 0 (*false*) when this attempt fails. The following code shows a common way to check whether an open() operation was successful. If it fails, the following code uses the die() function to output a programmer-specified message and end the program.

```
$infile = "mydata.txt";
open (INFILE, $infile) || die "Cannot open $infile : $!";
```

The second line contains some strange-looking items. For example, it uses the logical OR operator ("||") to decide whether the die() function is executed. The code evaluates the open() function first. If the open() attempt is successful, the die() function does not execute. Note also the use of the $! variable. The $! variable is a Perl special variable set to the last system message received by Perl. Thus, if open() generated any system messages (such as an explanation of why it could not open your file), the $! operator could be used to display it.

As previously mentioned, the die() function is used in this example to end the program when the open() function fails to open its file. Unfortunately, many Web servers direct these error messages to their Web server logfiles. As a consequence, the end user might still receive a generic Internal Server Error message. The best way to handle this possibility is with the module called CGI::Carp. (CGI::Carp is not officially part of the CGI.pm module, but it is commonly distributed with CGI.pm and, therefore, with newer versions of Perl.) To use this module, simply add the following line at the beginning of your program (after the use CGI ':standard'; line):

```
use CGI::Carp "fatalsToBrowser";
```

This line connects to the CGI::Carp module and forwards the die() message to the browser if the open() attempt fails. Figure 7.9 shows a sample output of a screen that the end user would receive if an open() failed using CGI::Carp and a die() function. (The program associated with Figure 7.10 also demonstrates how to place CGI::Carp in your program.)

☆ **TIP**   Custom `CGI::Carp` Messages

In addition to forwarding your error messages from `die()`, `CGI::Carp` outputs a default generic message that you can customize by calling an error subroutine. More details on the `CGI::Carp` module can be found at `http://stein.cshl.org/WWW/software/CGI/cgi_docs.html` or in Lincoln Stein's book, *Official Guide to Programming with CGI.pm*. Another in-depth reference is a book by Scott Guelich, Shishir Gundavaram, and Gunther Birznieks called *CGI Programming with Perl*.

Figure 7.9 An Open Error Message Generated from `CGI::Carp`

Using the File Handle to Read Files

As previously mentioned, a file handle is a name you pick to refer to the file once it is opened. (In Figure 7.8, the file handle is `INFILE`.) You cannot change or modify the file handle. You can use it only to refer to the particular file with which you are working. You can combine the file handle with the file input operator ("`<>`") to read a file into your program. For example, the following code opens a file called `mymdata.txt`, and then outputs the first and third lines of the file. It uses the Perl file input operator ("`<>`") to read each line into the `@infile` list variable. Finally, it uses the `close()` function to close the file when the program is finished and to release the connection to the file.

```
$infile="mydata.txt";
open (INFILE, $infile ) || die "Cannot open $infile: $!";
@infile = <INFILE>;        Reads entire file
                           into @infile
print $infile[0];
print $infile[2];
close (INFILE);
```

Working with Files

☆ **TIP**   **Close Files as Soon as Possible**

The preceding program code is fairly simple, so closing the file at the end of the program is not much of an issue. In general, however, it is a good idea to close a file as soon as possible, thereby releasing its resources and minimizing the chance of contention (that is, the problem of other programs or end users wanting to access the file).

If the file `mydata.txt` contained (and resided in the same directory as the previous program):

```
Apples are red
Bananas are yellow
Carrots are orange
Dates are brown
```

then the output of this program would be

```
Apples are red
Carrots are orange
```

Although this program works well with small input files, reading a very large file into the list variable `@infile` consumes a lot of computer memory. A better method is to read the file in one line at a time. The next example uses a `while` loop to read each line from `mydata.txt` one line at a time:

```
$infile="mydata.txt";
open (INFILE, $infile ) || die "Cannot open $infile: $!";
while ( <INFILE> ) {
    $inline=$_;
    print $inline;
}
close (INFILE);
```

Here, the `while` loop terminates when the end of the file is reached. The `$_` Perl variable is automatically set to the line being read in. Thus the fourth line sets `$inline` to the next line read, and the fifth line prints it out. Assuming the file `mydata.txt` contains the same data as before, these program lines would produce the following output:

```
Apples are red
Bananas are yellow
Carrots are orange
Dates are brown
```

Now let's look at a complete example of reading a file into a program. This example uses an input file called `indata.txt` that resides in the same directory as the program. Before the program executes, `indata.txt` contains the following four lines:

```
AC1000:Hammers:122:12
AC1001:Wrenches:344:5
AC1002:Hand Saws:150:10
AC1003:Screw Drivers:222:3
```

The CGI/Perl program opens the `infile.txt` file and uses a `while` loop to read each line in that file. It then uses the `split()` function to split the input into different scalar variables by using a colon ("`:`") as a field separator. Lines 10–11 output the variables that receive the values from the contents of the file. The output is shown in Figure 7.10.

```
1.  #!/usr/bin/perl
2.  use CGI ':standard';
3.  use CGI::Carp "fatalsToBrowser";
4.  print header, start_html('Inventory List');
5.  $infile="infile.txt";
6.  open (INFILE, $infile ) || die "Cannot open
        $infile: $!";
7.  while ( <INFILE> ) {
8.      $inline=$_;          ⟵ Set to next line in file
9.      ($ptno, $ptname, $num, $price ) = split ( /:/,
            $inline );
10.     print "We have $num $ptname ($ptno). ";
11.     print "The cost is $price dollars.", br;
12. }
13. close (INFILE);
14. print end_html;
```

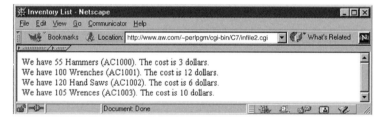

Figure 7.10 Output of a Program That Reads and Outputs a File

In this program:

☆ Line 3 uses the `CGI::Carp` module to direct error messages to the browser.

☆ Line 6 uses the `open()` function to connect to the file `infile.txt`, which must be in the same directory as the program. It uses `INFILE` as the file handle.

☆ Lines 7–12 use a `while` loop to loop through each line of the input file (line 7) and assign the next line read into the variable `$inline` using `$_` (line 8).

Line 9 uses the `split()` function to break the input line into pieces using a colon (":") as the field separator. This function copies the fields in the order in which they are encountered into the variables $ptno, $ptname, $num, and $price. Lines 10–11 use a print statement to output these values.

Specifying Filenames

As you have already seen, a filename in the `open()` function call is used to indicate the file to which your program should connect. To this point, this file must reside in the same directory as your program since the `open()` function call has not specified a directory path name to the file to open. By default, then, the file must reside in the same directory as the program being executed.

Alternatively, you can specify a full directory path name for the file to be opened. For example, the code in Figure 7.11 sets $infile to the full path name of the file used in Figure 7.11.

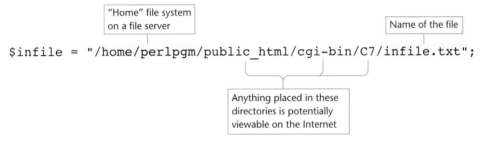

Figure 7.11 Format of a Full Path Name Specification for a File

Using a full file path name in this way, you can move your data files to a different location than that occupied by your program. This consideration is particularly important when you need to store data that shouldn't be viewable over the Internet. You *should not* store your data files in a location that is viewable by people over the Internet—there is too much potential for tampering by people you do not know. A much better solution is to move your files to a location that is not viewable by users accessing your pages from the Internet. Figure 7.12, for example, sets a file path that is not viewable over the Internet on my Web server. (The file system structure of my account on my ISP's Web server is shown in Figures 2.5 and 2.6.)

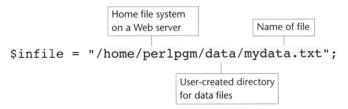

Figure 7.12 Format of a File Specification for a Location Not Viewable from the Internet

Even with this strategy, you should still ensure that the permissions assigned to the file and directory do not allow anyone other than your user id to write to them. (A common method is to set data files to the 644 permission settings. See Chapter Two and Appendix A to review permissions). The following Perl statements open the file mentioned previously from a Perl program:

```
$infile = "/home/perlpgm/data/mydata.txt";
open (INFILE, $infile ) || die "Cannot open $infile : $!";
```

☆WARNING Using Programs Available from the Internet

Be careful with *any* program using a file that is viewable over the Internet, including CGI/Perl programs that are offered for free on a Web site that "shares" programs. For example, you might want to use a guest book application that keeps its guest book file in a publicly viewable area. You should change this program to make it more secure.

Writing to Files

So far, all of our `open` statements have been used to read files. When you want to write to files, you need to indicate an **open mode** to the `open()` function. Three open modes are used to open a file:

☆ **read-only:** This mode is the default when no mode is specified. To explicitly specify it, put the character < before the filename in the `open()` function. For example,

```
open(INFILE, "<myfile.txt") || die "Cannot open: $!";
```

☆ **write-only-overwrite:** This open mode allows you to write to a file. If the file exists, it overwrites the existing file with the output of the program. To specify this mode, use > at the beginning of the filename used in the `open()` function. For example,

```
open(OFILE, ">myfile.txt") || die "Cannot open: $!";
```

☆ **write-only-append:** This open mode allows you to write and append data to the end of a file. If the file exists, it will write the program's output to the end of the existing file. If the file does not exist, it will create the file for you. To specify this mode, use >> before the filename in the `open()` function. For example,

```
open(OFILE, ">>myfile.txt") || die "Cannot open: $!";
```

Once you open the file for write-only-overwrite or write-only-append mode, you can write to your file by using a file handle in a `print` statement. For example, the following code writes the line `My program was here` to the file referenced by the file handle called `OFILE`:

```
print OFILE "My program was here";
```

Locking before Writing

Web applications have the potential to allow many end users to execute the same program simultaneously. If two programs want to write to the same file at the same time, the programs could possibly **corrupt** the file. A corrupted file is usually an unintelligible mixture of output that is useless to your program.

Perl provides a `flock()` function that can be used to ensure that only one Perl program at a time can write data. The following code uses a `flock()` function call to lock the file handle `OFILE`. The two specified establishes an exclusive lock on the file to ensure only one program can write to the file at once.

```
flock(OFILE, 2);
```

The following code opens a file handle in write-only-append mode, uses `flock()` to get exclusive access to the file, and writes a line to the file:

```
$outfile=">>/home/perlpgm/data/mydata.txt";
open (OFILE, $outfile ) || die "Cannot open $outfile:
    $!";
flock( OFILE, 2 );
print OFILE "AC1003:Screw Drivers:222:3\n";
close (OFILE);
```

These Perl lines will append the following line to the file `mydata.txt` stored at `/home/perlpgm/data/mydata.txt`:

```
AC1003:Screw Drivers:222:3
```

☆ **TIP**   **Remember the Newline Character**

Use the \n character to output a newline character into the file. If you omit the newline character, the file would have the following appearance if you executed the example program twice:

```
AC1003:Screw Drivers:222:3AC1003:Screw Drivers:222:3
```

Because the example program does use a newline character, your file will have the following appearance if you execute the program twice:

```
AC1003:Screw Drivers:222:3
AC1003:Screw Drivers:222:3
```

Putting It All Together

A good application for the write-only-append mode involves logging information. The next example program opens a file and appends end-user comments to the end of it. It logs the following information:

1. The **date** is obtained from the `localtime(time)` function. (This function was described in Chapter Three, "Basic Perl Functions.") It returns the current seconds, minutes, hour, day, month, and year. The months are numbered from 0 to 11, so the program adds 1 to the month value to get the current

month. Also since `localtime()` returns the number of years since 1900 (that is, for 2001 it would return 101, and for 2002 it would return 102), it adds 1900 to the year to get the current year.

2. The program uses **HTTP_REFFERER** (see Chapter Six, "Environmental Hash Lists") to log the TCP/IP address of the calling Web page.

3. The **end-user comments** are input by the end user using the input form.

The top screen in Figure 7.13 shows the form that sends comments to the example program. The bottom screen shows the program's output.

```
 1. #!/usr/bin/perl
 2. use CGI ':standard';
 3. use CGI::Carp "fatalsToBrowser";
 4. print header, start_html('Logger');
 5. $comments = param('ucomments');
 6. $logfile=">>/home/perlpgm/logfiles/mydata.txt";
 7. open (OUTFILE, $logfile ) || die "Cannot open
       $infile: $!";
 8. $remrefer=$ENV{'HTTP_REFERER'};
 9. ( $sec, $min, $hr, $Day, $mon, $year ) =
       localtime(time);
10. $year=$year+1900;
11. $mon = $mon + 1;
12. print OUTFILE "$mon/$Day/$year:$hr:$min:$remrefer:
       $comments\n";
13. print 'Just Logged:',br,"$mon/$Day/$year:$remrefer:
       $comments";
14. close (INFILE);
15. print end_html;
```

Get TCP/IP address of the end user's machine

Output log data

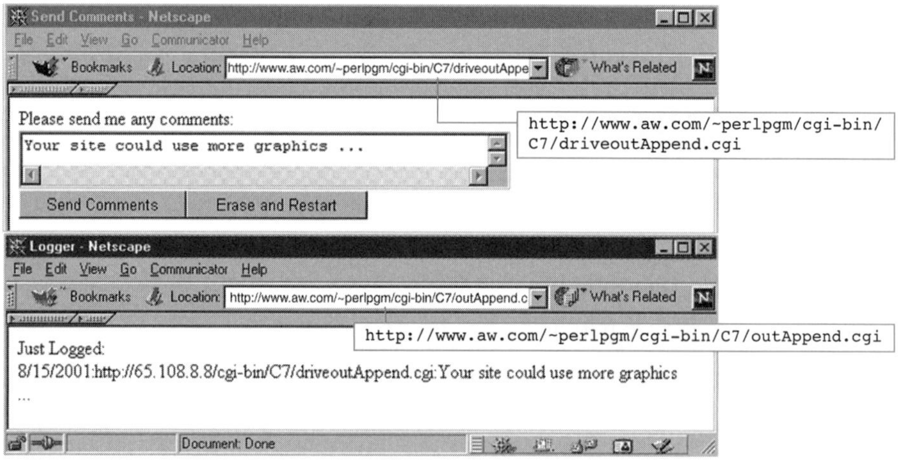

Figure 7.13 Output of the Logging Program

In this program:

☆ Lines 6–7 identify the location of the logfile (`/home/perlpgm/logfiles/mydata.txt`) and then open this file in append mode.

☆ Lines 9–11 get the day, month, and year. Line 10 adds 1900 to the year, because `localtime()` returns the number of years since 1900. Line 11 adds 1 to the month, because months are numbered from 0 to 11 in the output of `localtime()`.

☆ Lines 12–13 output the logging information first to the logfile (line 12) and then to the browser (line 13).

☆ **TIP   More on Using Field Delimiters with File Data**

This example uses a colon (":") to separate the date, `HTTP_REFFERER`, and comments fields. Using a field separator such as a colon consistently makes it easier to read and interpret the data later, because you can read one line at a time and use `split()` to get each input field.

☆ **WARNING   These Examples Are Just That—Examples**

All of the examples in this book are intended to illustrate specific points about working with CGI/Perl. Carefully consider security issues before writing any program that allows end users to write to files across the Internet. For example, the preceding program needs some measures to ensure that the logfile does not fill up because a hacker consumes all of the disk space on the server by logging comment after comment. Making an application secure is your responsibility as a developer. For more information on security, review the WWW Consortium's CGI security FAQs at `http://www.w3.org/Security/Faq/www-security-faq.html`.

Reading and Writing Files

Many programming problems require a program to read data from a file during its execution. The next program demonstrates a simple page counter. This example uses a `counter` subroutine that starts on line 9. This subroutine opens a counter file at `/home/perlpgm/logfiles/counter.txt` for reading, then reads and increments its counter value. Next, it reopens the counter file to write the new page count value. After the program closes the file, the new counter value is returned to the calling program. Figure 7.14 shows the output from this program.

```
1. #!/usr/bin/perl
2. use CGI ':standard';
3. use CGI::Carp "fatalsToBrowser";
4. print header, start_html('My Page');
5. print '<FONT SIZE=5>', "WELCOME TO MY SITE
      </FONT>";
6. $ct = &counter();
7. print br, '<FONT COLOR=BLUE>', "You Are Visitor $ct
      </FONT>";
```

```
 8. print end_html;
 9. sub counter {
10.     $ctfile="/home/perlpgm/logfiles/counter.txt";
11.     open (CTFILE, "<" . $ctfile ) || die "Cannot open
            $infile: $!";
12.     @inline = <CTFILE>;
13.     $count=$inline[0] + 1;
14.     close (CTFILE);
15.     open (CTFILE, ">$ctfile" ) || die "Cannot open
            $infile: $!";
16.     flock (CTFILE, 2);
17.     print CTFILE "$count";
18.     close (CTFILE);
19.     return $count;
20. }
```

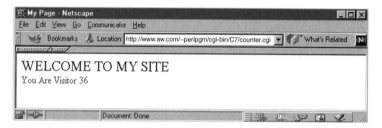

Figure 7.14 Output of a Simple Counter Program

In this program:

☆ Line 6 calls the `counter()` function and sets `$ct` to the return value. The variable `$ct` is used in the output in line 7.

☆ Lines 10–11, which are inside the `counter()` function, open the counter file for reading.

☆ Line 12 reads in the input file that contains the current page count value using the file `CTFILE`. Next, line 13 increments the page count value.

☆ Lines 15–18 reopen the file in *write-only-overwrite* mode. The new value of `$count` is output in line 17 after the file is locked in line 16. Line 18 closes the `CTFILE` file handle that releases the lock.

☆ Line 19 returns the count value to the calling program.

☆**TIP**   **A Variation on Counters**

One fanciful way to display page count values is to create (or obtain) graphic files that represent each digit you want to display and then use those graphic files to output the current page count. For example, you may have files called `one.gif`, `two.gif`, `three.gif`, and so on. If you want to display the number 35, for example, you could display `three.gif` and `five.gif` next to each other.

Working with Files

Yet Another File Read/Write Example

The next example also performs reads and writes with files. This simple application creates a Web survey focused on the favorite tools at *Harry's Happy Hardware*. This survey program is called from a form (`http://www.aw.com/~perlpgm/cgi-bin/C7/drivesurvey.cgi`) shown on the top of Figure 7.15 This calling form creates radio buttons with the CGI variable `tools` with one of the following values: `hammer`, `wrench`, `sdriver`, or `fryingpan`.

Lines 6–9 of the program open the file that contains the current survey data and read the file contents into a variable. Because the data kept in this file are delimited with colons ("`:`"), the `split()` function is used to get the current vote count for each tool field from the input file (line 10). Once the current vote totals are available, the program can add one vote to the total for the tool just selected (lines 11–22) and display the results (line 24) and then save the new values (lines 25–28).

```perl
1.  #!/usr/bin/perl
2.  use CGI ':standard';
3.  use CGI::Carp "fatalsToBrowser";
4.  print header, '<FONT SIZE=5 COLOR="BLUE">',"Survey
        Results</FONT>";
5.  $tool = param( 'tool' );
6.  $ctfile="/home/perlpgm/data/survey.txt";
7.  open (SURVFILE, "<" . $ctfile ) || die "Cannot open
        $infile: $!";
8.  @inline = <SURVFILE>;
9.  close (SURVFILE);
10. ( $hammer, $wrench, $sdriver, $fpan ) = split ( /:/,
        $inline[0] );
11. if ( $tool eq "hammer" ) {
12.     $hammer = $hammer + 1;
13. } elsif ( $tool eq "sdriver" ) {
14.     $sdriver = $sdriver + 1;
15. } elsif ( $tool eq "wrench" ) {
16.     $wrench = $wrench + 1;
17. } elsif ( $tool eq "fryingpan" ) {
18.     $fpan = $fpan + 1;
19. } else {
20.     print 'ERROR: Illegal call';
21.     exit;
22. }
23. $ct=$hammer + $sdriver + $wrench + $fpan;
24. print br, "Hammers=$hammer wrench=$wrench
        sdriver=$sdriver fpan=$fpan Total votes=$ct";
25. open (SURVFILE, ">$ctfile" ) || die "Cannot open
        $infile: $!";
26. flock (SURVFILE, 2);
27. print SURVFILE "$hammer:$wrench:$sdriver:$fpan";
28. close (SURVFILE);
```

Split the input line delimited by colons

Increment the votes for the tool picked by the end user

Write updated results

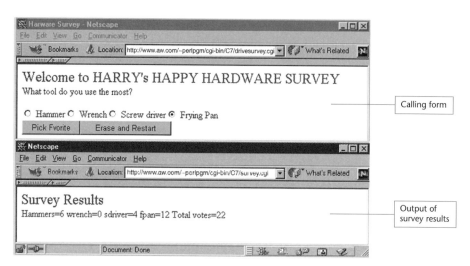

Figure 7.15 Output from the Survey Program

In this program:

☆ Line 5 gets the value of the CGI variable `tool` from the calling form.

☆ Lines 7–9 open the survey file and read the file's contents.

☆ Line 10 uses the `split()` function to parse the input data file into fields using a colon as a field separator.

☆ Lines 11–22 use the value of `$tool` (received from the calling form) to decide which tool the end user picked. That tool's vote total is then incremented.

☆ Line 23 calculates the total votes received.

☆ Line 24 outputs the new survey totals.

☆ Lines 25–28 reopen the survey file, lock it, and save the new results.

☆ Summary

▷ Perl supports a set of operators and functions that are useful for working with string variables and verifying input data. The `match` operator is used to look for patterns in strings. The `substitute` operator can search for a pattern and actually change strings. The `split` function uses a pattern to split the string into as many pieces as there are matches with the pattern.

▷ Perl uses regular expressions to greatly enhance its pattern matching capabilities. Regular expressions enable a program to look for specific characters (such as numbers, words, or letters) in specific places in any string. You can use them to verify form input, thereby providing a first line of defense against accidental or malicious input.

▷ Working with files enables a program to store data. As files can be used to remember data between times when a program executes, they greatly expand the types of problems that can be solved.

▷ Files can be opened in read-only, write-only-append, or write-only-overwrite mode. You cannot read and write from the same file simultaneously.

▷ The location of a program's data files should never be visible to other users over the Internet.

▷ Special care should be taken to lock a file before writing to it (using the `flock()` function).

☆ Online References

Articles on Writing Regular Expressions in Perl
`http://perl.about.com/`

World Wide Web Consortium's Frequently Asked Questions Dealing with Security
`http://www.w3.org/Security/Faq/www-security-faq.html`

Lincoln Stein's Site Containing `CGI.pm` Information
`http://stein.cshl.org/WWW/software/CGI/cgi_docs.html`

☆ Review Questions

1. Write a statement that checks whether the value of $name contains the sequence ABC. Write a statement that checks whether the value of $name contains either ABC or DEF.

2. Show two possible values for $name that would make the following test condition *true*. Show one possible value for $name that would result in it being *false*.

   ```
   if ( $name =~ m/^..[\d][\d]/ ) {
   ```

3. What is the output of the following code?

   ```
   $tester = "Exercises";
   $tester =~ s/E/e/g;
   print "Tester= $tester";
   ```

   What would the output be if the second line was changed to the following code?

   ```
   $tester =~ s/e/E/g;
   ```

4. What is each of the following character classes used for: \s, \S, \w, \W, \d?

5. What is each of the following character quantifiers used for: ^, $, +, *, .?

6. Suppose you wanted the program from Figure 7.5 to accept as input only dates in October. How would you change line 5 of this program (shown below)?

   ```
   if ( $date =~ m{^\d\d/[0-3]\d/2\d\d\d$} ) {
   ```

7. What is the output of the following code?

   ```
   $line = "XYZ123:12.50:22:Big and Green";
   @parsed   =   split( /:/, $line );
   print "$parsed[1] $parsed[2]";
   ```

8. What is a file handle? What is the $! variable used for and when is it set?

9. What are the three modes in which you can open a file? Which mode is the default? What character sequence is used to specify each mode in the **open** function (before the filename)?

10. Why is it necessary to lock a file before you write to it? What function do you use to lock it?

☆ Hands-On Exercises

1. Create a form that asks the end user to enter a phone number. Use regular expressions to test for one of the following phone number formats:

   (a) Allow only seven digits. Do not allow dashes or other characters to be specified.

   (b) Allow an optional dash between the third and fourth digits—that is, 345-1234.

(c) Allow an optional dash or space between the third and fourth digits—that is, `345 1234`, `3451234`, or `345-1234`.

2. (a) Create a form that asks the end user to create a user ID and password. The user ID and password must conform to set of rules to be valid (see below). Generate an appropriate message upon receiving an invalid user ID or password. Use the following rules for these input fields:

   (i) User IDs must start with a character (a–z) and be at least three characters long. Capital letters are not allowed anywhere in the user ID (for example, as in `hotDog` or `myLogin`). User IDs also cannot include spaces, dashes, or any other special characters (such as "`!`", "`@`", "`#`", "`$`", or "`%`"). Finally, user IDs cannot be one of the "reserved" user IDs, which include `root`, `admin`, and `operator`.

   (ii) The password field must be at least six characters long. Passwords must be valid letters or numbers and cannot include spaces, dashes or any other special characters (such as "`!`", "`@`", "`#`", and "`$`").

   (b) Extend the program so that when a valid user ID and password is received, it checks a file on your server to see whether the user ID exists. If it does, determine whether the password matches. Generate a Web page that lets the end user know if a match has been found. The password file can contain a simple list of valid user IDs and passwords.

3. Read the file generated by the example from Figure 7.13. A sample file can be found at `http://www.aw.com/~perlpgm/AppendComments.txt`. Produce a report that counts the number of lines in the file and indicates how many lines show an `HTTP_REFFER` from `http://www.aw.com/~perlpgm/cgi-bin/C7/driveoutAppend.cgi`.

4. Create a program that reads a file and produces a Web-based report for each "product" in the file. The file will be a set of four fields, each separated from the next by a colon ("`:`"), with the following format:

   `Part Number:Number Sold:Price:Number Available:Cost`

   For each line in the file, the report should indicate:
   ☆ The product number
   ☆ The *total revenue* it generated—that is, `Price * Number Sold`
   ☆ The *total cost* of the inventory remaining—that is, `Number Available * Cost`

   For example, with the input

   `AX1001:2:10:20:5`

   the output would be

   `Part Number: AX1001 Total Revenue: 20`
   `    Inventory Cost: 100`

   A sample input file can be found at `http://www.aw.com/~perlpgm/7.4Input.txt`. Make sure you use regular expressions to validate each input field received.

5. Write a guest book application that enables a Web-based end user to leave an e-mail address and comments about your site. Save the comments in a file. Use semicolons as the field separator. (*Hint*: If the end user enters a semicolon as part of his or her comments, you must change it to something else to keep your field separator working.)

6. Write an application that creates a survey containing at least four choices. Make sure that the application can handle illegal input. Save the results to a file.

   Optional: Provide a supersecret input sequence that resets the survey results in the file. This input sequence would not appear on the end user's form but could be set only by specifying it from a special form or by entering it from a URL.

7. Modify the file counter example from Figure 7.14 to use graphic files for each digit displayed in the counter. You will need 10 files—`zero.gif`, `one.gif`, `two.gif`, and so on. When you output a counter number, use the proper graphic file for each digit (placing the numbers—that is, appropriate graphic files—next to each other). For example, if the current page hit count was 34, you could output `three.gif` followed by `four.gif`.

CHAPTER EIGHT

Managing End-User Sessions

This chapter discusses the use of *hidden form fields* and *browser cookies* to remember end-user data. Hidden fields are first discussed as a way to build multiple-form Web applications that retain end-user input data from screen to screen. The chapter provides some examples illustrating how to build these applications and discusses the complexities and challenges of developing such sessions. Browser cookies are then discussed primarily as a way to store end-user preferences when viewing your site.

Chapter Objectives

- Discover how to use hidden fields to build multiple-screen end-user sessions
- Understand the complexities involved in creating Web applications with multiple-screen sessions

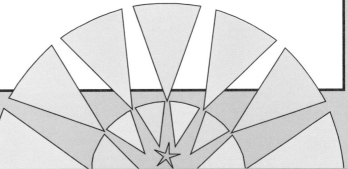

☆ Recognize the advantages and limitations of browser cookies

☆ Learn how to use browser cookies to track data about the end user

◎◎ Multiple-Form Applications

To this point, all of the form applications that we have developed have been only one or two screens long. Sometimes, however, you might need to write a CGI/Perl application that presents a **multiple-form Web session**. A multiple-form Web session leads the end user through a series of HTML forms, all of which work together. A shopping cart and a multiple-page Web survey are two examples of multiple-form Web sessions. Each screen must retain some data from screen to screen so that if a mistake is made on the third screen, for example, the end user does not have to reenter the data on the first and second screens.

As an example, consider an application that gathers order information with three screens:

☆ *Order information:* This screen gathers a product code and a quantity to be ordered.

☆ *Customer information:* This screen gathers the customer's name and address.

☆ *Billing information:* This screen gathers the customer's method of payment and other billing information.

If the customer makes a mistake while entering his or her billing information (on the third screen), you need some way to ask for the billing information again while still remembering the customer name and order information from the first two screens.

One way to retain data between forms is by using **hidden fields**. (Hidden fields were first introduced in Chapter Four.) Hidden fields are form elements that are not visible on the form. They enable the form designer to set CGI variable names and values from one form, and then retrieve them from the next form. We next describe how to set a hidden field and then see how they can be used.

Using Hidden Fields

Recall from Chapter Four that the format of hidden fields within a form looks like the following:

```
<INPUT TYPE="hidden" NAME="preference"
       VALUE="Likes Hardware">
```

CGI variable name

CGI variable's value

Even though the hidden fields aren't displayed on the screen, the CGI variable name and its value will still be available to the receiving CGI/Perl program when the form is submitted. One use of hidden fields is for maintaining data entered in previous screens. Of course, your programs can set whatever CGI variables and variable values that it needs.

The following program creates a hidden field. It provides an initial form in a series of forms that gather product order information. This form looks like any

⭐**WARNING** **Hidden but Not Completely Invisible**

Hidden fields are hidden but not completely invisible to the end user. In fact, any end user can view them by looking at the HTML source (for example, by doing a `view->source` operation in Netscape). For this reason, you shouldn't store any data in them that you don't expect the end user to be able to view.

other form to the end user; that is, it is not obvious that hidden fields are being set. Line 14 sets a hidden field to a CGI variable called STATE with a value of GET_INPUT. When the form processing program at `http://www.aw.com/~perlpgm/cgi-bin/C8/orderproduct2.cgi` starts, it can get the value of this variable, just as it gets the value of any other form CGI variable, by using the `CGI.pm param()` function as follows:

`$state=param('STATE');`

The code for this form that sets the CGI variable in a hidden field follows. Figure 8.1 shows the output.

```
 1. #!/usr/bin/perl
 2. use CGI ':standard';
 3. print header, start_html('Order Product');
 4. print '<FORM ACTION="http://www.aw.com/~perlpgm/cgi-
          bin/C8/orderproduct2.cgi" METHOD="POST" >';
 5. @Products=('Hammers', 'Hand Saws', 'Wrenches');
 6. print 'We have the following products available: ';
 7. print "@Products";
 8.
 9. print br, 'Please select a product ';
10. print '<INPUT TEXT TYPE="text" SIZE="15"
          MAXLENGTH="20" NAME="product">';
11. print ' Please enter quantity ';
12. print '<INPUT TEXT TYPE="text" SIZE="15"
          MAXLENGTH="20" NAME="quantity">';
13.
14. print br, '<INPUT TYPE="hidden" NAME="STATE"
          VALUE="GET_INPUT"> ';
15. print br, '<INPUT TYPE=SUBMIT VALUE="Order">';
16. print '<INPUT TYPE=RESET VALUE="Erase and
          Restart">';
17. print '</FORM>', end_html;
```

Set the CGI variable STATE in a hidden field

In this program:

⭐ Line 5 uses a list variable to hold the products available.

⭐ Lines 10–12 set the visible form text fields.

⭐ Line 14 sets a hidden field and establishes the CGI variable called STATE with the value `GET_INPUT`. This CGI variable's value will be available to the receiving program at `http://www.aw.com/~perlpgm/cgi-bin/C8/orderproduct2.cgi`.

Figure 8.1 An Initial Input Form That Sets a Hidden Field

Receiving and Using Hidden Fields

The preceding program sends its output to a program located at `http://www.aw.com/~perlpgm/cgi-bin/C8/orderproduct2.cgi`. Suppose that this second CGI/Perl program should generate a form to ask for additional information such as a customer name and billing code. If the end user makes a mistake in entering data into one of these fields, you don't want the end user to have to backtrack and reenter data on the first form. Instead, you want to show an error message and redisplay the second form. Figure 8.2 shows the desired flow of these two forms, which involves two CGI/Perl programs:

☆ `orderproduct.cgi`: This program generates the first form shown in Figure 8.1. It requests a product name and a quantity to order. When these data are submitted, the second form (generated from `orderproduct2.cgi`) is started.

☆ `orderproduct2.cgi`: This program is called after the user clicks the submit button on the `orderproduct.cgi` form. It asks for a customer name and billing code and then verifies these fields. If the end-user makes a mistake (like enters an invalid code), it does not force him or her back to the first form to reenter the product number and quantity again. Instead, the program remembers the data from the first form and starts itself all over again. This time, however, it notifies the end user of the error and asks him or her to enter a name and customer code again.

Same Program Different State

As shown in Figure 8.2, `orderproduct2.cgi` could potentially be called two or more times in a row:

☆ The first time to get the input data from `orderproduct.cgi` and then to ask the end user for a customer name and customer billing code.

☆ The second time to verify its own form (the customer name and billing code just received) and decide whether an error occurred. If an error is detected,

the program can then *redisplay the same form and ask for new input.* If the
input is acceptable, it thanks the end user and exits.

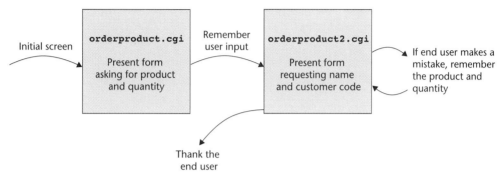

Figure 8.2 Screen Flow for a Multiple-Form Application

The `orderproduct2.cgi` program uses a CGI variable called `STATE` to
determine whether it is being called for the first or second time. The variable is
originally set by `orderproduct.cgi` as a hidden field. The CGI variable `STATE`
might have either of two valid values:

☆ `STATE=GET_INPUT`: If the variable is set to this value, then the program is
being started for the first time. Therefore, it should create its next form by
asking for a customer name and customer code. First, however, it uses hidden
fields to retain the product number and quantity for future use. Only then
does it set the `STATE` variable to a new value, `VERIFY_INPUT`, and call
itself again.

☆ `STATE=VERIFY_INPUT`: If the program is in this state, then the program
assumes that it is being called for the second (or more) time. Therefore, it
gets its expected CGI variables and verifies whether they contain any input
errors. If mistakes were made, the program displays an error message and
then redisplays its form. If the variables are error-free, it thanks the customer
and exits.

Figure 8.3 shows the screens generated by `orderproduct2.cgi` the first time
it is called from `orderproduct.cgi` (top screen), the second time it is called
and receives invalid input (middle screen), and when the end user enters valid
input (bottom screen). Note that the final screen is able to retain the initial data
entered (a product name of `Hammers` and a quantity of `144`) originally set in
`orderproduct.cgi` in Figure 8.2.

The Details of `orderproduct2.cgi`

As previously noted, Figure 8.3 shows the output of `orderproduct2.cgi` when
it is called with invalid and valid input. We will examine the programming code
for `orderproduct2.cgi` in three stages:

1. The *main portion* of the program starts the program and decides which subroutine to call depending on the value of the CGI variable `STATE`.

2. The `askname()` subroutine generates a form that asks for a name and customer billing code.

3. The `checkname()` subroutine generates a form to verify the customer name and customer billing code.

We will explain each of these program sections in turn.

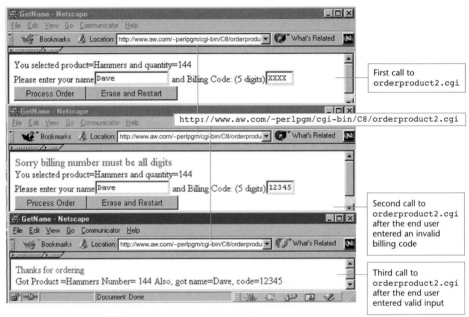

Figure 8.3 Output of the `orderproduct2.cgi` Program

The Main Program Section

The programming statements shown below constitute the main body of the `orderproduct2.cgi` program. They first set the HTML FORM ACTION argument to call itself again (Line 4) when the form is submitted. They then access the CGI variables `product`, `quantity`, and `STATE` (Lines 6–8) using the `CGI.pm` `param()` function. The first time `orderproduct2.cgi` is called, these CGI variables are set by `orderproduct.cgi` (with `STATE` as a hidden field). Based on the value of the CGI variable `STATE`, the main portion of `orderproduct2.cgi` decides which action the program should take:

☆ *Generate a form.* Lines 10–11 decide whether `orderproduct2.cgi` was called to produce a form by checking whether `$state` has the value `GET_INPUT`. If so, the program calls `askname()`.

☆ *Verify the form.* Lines 12–13 decide whether the program was called to verify its own form. If `$state` has the value `VERIFY_INPUT`, the program then calls `checkname()` to verify its own form.

⭐ *Generate an error message.* Line 14 decides whether the value of **STATE** somehow got messed up. The program does not expect this condition to occur. If `$state` does have a bad value, however, it prints a message and terminates.

```perl
1.  #!/usr/bin/perl
2.  use CGI ':standard';
3.  print header, start_html('GetName');
4.  print '<FORM ACTION="http://www.aw.com/~perlpgm/
      cgi-bin/C8/orderproduct2.cgi" METHOD="POST">';
5.  @Products=('Hammers', 'Hand Saws', 'Wrenches');
6.  $prod=param('product');
7.  $number=param('quantity');
8.  $state=param('STATE');
9.
10. if ( $state eq 'GET_INPUT' ) {
11.     &askname();
12. } elsif ( $state eq 'VERIFY_INPUT' ) {
13.     &checkname();
14. } else { print "ooops Get help! state=$state"; }
```

Get CGI variables passed in

Call to get the user information

Call to verify the information entered by the customer

An error in $state

⭐**WARNING** **Allow for Erroneous State Values**

Whenever you write a program that uses a variable to set the "state" of the program, you should always include a final check for bad variable values, as in Line 14 of the preceding program. Even though you don't expect such a line to execute, your program might be called by a different form (not your own) over the Internet. You want to catch these mistakes immediately.

The askname Subroutine

The `askname` subroutine is called from the main body of the program when the value of **STATE** is set to **GET_INPUT**. It generates a form that asks the end user to input a customer name and billing code (top screen of Figure 8.3). This subroutine performs two major tasks:

⭐ *Saving state:* Lines 18–20 set hidden form fields to save the values for the CGI variables **product**, **quantity**, and **STATE**. Performing this task enables the program to have access to these values the next time it is called (along with the customer name and billing code it will gather).

⭐ *Generating the visible form fields.* Lines 22–29 generate the "visible" form fields that ask the end user for a name and billing code. Line 4 in the main body of the program, as you will recall, has already set the form's action value to call itself again (at `http://www.aw.com/~perlpgm/cgi-bin/C8/orderproduct2.cgi`) when the form is submitted.

The code for the `askname` subroutine follows:

```
15. sub askname   {                    ┌─────────────────────────────────────┐
16.                                    │ Save product, quantity, and STATE   │
17.     print "You selected product=$prod and quantity=
                $number";
18.     print br, "<INPUT TYPE=\"hidden\" NAME=\
                "product\" VALUE=\"$prod\"> ";
19.     print "<INPUT TYPE=\"hidden\" NAME=\"quantity\"
                VALUE=\"$number\">";
20.     print '<INPUT TYPE="hidden" NAME="STATE"
                VALUE="VERIFY_INPUT"> ';
21.
22.     print 'Please enter your name';
23.     print '<INPUT TEXT TYPE="text" SIZE="15"
                MAXLENGTH="20" NAME="name">';
24.
25.     print ' and Billing Code: (5 digits)';
26.     print '<INPUT TEXT TYPE="text" SIZE="5"
                MAXLENGTH="5" NAME="code">';
27.
28.     print br, '<INPUT TYPE=SUBMIT
                VALUE="Process Order">';
29.     print '<INPUT TYPE=RESET
                VALUE="Erase and Restart">';
30.                                    ┌──────────────────────┐
31.     print end_form, end_html;      │ Get user information  │
32. }                                  └──────────────────────┘
```

☆ **TIP**   **Using the Backslash to Escape**

Note the use of the backslash ("\") in lines 18-19 but not in line 20. The backslash is needed in lines 18-19 because those lines use double quotation marks to output the values of $prod and $number. Line 20 does not output any variable's value, so it can use single quotation marks and does not need the backslashes. (Chapter 2 initially covered the use of double and single quotation marks.)

The checkname Subroutine

The checkname subroutine is used to verify the name and code fields. It assumes that askname() has already been run and made the CGI variables name and code available to it. Lines 35 and 36 shown below get these variables using the CGI.pm param() function. This subroutine verifies the input and takes two different actions depending on whether the input is valid:

☆ *Invalid input:* After getting the CGI variables name and code, line 37 uses a very simple regular expression to determine whether the end user entered five digits. If not, it outputs a message indicating the error and then calls askname(). As noted previously, askname() will save any state information and output a form asking for a new name and billing code.

☆ *Valid input:* If valid input was found, then lines 42–44 output a message indicating that the input was received and exit the program.

```
33. sub checkname  {
34.
35.     $code=param('code');          Ensure $code is 5 digits
36.     $name=param('name');
37.     if ( $code !~ /^\d\d\d\d\d$/ ) {
38.         print '<FONT COLOR="RED" SIZE=4> Sorry billing
                 number must be all digits</FONT>', br;
39.         &askname();                Everything looks okay; output data and exit
40.     }
41.     else {
42.         print '<FONT COLOR="BLUE"> Thanks for ordering
                 </FONT>', br;
43.         print "Got Product =$prod Number= $number";
44.         print " Also, got name=$name, code=$code";
45.     }
46. }
```

Call askname again to gather information again

☆ **WARNING**   **Minimal Error Checking**

Like other examples in this book, the entire application (`orderproduct.cgi` and `orderproduct2.cgi`) given here intentionally keeps the checking of form fields simple to minimize the program's complexity. If this example were a real application, you would use much more checking of input fields.

Building More Sophisticated Applications

Using hidden fields to store session data enables you to create more complex Web applications. As an example, Figure 8.4 shows an application with four forms that gathers survey information. Each form displays its initial fields and then calls itself to verify its own fields. This code can be implemented using the same general technique as the `orderproduct2.cgi` program from Figure 8.3. Each form could use a different CGI/Perl program that uses a hidden variable to set a "state." Alternatively, the forms can be placed within a single program that knows how to generate all of the forms based on the state information.

Beyond storing and retrieving data in hidden fields, you can use some techniques to create even more complex applications. These techniques include the following:

☆**TIP**   **Using One Form**

Chapter Six describes how to generate multiple forms from one program by using the `CGI.pm param()` function and subroutines.

☆ *Using files for storing state information.* Files can be used in conjunction with hidden fields to store and retain session data.

☆ *Using files and databases for storing initial data and form results.* Files and databases can be used for initial form input and long-term storage of form results. Such information could include initial input to applications and stored survey results or product orders.

⭐ *Sending e-mail from forms.* Forms can cause e-mail to be sent to a transaction-handling e-mail account or back to the customer to confirm the order.

Each of these techniques will be described next.

☆**TIP**   **Develop a Design Diagram before You Code**

When you are designing multiform Web applications, it is good idea to start with a diagram such as that shown in Figure 8.2, 8.4, or 8.5. These form-state diagrams can clarify to you (and to your end users) how the final application should work before you start coding.

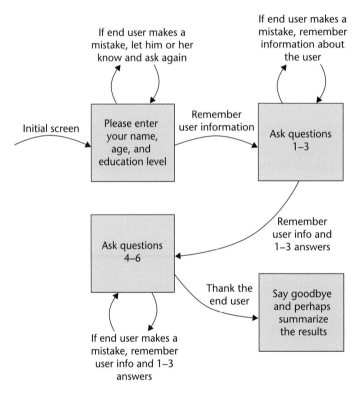

Figure 8.4 Screen Flow for an Example Survey Application

Using Files for Saving State

An alternative to using hidden fields exclusively for managing user sessions is storing user-specified data in a session file. When the user submits the first screen, his or her session can be assigned a session ID. Any input data can then be stored in a file corresponding to that session ID. Each new form would receive the session ID in a hidden field and use it to open its respective file with session input data.

Using files to store session states does increase the complexity of your session application. For example, you need to figure out how to generate session IDs and keep them secure from malicious hackers. Even with these considerations, using files for session management offers some advantages:

☆ *Revisiting states.* Using files to store session information can provide a consistent way for screens to "remember" session data, even when two screens do not normally call each other. Figure 8.5 shows an example "check-out" session application that allows users to jump from "Confirm Order" back to "Browse Product Catalog," while retaining the data already entered (that is, orders and billing information).

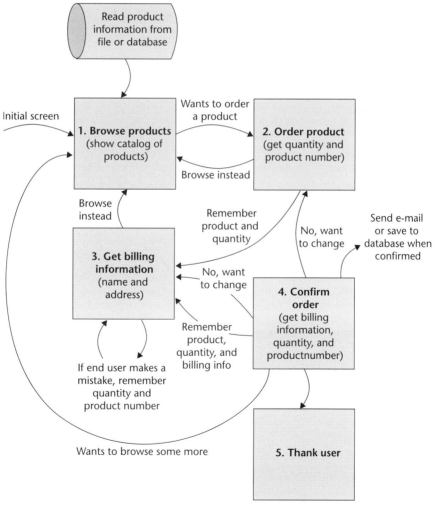

Figure 8.5 Screen Flow for a Multiple-Screen Check-out Application

Remembering data between sessions. You may want to remember data about the end user or a particular session even after the end user leaves your site. For example, you may want to enable end users to add items to their shopping carts and then leave your site without checking out. When they return, the application might still have the previously selected items in the cart. This type of "memory" can be implemented by storing some end user data in data files. It may also involve the user signing in (upon reentering the site) and/or the use of browser cookies (described later in this chapter).

☆ TIP   End-User Sign-On

Creating sessions that securely transmit, confirm, and store passwords is not covered in depth in this book. A variety of programs available for free and purchase on the Internet provide this functionality.

Storing Orders in Files

Sometimes after you complete a set of session screens, the session results need to be stored somewhere for later use. For example, after the application in Figure 8.5 confirms the order, it either (1) saves the data in a file or database or (2) sends an e-mail with the order information. Sending e-mail is covered in the next section. Let's briefly look at the issues involved in saving data in files or databases.

In Chapter Seven, we discussed the use of files for reading and writing data. A key aspect of storing data in files is employing a **field delimiter** such as a comma, tab, or vertical bar ("|"), which ensures that the fields can be identified and retrieved easily. For example, the `split()` function (discussed in Chapter Seven) can be used to quickly parse file lines into fields via field delimiters. Files work well when traffic is moderate in volume and the amount of data to be saved is relatively small. They are simple to use, can be edited with text editors (to add fields or records or fix a damaged line), and can be implemented quickly.

At some point, however, your site may need to store data in a database. Databases can provide faster access, higher security, and greater data integrity than do files. Perl supports a special `DBI` module for working with a variety of databases, including most major databases (such as Oracle, Informix, and Access) and some free ones (such as Mysql). (Check with your ISP to find out which database is available or obtain and install a database yourself if you can.) While the details of using `DBI` are beyond the scope of this book, suffice it to say that you can use DBI to connect to a database and then insert, update, and delete data in that database. You are also likely to organize your data into hash lists (discussed in Chapter Six), because the Perl `DBI` uses hash lists as a convenient way to read from and write to databases.

Sending E-mail from a Form

It is sometimes useful to send e-mail providing survey results or confirming order information. The **sendmail** program is a popular way to send e-mail from a UNIX Web server. The `sendmail` program has been available on UNIX systems since the 1980s; indeed, it comes as a preinstalled utility on most UNIX servers. You can use it to send e-mail via programs or interactively when logged into the Web server. (The `sendmail` program is also available for Windows NT systems.)

☆TIP Why Not Use the `mailto` Option with the HTML <FORM> Tag?

You may recall that the HTML <FORM> tag allows you to specify an e-mail address to which to mail results. With a mail program such as `sendmail`, you have many more options. You can decide when to e-mail results (for example, after the form fields have been validated or after several screens of input from a set of forms) and how to format the body of the message. You could also include environmental variables in the e-mail if desired. (Environmental variables are described in Chapter Six.)

To use `sendmail`, you need to know the directory path to the file where this program is stored. On a UNIX system, it is usually stored in */usr/lib/sendmail*. Other locations are also possible, so you should always verify `sendmail`'s location. Either ask your ISP or check out this location for yourself. If you can Telnet to your Web server, on many UNIX systems you can execute the `whereis` command to identify the location of `sendmail`. For example,

```
whereis sendmail
```

Here, we will use /usr/lib/sendmail as the path to `sendmail`.

☆TIP Blat for NT

A public domain utility called Blat can be used to send e-mail for Windows NT systems; it is available at `http://gepasi.dbs.aber.ac.uk/softw/Blat.html`. Its use is similar to that of `sendmail`, except that mail messages must be stored in an external file.

Using `sendmail`

When you want to send an e-mail message from a CGI/Perl program, you need to first connect to the `sendmail` program using `open()`. Figure 8.6 shows an example statement that opens a connection to `sendmail`.

Use the name `MAIL` like a file handle to output to the `sendmail` program

The vertical bar indicates to open an external program (in this case, the `sendmail` program)

```
open ( MAIL, "|/usr/lib/sendmail -t") ||
       die "Cannot start send mail: $!";
```

Use the `-t` `sendmail` option

Figure 8.6 Opening a Connection to the `sendmail` Program

Some of the key elements from the line of code in Figure 8.6 are described below:

☆ **`MAIL`** is the name that you give to the connection to the `sendmail` program. You use it much like a file handle when you want to print output to the `sendmail` connection.

☆ The **sendmail** path is the full directory path to the `sendmail` program. The vertical bar (" | ") is specified before the `sendmail` path. It is used when establishing an open connection to an external program. The `-t` option instructs `sendmail` to get the destination e-mail address and subject lines from the "To:" and "Subject:" data that we will send to it.

☆ Like the `open` function from Chapter Seven, the `die` function is executed only if a connection to the `sendmail` program cannot be established.

The following program segment shows the basic steps needed to use `sendmail`. It opens a connection to the `sendmail` program, specifies the e-mail address with the "To:" line, sets an e-mail subject line, and then creates the body of the e-mail. When the handle MAIL is closed, the e-mail is sent. Note that the character \n is required at the end of lines 3–5 for `sendmail` to work correctly.

```
1. open ( MAIL, "|/usr/lib/sendmail -t" ) || die "Cannot
        start sendmail: $!";
2.    $email='myhandle@myhandle.com';
3.    print MAIL "To: $email \n";
4.    print MAIL "Subject: New Order\n";
5.    print MAIL "Product =$prod Number= $number\n";
6.    close (MAIL);
```

☆TIP   **Forwarding Error Messages**

Chapter Seven discusses the use of CGI::Carp to forward error messages. You should also use this module when you work with sendmail. To use this module, simply add the following line at the beginning of your program (after use CGI ':standard';):

```
use CGI::Carp "fatalsToBrowser";
```

The following example presents a modified version of the form application originally shown in Figure 8.3. Here, the `checkname()` subroutine has been changed so as to send an e-mail via `sendmail` (lines 11–18). Figure 8.7 shows the output of the new `checkname()` subroutine with a complete order product application. Figure 8.8 shows the e-mail received at my site (perlpgm@www.aw.com).

```
1. sub checkname   {
2.
3.    $code=param('code');
4.    $name=param('name');
5.    if ( $code !~ /^\d\d\d\d\d/ ) {
6.       print '<FONT COLOR="RED" SIZE=4> Sorry billing
            number must be all digits</FONT>';
7.       &askname();
8.    }
9.    else {
```

```
10.        print '<FONT COLOR="BLUE"> Thanks for
              ordering</FONT>', "$name", br;
11.        open ( MAIL, "|/usr/lib/sendmail -t" )
              || die "Cannot start sendmail: $!";
12.
13.        $email='perlpgm@www.aw.com';
14.        print MAIL "To: $email \n";
15.        print MAIL "Subject: New Order\n";
16.        print MAIL "Got Product =$prod
              Number=$number\n";
17.        print MAIL " Also, got name=$name,
              email=$email, code=$code \n";
18.        close (MAIL);
19.        print '<FONT COLOR="BLUE"> Just sent email to
              </FONT>', "$email";
20.
21.     }
22. }
```

Open
and
send
mail

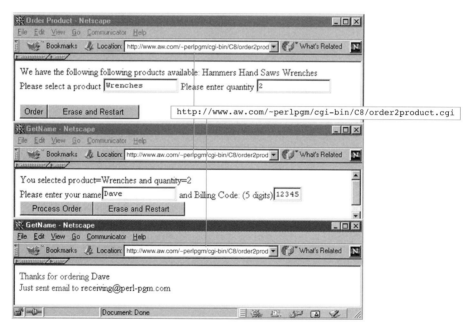

Figure 8.7 Output of a Program with a Revised `checkname()` Subroutine

In this program:

☆ Line 11 opens a connection to the `sendmail` program.

☆ Line 13 identifies the recipient's e-mail address.

☆ Lines 14–17 send the content of the e-mail message. (Remember to include the \n character at the end of the line.)

☆ Line 18 closes the MAIL handle and actually sends the mail.

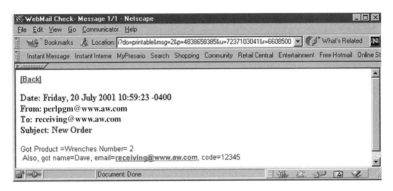

Figure 8.8 Received E-mail from the Revised Order Entry Program

⊚⊚ Using Cookies to Save Information

Browser cookies were developed by Netscape as a way for Web sites to "remember" visitor information. Today, they are implemented in both Netscape and Internet Explorer. Browser cookies are small pieces of data that can be saved by a Web site application when an end user visits the Web site. They are stored on the visitor's hard drive in a special "cookie" file. When the visitor returns to the Web site, that site's Web application program can read the browser cookie data that it previously stored and use it to "remember" something about the visitor.

As long as the end user's browser supports the use of cookies and that feature is enabled, the Web site can store any data it wants (with some size and volume restrictions). Cookies are typically used for tasks such as saving visitor preferences, managing sessions with state information, and recording the frequency with which the end user visits the site. For example, suppose you visit a site that sells books. While there, you fill out a form and indicate you prefer to read mystery novels. The site might then set a cookie to remember that you like mysteries. The next time you visit, the site might automatically suggest several mystery novels.

☆WARNING **You Are Probably Accepting Cookies Already**

The default settings on the Netscape and Internet Explorer browsers are to accept all cookie data being sent. Thus, unless you disable this feature, you allow cookie data to be sent to your hard drive.

Cookie Limitations

Before examining how to set and read cookies, you should understand some of their limitations. These limitations include the following:

☆ *Cookies can be easily disabled.* Both Netscape and Internet Explorer provide methods for end users to disable cookies and refuse to allow sites to set them. For example, in Netscape you can disable cookies by clicking Edit, Preferences, Advanced. (See Figure 8.9.)

☆ *People move around.* Cookies don't make much sense on computers that have multiple users (such as a library or computer lab). A cookie that stores a preference for one of the computer's users is not likely to be relevant for another user. Furthermore, people who visit a Web site from different computers (for example, at home, work, and school) probably have different cookie settings.

☆ *Not all browsers support cookies.* Although it is becoming less common, not all browsers support cookies. If your site requires cookies to view it, you might exclude people with older browsers or people who disable cookies.

☆ *Cookies can be easily deleted.* Because cookie data are stored in one or more files on the end user's computer, an end user might accidentally or intentionally delete the data. Also, both Netscape and Microsoft Internet Explorer have measures to limit the number of cookies and size of cookie files. For example, Netscape limits the number of cookies per site to 20 and to no more than 300 in total. Cookies in excess of 300 are discarded.

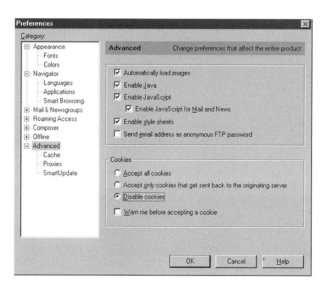

Figure 8.9 Disable Cookie Screen in Netscape 4.7

Why Some People Don't Like Cookies

Some end users do not want Web sites to store cookie data on their hard drives using browser cookies and prefer to run their Web browsers with browser cookies disabled. They commonly cite two objections to accepting cookie data:

⭐ *Anonymity.* Some people prefer to browse the Web anonymously without allowing Web sites to track their preferences and movements at any given site. For example, a Web site might give the user's computer a cookie with a unique ID on it, then on its server record when that ID logs in, which pages it visits, and even which page that ID was viewing just before coming to the site.

⭐ *Potential use in market research.* Some Web marketing research companies use cookie data to develop profiles of Web usage patterns. They then sell these patterns to interested Web companies for their informational purposes. Some people prefer not to have their surfing data included in these surveys (especially given that cookie data can be gathered for the most part without their knowledge).

⭐**SHORTCUT**   **View Your Own Cookie Data**

On PCs running Windows, you can look at your cookie files. If you are using Netscape or Internet Explorer on a Windows PC, click Start, Find, Files and Folders, and then enter `cookie` in the search box. Netscape stores cookies in a file called `cookies.txt`. Internet Explorer stores them in a `Cookies` directory.

Setting and Understanding Cookies

Despite these limitations and concerns, cookies can be useful to Web site designers. Many sites use them to track end-user browsing preferences. Some use cookies instead of hidden fields to maintain session states. Still other sites use them to track customer browsing patterns at the site. This section discusses how to set a cookie and then describes how to read previously set cookies.

Setting a Cookie

A Web application program can request that a browser cookie be saved in memory or onto disk. Browser cookies set in memory are deleted when the end user exits from the browser. Those saved to disk are retained (on disk) until some defined expiration date. Figure 8.10 shows the basic syntax for setting a cookie into memory from a CGI/Perl program.

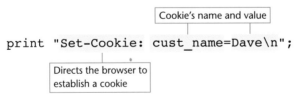

Figure 8.10 Syntax for Setting a Memory-Only Cookie

The line of code in Figure 8.10 must be output *before* the MIME Content-type line is output to the browser. You can select whatever cookie variable name and value you desire when you set a cookie. As shown in Figure 8.10, no spaces can appear between the name, equals sign ("="), and value. Also, the \n character is required at the end of the line.

☆ **TIP**   **Cookies for Session Management**

One use of memory-only cookies is to store session-state information instead of using hidden fields. Session management was discussed earlier in this chapter.

When you want to save a cookie onto the end user's hard disk, you need to specify an expiration date. For example, the line of code in Figure 8.11 directs the browser to set a cookie that expires on July 4, 2003, at 00:00:00 GMT.

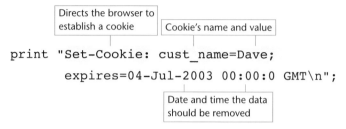

Figure 8.11 Setting a Cookie That Will Be Saved to Disk

When you set a cookie with an expiration date and time, you must use dashes ("–") to separate the parts of the date: a two-digit day (for example, 01), followed by a three-letter month for example, Dec), followed by a four-digit year.

☆ **TIP**   **Setting Cookie Expiration Dates**

One method to set session expiration dates is to use the `localtime()` function. Recall that the `localtime()` function can be used to get the current month, day, and year. You can add to these values to set a cookie's expiration date. Chapter Three discusses the `localtime()` function in more detail.

The following example program asks for end-user preferences and then sets a cookie on the end user's hard drive. This program is called from a form whose output is shown at the top of Figure 8.12 (the code creating this form is not provided here). The program receives the CGI variables `name` and `prefers` from the calling form and then sets two cookies. Note that lines 3–6 are all executed before the MIME Content-type header line is output (that is, before the `header` function call in line 8). Lines 3–4 get the parameters from the previous screen (shown at the top of Figure 8.12) and then lines 5–6 set the cookies using the syntax shown in Figure 8.11. The output from the program appears in the bottom screen in Figure 8.12.

```
1. #!/usr/bin/perl
2. use CGI ':standard';
3. $name=param('name');
4. $prefers=param('prefers');
5. print "Set-Cookie: cust_name=$name;
          expires=04-Jul-2003 00:00:0 GMT\n";
6. print "Set-Cookie: cust_prefer=$prefers;
          expires=04-Jul-2003 00:00:0 GMT\n";
```

Set two cookies

```
7.
8. print header, start_html('set cookie');
9. print br, "Thanks $name Lets now look at $prefers
         . . . ";
10.
11. print end_html;
```

MIME content-type after setting cookies

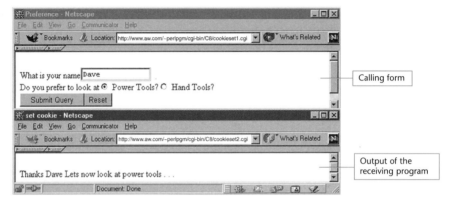

Calling form

Output of the receiving program

Figure 8.12 A Program That Sets Two Cookies to the End User's Hard Drive

In this program:

☆ Lines 3–4 get the CGI variables `name` and `prefers`.

☆ Lines 5–6 set two cookies that expire July 4, 2003.

☆ Lines 8–11 output an HTML document.

It is worth noting three things from the above example.

1. Unless the end user explicitly sets the browser settings to be notified when a site sets a cookie, the end user probably won't realize that a cookie was set.

2. If the end user disables cookies, the program will not know it. It is possible for CGI/Perl applications to detect whether cookies are enabled, but they must set a cookie and then try to read that cookie again to make this determination.

3. While you are testing the use of cookies, it is helpful to set your browser setting to "Warn me before accepting a cookie." (Both Internet Explorer and Netscape support this setting.) This setting will create a pop-up warning box for every cookie that was set, like that shown in Figure 8.13.

☆**TIP   Many Sites on the Internet Use Cookies**

If you set your browser to warn you every time a cookie is set and then browse the Internet, you will quickly learn which sites are setting cookies to your hard drive. Cookies are so popular, however, that you will likely become inundated by these pop-up warnings.

Using Cookies to Save Information

Figure 8.13 Pop-up Warning Box When the "Warn me before accepting cookies" Setting Is Enabled in Netscape

Reading Cookies

The easiest way to read a cookie is with the `CGI.pm` function called `cookie()`. To use the `cookie()` function, simply call the function with the cookie name for which you are searching. For example, the code in Figure 8.14 gets a cookie called `prefer` and assigns it to the Perl variable `$uprefer`.

Figure 8.14 Sample Format of the `CGI.pm` cookie Function

☆**TIP**   **An Alternative Way to Read Cookies**

You could obtain cookie names and values from a `%ENV` hash variable called `HTTP_COOKIE`. It returns a list of semicolon-separated name/value pairs of cookies. For example,

`$cookies=$ENV{'HTTP_COOKIE'};`

sets the variable `$cookies` to all of the cookie names and values separated by semicolons.

☆**SHORTCUT**   **Using `CGI.pm` to Read Cookies**

The `CGI.pm` module also provides a function to set cookies. Its syntax is not shown here because it uses the more difficult variable/value pair method. Nevertheless, it has a very useful short-hand method for setting retention time periods. For more information, see `http://stein.cshl.org/WWW/software/CGI/cgi_docs.html` or Lincoln Stein's book *Official Guide to Programming with CGI.pm*.

The following program reads the cookie values set in the program for Figure 8.12. It creates one message if the user has a cookie previously set (shown at the top of Figure 8.15). It creates a different message if the user either has cookies disabled or has not visited the site before (shown at the bottom of Figure 8.15).

```
 1. #!/usr/bin/perl
 2. use CGI ':standard';
 3. print header, start_html("Welcome ");
 4. $cust_name=cookie( 'cust_name');          ┐── Read two cookies
 5. $prefers=cookie('cust_prefer');           ┘
 6. print '<FONT COLOR="BLUE">';
 7. if ($cust_name) {  ─────────────────── Tests the value of cust_name cookie
 8.     print "Welcome back $cust_name to our humble
           hardware site.";
 9. } else {
10.     print '<FONT COLOR="RED"> ';
11.     print 'Welcome to our humble hardware site.
           </FONT>';
                                      ─── Test the value of cust_prefer cookies
12. }
13. if ( $prefers eq "hand tools" ) {
14.     print br,'We have hammers on sale for 5
           dollars!';
15. } elsif ( $prefers eq "power tools" ){
16.     print br, 'We have power drills on sale for 25
           dollars!';
17. } else {
18.     print br, '<FONT COLOR="RED">';
19.     print ' We have drills and hammers on special
           today!</FONT>';
20. }
21. print "</FONT>", end_html;
```

Program output when cookies are enabled and a previous preference was mentioned

Welcome - Netscape
File Edit View Go Communicator Help
Bookmarks Location: http://www.aw.com/~perlpgm/cgi-bin/C8/readcoo   What's Related

Welcome back Dave to our humble hardware site.
We have power drills on sale for 25 dollars!

http://www.aw.com/~perlpgm/cgi-bin/C8/readcookie.cgi

Welcome - Netscape
File Edit View Go Communicator Help
Bookmarks Location: http://www.aw.com/~perlpgm/cgi-bin/C8/readcoo   What's Related

Welcome to our humble hardware site.
We have drills and hammers on special today!

Document: Done

Program output if cookies are disabled or the user has not visited the site before

Figure 8.15 Output of a Program That Reads Cookie Values

In this program:

☆ Lines 4–5 use the CGI.pm cookie() function to get the cookie values.

☆ Line 7 tests whether $cust_name has a value. If it does (which means that the program did retrieve a value from the cookie), the program outputs a personalized message.

Lines 13–20 test the value of `$prefers`. Depending on its value, the program prints out information on a sale that it wants to highlight. If the value of `$prefers` does not match any known values, the program prints out a default message.

Some Advanced Cookie Options

A few more options for the Set-Cookie browser command are worth mentioning. By default, cookies are set so that they can be retrieved only from the directory in which they were set and only by the computer that set them. If you want to read the cookie from a different file system directory than where it was set, then you must specify the `path` option. For example, you might set the cookie from a program in `http://www.aw.com/~perlpgm/cgi-bin/C7` and then read it from a program in `http://www.aw.com/~perlpgm/cgi-bin/C8`. The following code enables any directory on the system that set the cookie to read it:

```
print "Set-Cookie: cust_name=$name; expires=04-Jul-2003
     00:00:0 GMT; path=/\n";
```

You might also want to enable any server within your domain to be able to read the cookie. Perhaps one server sets the cookie while taking the order and another server reads it while processing the order. You use the `domain` option of the Set-Cookie command to enable different computers within your domain to read the cookie. For example,

```
print "Set-Cookie: cust_name=$name; expires=04-Jul-2003
     00:00:0 GMT; domain=.mysite.com\n";
```

indicates that the cookie could be read at any computers with domain name that ends in `.mysite.com`. Thus, if the domain `mysite.com` included two computers called `www.mysite.com` and `orders.mysite.com`, then either of them could read the cookie specified above.

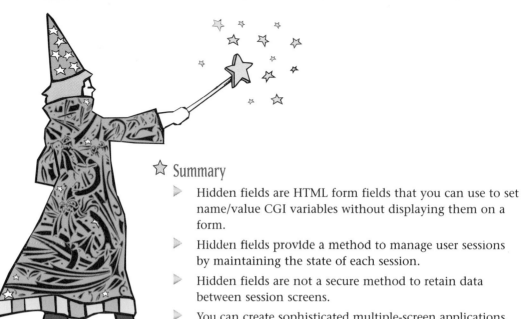

☆ Summary

▷ Hidden fields are HTML form fields that you can use to set name/value CGI variables without displaying them on a form.

▷ Hidden fields provide a method to manage user sessions by maintaining the state of each session.

▷ Hidden fields are not a secure method to retain data between session screens.

▷ You can create sophisticated multiple-screen applications, such as shopping carts and surveys, by using hidden fields.

▷ Cookies provide a way for Web server applications to store small pieces of data on the end user's machine.

▷ Cookies can be easily refused by the end user and therefore cannot be relied upon to always be available to the CGI/Perl program.

▷ Data set by cookies can be available for long periods of time, even when the end user leaves the site and comes back months later.

☆ Online References

Information about the Blat Program for NT Systems
`http://gepasi.dbs.aber.ac.uk/softw/Blat.html`

A Storehouse of Information About Browser Cookies
`http://www.cookiecentral.com/`

Lincoln Stein's Site about `CGI.pm`
`http://stein.cshl.org/WWW/software/CGI/cgi_docs.html`

Free and For-Purchase CGI Programs
`http://www.cgi-resources.com/`

☆ Review Questions

1. What is a hidden field? How is it set?

2. What are the three major tasks executed by the main program section from the program output shown in Figure 8.3? Which subroutine is executed the first time the program is called?

3. Under what conditions can line 14 of the program from Figure 8.3 be executed? This line follows:

   ```
   } else { print "ooops Get help! state=$state"; }
   ```

4. What are the two major tasks that the `askname` subroutine perform? Which three CGI variables does it set?

5. What are the two major tasks accomplished in the `checkname` subroutine from the program from Figure 8.3?

6. What are two advantages of using files to save state information rather than exclusively using hidden fields?

7. What are the advantages and disadvantages of using files to store data?

8. What are the advantages of using databases to store data? Which Perl module do you use to work with databases?

9. What is a browser cookie? What are four disadvantages of using such cookies?

10. Why don't some people like cookies? What argument must you use to set a cookie that will be retained after the end user leaves your site?

☆ Hands-On Exercises

1. Create a CGI/Perl survey that implements the session shown in Figure 8.2. It should have the following pieces:
    (a) On the first screen, ask the end user's name and age. If the user fails to enter one of these answers, generate an error message and ask for input again. (Make sure the end user's age is between 5 and 100.)
    (b) On the second screen, ask two questions:
        i. Do you prefer to work with hammers or power drills?
        ii. Do you prefer to do your own fix-it jobs or hire someone else?

    If the end user fails to enter information in one of these fields, generate an error message and ask the question again. (Also, retain and input data from the first screen.)
    At the end of the survey, display output summarizing the results. (*Hint*: Use parts of the program from Figure 8.3 to develop this application.)
    Optional: Use an e-mail program to send the results to yourself.

2. Create a CGI/Perl survey application that implements the screen flow shown in Figure 8.4. It should have four screens:
    (a) An initial screen to collect a name and code number.
    (b) A second screen that asks three survey questions. If the end user makes a mistake (such as not answering a question), enable him or her to reenter the data without going back to the first screen.
    (c) A third screen that asks three more survey questions. If the end user makes a mistake (such as not answering a question), enable him or her to reenter the data without going back to the first or second screen.
    (d) A final screen that summarizes the end user's answers and thanks him or her for participating in the survey. The end user's name should be output on this screen as well.

3. Modify the program from Figure 8.3 as follows:
    (a) Use a file for input of the initial order. This file will have the following format:

        `PARTNO:PART:NUMAVAIL:COST:`

Use the following as initial data in the file:

```
AC1000:HAMMER:12:5
AC1001:WRENCHES:10:5
AC1002:PLIERS:22:4
AC1003:SCREW DRIVERS:100:5
```

(b) Allow only four valid customer billing codes:

```
12345
23456
34567
45678
```

(c) Validate all fields while accepting only the billing codes and product numbers mentioned in parts (a) and (b). Do not allow a request for more of an item than is available in inventory. (For example, do not allow anyone to order more than 12 hammers.)

(d) When the order is complete, e-mail an appropriate message to your e-mail address.

4. Create a form to allow an end user to send feedback about your site. When the end user enters feedback and submits the form, get his or her TCP/IP address and browser type (using environmental variables). Then, use `sendmail` to mail the end user's input to yourself. Format this information so that it is easily readable by you when you receive the e-mail.

5. Create an HTML form that allows end users to specify a preferred background color when visiting your Web site. Notify end users that only red, yellow, green, and white can be used (and enforce that limitation). When a user selects a color, generate another screen that thanks the Web site visitor. Set the background to that color (if a valid one was selected) and set a cookie with this preference. Use this color when the end user visits your site again.

6. Create a "dice" guessing game. The initial form should ask the end user's name, a guess of the dice (from 1 to 6), and the number of "points" the user wants to bet (from 1 to 100). Give the end user 100 points initially.

(a) When the end user submits a guess and bet, generate a new form with a random number from 1 to 6. If that number matches the end user's guess, add his or her "bet" to the point total. If it is wrong, deduct the "bet" from the point total.

(b) Ask the end user for another guess and bet.

(c) The game is over when the end user's point total is 0.

(d) Do not let the end user guess more than his or her remaining point total. If the end user does guess more than this point total, generate an error message, remember the point total, and let the end user guess again.

(e) If the end user fails to fill out a field, notify him or her and allow the end user to reenter data.

APPENDIX A: SOME BASIC UNIX COMMANDS

◎◎ Some Basic UNIX Commands

Chapter Two describes the UNIX commands that you can use to navigate a UNIX Web server and set access permissions (if you have Telnet access to a UNIX web server). This section expands on these commands and shows some additional useful UNIX commands.

The more command

The UNIX **more** command is used to list out the contents of a file on a UNIX web server. It will pause when it fills up your current window (to continue hit the space bar). Figure A.1 shows the output of the UNIX more command executed on a file called **test.cgi**. Note how the last line pauses when the current screen is filled up.

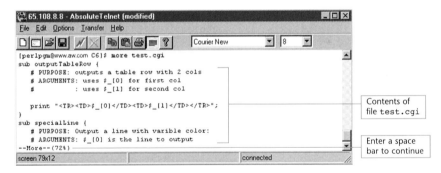

Figure A.1 The output of a UNIX more command

The ls Command Revised

As indicated in Chapter Two, the **ls** command lists the files and directories in the current working directory. If you include the **-xF** arguments (**ls -xF**), it will list the files in multiple columns (rather than a single column) and indicate directories with a trailing slash character ("/") and executable files with a trailing asterisk ("*"). Figure A.2 shows the output of an ls -xF command. The directories shown below are C, C2, C3, C4, C5, C6, C7, C8, and test. The executable files are FirstHTML.cgi, first.cgi, simple.cgi, simple1. cgi, simple2.cgi, simple3.cgi, and test.cgi.

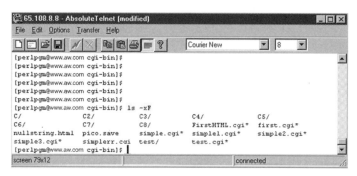

Figure A.2 The output of an `ls -xF` command

You can use the **−1** argument (**ls −1**) to instruct UNIX to create a long listing that includes information about the file access permissions, file size, and the last modification date of the file. Figure A.3 shows an example `ls −1` command executed for the file `simple1.cgi` and a description of the output.

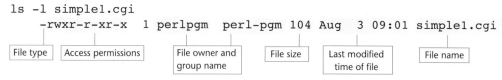

```
ls -1 simple1.cgi
     -rwxr-r-xr-x  1 perlpgm  perl-pgm 104 Aug  3 09:01 simple1.cgi
```

Figure A.3 An Example of an `ls −1` UNIX command

The *file type* indicates if the file is a directory or regular file. If this first character is a "**−**" then the file is a regular file, if it is a "**d**", then it is a directory. The *access permissions* are the next nine characters and they define the read, write, and execute permissions of the file's owner, file's group, and everyone else. For example, Figure A.4 shows a regular file (since the first character is a "**−**"), with read, write, and execute permissions ("**rwx**") for the file's owner, and read and execute ("**r−x**") permissions for the file's group and everyone else.

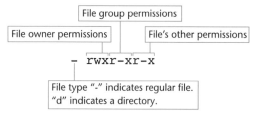

Figure A.4 File type and Access Permission Output from an `ls −1` command

The `ls −1` command is helpful when used in conjunction with the `chmod` command (used to change file access permissions and originally described in Chapter Two). For example, Figure A.5 shows an `ls −1` command on the file `simple.cgi` (showing `rw−r−r−−` permissions), followed by a `chmod` command, followed by another `ls −1` command (now showing `−rwxr−xr−x` permissions).

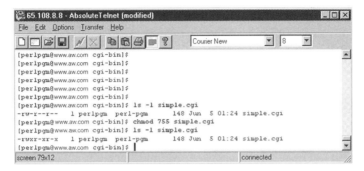

Figure A.5 The `ls -l` UNIX command used with `chmod`

The **-ltr** arguments to the **ls** command (`ls -ltr`) are useful to create a long listing of all your files in a directory and sort the files by modification times (with the most recently modified file output last). For example, Figure A.6 shows an `ls -ltr` command. It indicates that `t1.cgi` was the file most recently modified and `test2.cgi` was the file modified the longest ago.

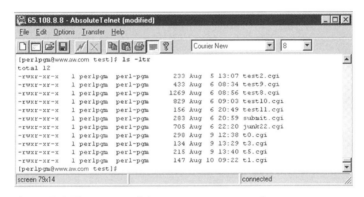

Figure A.6 The output of the `ls -ltr` command

The cp Command

The `cp` command copies a file from a source file to a destination file. It has the following general format:

```
cp file1.txt newfile1.txt
```

The **cp** can be particularly useful to make a copy of an existing file before you start altering it (so you have a backup copy). For example Figure A.7 shows an `ls -xF` command output, followed by a `cp` command that copies `simple.cgi` to `oldsimple.cgi`, followed by another `ls -xF` command. Now `oldsimple.cgi` is a backup copy of `simple.cgi`.

Figure A.7 Using cp to copy UNIX files

APPENDIX B: ANSWERS TO ODD-NUMBERED REVIEW QUESTIONS

Chapter One

1. CGI is an interface standard between application programs and Web servers. Perl is a programming language that can be used to develop Web application programs (and non-Web application programs).

3. Both are written in a computing language and are stored as files. Web application programs interact with Web browsers.

5. A browser sends a request and input data across the Internet to a Web server. The Web server receives this request and executes a Web application program; it sends any input data using CGI. The program executes and then returns the results to the Web server. The Web server forwards the results across the Internet and back to the browser. The browser displays the result in its window.

7. A Web server can refer both to a computer and the software that runs on that computer. A Web server provides data files and executes Web applications on demand.

Chapter Two

1. A home directory is created for you on your ISP's Web server as a place to store your files and directories. It is usually created when your account is created.

3. Read, write, and execute access. You set them for your user ID, your group, and any one else. A good access permission for CGI/Perl programs is 755—that is, read, write, and execute access for your user ID and read and execute access for everyone else.

5. Syntax checking verifies that the statements in a program are grammatically valid. The `perl -c` command is used to check syntax.

7. This line lets the browser know to expect output of type `text` or HTML from the CGI/Perl program.

9. /home/perlpgm/public_html, /home/perlpgm, /home/perlpgm/public_html/cgi-bin

◎◎ Chapter Three

1. `$1st_counter`, squared

3. `if`, `elsif`, `else`; only the `if` statement can be used by itself.

5. It will output 0, 1, 2, 3, and 4 randomly.

7. `print "$name was \"deleted\" from our database";`

9. `use CGI ':standard';`

◎◎ Chapter Four

1. No argument, positional argument, name-value argument

3. These tags create the starting portion of an HTML document.

    `print start_html('My First Document');`

5. The `NAME=` argument from a form element sets the variable name. The `CGI.pm param()` function can be used to receive the value.

7. The CGI variable name is `Q1`; its value would be `Got Two`.

9. The code connects to the `CGI.pm` Perl module using standard mode (instead of object-oriented mode). It enables the program to use the functions in the `CGI.pm` module.

◎◎ Chapter Five

1. `Jones, Jefferson, Johnson`

3. It is set to the subscript number of the last item in your list. You can use it to get the length of your list variable and access the last item.

5. `sublist=9 6 8`

7. `for`, `foreach`, `while`, `until`. The `foreach` statement might be the most convenient, but all four constructs can be used.

9. Initialization expression (gives the initial value of a loop control variable), loop-ending expression (loop end condition), iteration expression (expression to evaluate after each iteration)

◎◎ Chapter Six

1. Cross referencing one piece of information with another; when the access time needed to look up information is important

3. (a) There are 25 days left in Apr. Apr has 30 total days.

(b) There are 27 days left in Jul. Jul has 31 total days.

(c) Hmmm, there aren't 12 days in XXX.

5. `$x=wrench.gif; $y=3; $z=5`

7. `$_[2]; $_[0]; $size=@_`

9. Easier to make changes to parameters; easier to maintain. With no arguments, calls `build_form()`. With four arguments, calls `handle_form()`.

◎◎ Chapter Seven

1. `if ( $name =~ m/ABC/ ) {, if ( $name =~ m/ABC|DEF/ ) {,`

3. `Tester= exercises Tester= ExErcisEs`

5. "`^`" matches when the character following it starts a string; "`$`" matches when the preceding character ends the string; "`+`" matches one or more occurrences of the preceding character; "`*`" matches zero or more occurrences of the preceding character; "`.`" is a wildcard symbol that matches any one character.

7. `12.50 22`

9. Read-only, write-only-overwrite, write-only-append. Read-only is the default. Read-only uses "`<`", write-only-overwrite uses "`>`", and write-only-overwrite uses "`>>`".

◎◎ Chapter Eight

1. A hidden field is a form element. It can be set with the following CGI/Perl statement:

   ```
   print '<INPUT TYPE="hidden" NAME="preference"
   VALUE="Likes Hardware"> ';
   ```

3. Line 14 can be executed if the `STATE` variable gets an illegal value, perhaps from an end user who accesses your site using his or her own form or who enters the URL by hand and specifies the CGI variable on the URL line.

5. Determines whether the input was valid; outputs a final message once valid input is received.

7. Files can be simple to use and can be edited by hand (with a text editor). Accessing data in files will be slower than using a database when the volume of data is large.

9. Cookies are small pieces of data that can be stored on a visitor's hard drive. Cookies can be disabled, people move around, not all browsers support them, and they can be deleted easily.

INDEX

$ (dollar sign), 38–39, 163
; (semicolon), 47, 110
" " (quotation marks), 57–58
= (equal sign), 60
@menu list variable, 101–102
@_ variable, 140, 141
|| (OR operator), 118, 171
% (percent sign), 124
%ENV hash, 130, 207
(pound sign), 139
/ (slash), 155, 165
( ) (parentheses), 159
^ (caret symbol), 160, 163
\d, 163, 165
\D, 163
\n, 177, 200, 204
\s, 162
\S, 162
\w, 162
\W, 163
+ (plus sign), 164
. (wildcard symbol), 164
* (asterisk), 164
{ } (curly brackets), 165
<> (file input operator), 172
: (colon), 174
\ (backslash), 194
| (vertical bar), 200
& (ampersand), 60

absolute value (abs) function, 55
access permissions
    changing, 24–26, 27
    of ISP, 9
    ls -l command and, 214
    verifying, 32
alternation operator, 159,
    160–162
American Standard Code for
    Information Interchange
    (ASCII), 50–51, 63
ampersand (&), 60
AND operator, 118
Apache Web server software, 7
applications, Web. *See also*
    multiple-form applications
    building, 195–202

with CGI, 5–6
    cookies, 202–209
    defined, 4
    locking before writing, 177
arguments
    for form buttons, 77–78
    of <FORM> tag, 76–77
    to ls command, 214–215
    name-value, 73–75
    numerical, 55–56
    passing to subroutines,
        140–141
    positional, 71–73
    print function and, 57–58
    for program file combination,
        144–146
    sending to Web pages, 60–62
arrays, 74. *See also* list variables
ASCII (American Standard Code
    for Information
    Interchange), 50–51, 63
askname subroutine, 192,
    193–195
asterisk (*), 164

b function, 72
backslash (\), 194
billing information, 188, 190,
    197
binding operators
    for checking browser types,
        133
    for pattern matching, 154
    for returning values, 142, 143
Birznieks, Gunther, 172
Blat program, 199, 210
browser. *See* Web browser
browser cookies, 202–209
    advanced options for, 209
    limitations of, 202–203
    objections to, 203–204
    reading, 207–209
    setting and understanding,
        204–207
buttons, 77–78. *See also* radio
    buttons

C argument, 77
caret symbol (^), 160, 163
case sensitivity, 38, 129
cd command, 30
cd dir_name command, 19
cgi-bin directory, 29, 31
CGI (Common Gateway
    Interface)
    defined, 5–6
    ISP and, 8
    variables, 59–60, 89–90
CGI/Perl programs
    check boxes and, 84–86
    generating HTML statements
        from, 32–33
    HTML forms and, 79–81
    output text area from, 84
    password box creation in,
        81–83
    for radio buttons, 86
    for selection list, 87–88
    using hidden fields in,
        188–194
    using sendmail in, 199–202
CGI Programming with Perl
    (Guelich, Gundavaram, and
    Birznieks), 172
CGI::Carp, 171–172, 174, 200
CGI.pm module
    to combine program files,
        144–146
    cookie function of, 207–209
    debug mode of, 89–90
    generating HTML documents
        with, 68–75
    list items and, 98, 99
    param ( ) function of, 58–59,
        189–190, 194–195
    resource for, 63, 91
    start_html function and, 75
character class operator, 159–160
character classes, special,
    162–163
character quantifiers, 163–164
character strings, 44–46
check boxes, 84–86, 104
check-out application, 197–198

◎◎ Perl Functions and Related Statements

The following tables present the Perl functions, the CGI.pm functions, and related statements used in this book.

Perl Functions Used in This Book

Function	Effect
`$x=sqrt($n);`	Returns the square root of the value of $n to $x.
`$x=abs($n);`	Returns the absolute value of the value of $n to $x.
`$x=int(rand(10));`	Returns a random number from 0, 1, 2, ... 9 to $x.
`@ltime = localtime(time);`	Returns a list with values *seconds, minutes, hour, day, month, year, week day, day number of year,* and *time zone.*
`$n=3; print("N=$n");`	Creates the output of N=3.
`$ret = pop(@List1);`	Removes the *last* item from the list variable @List1 and sets $ret to its value.
`push(@List1,'NewOne');`	Adds an item with value NewOne to the *end* of the list variable @List1.
`$ret = shift(@List1);`	Removes the *first* item from the list @List1 and sets $ret to its value.
`unshift(@List1, 'NewOne');`	Adds an item with value NewOne onto the *beginning* of the list variable @List1.
`@kitems = keys(%hlist);`	Returns a list of all *keys* in hash list %hlist.
`@litems = values(%hlist);`	Returns a list of all *values* in hash list %hlist.
`@newl = split( /,/, $line );`	Splits $line using comma "," as a field separator. Returns a list of all matches to list variable @newl.

Some Special CGI.pm Functions

Function	Effect
`$mygrade = param('mygrade');`	Returns the value of the CGI variable mygrade to variable $mygrade.
`$pref=cookie('pref');`	Returns the value of a cookie called pref to variable $pref.